# Advanced JavaS

Speed up web development with the powerful
features and benefits of JavaScript

Zachary Shute

## Advanced JavaScript

Copyright © 2019 Packt Publishing

Author: Zachary Shute

Reviewer: Houssem Yahiaoui

Managing Editor: Aritro Ghosh

Acquisitions Editor: Aditya Date

Production Editor: Samita Warang

Editorial Board: David Barnes, Ewan Buckingham, Shivangi Chatterji, Simon Cox, Manasa Kumar, Alex Mazonowicz, Douglas Paterson, Dominic Pereira, Shiny Poojary, Saman Siddiqui, Erol Staveley, Ankita Thakur, and Mohita Vyas

First Published: January 2019

Production Reference: 1310119

ISBN: 978-1-78980-010-4

# Table of Contents

# Testing JavaScript 171

# Functional Programming                                               203

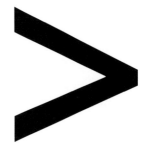

# Preface

**About**

This section briefly introduces the author, the coverage of this book, the technical skills you'll need to get started, and the hardware and software required to complete all of the included activities and exercises.

## About the Book

JavaScript is a core programming language for web technology that can be used to modify both HTML and CSS. It is frequently abbreviated to just JS. JavaScript is used for processes that go on in the user interfaces of most web browsers, such as Internet Explorer, Google Chrome, and Mozilla Firefox. It is the most widely-used client-side scripting language today, due to its ability to make the browser do its work.

In this book, you will gain a deep understanding of JavaScript. You will learn how to write JavaScript in a professional environment using the new JavaScript syntax in ES6, how to leverage JavaScript's asynchronous nature using callbacks and promises, and how to set up test suites and test your code. You will be introduced to JavaScript's functional programming style and you will apply everything you learn to build a simple application in various JavaScript frameworks and libraries for backend and frontend development.

## About the Author

**Zachary Shute** studied computer and systems engineering at RPI. He is now the lead full-stack engineer at a machine learning start-up in San Francisco, CA. For his company, Simple Emotion, he manages and deploys Node.js servers, a MongoDB database, and JavaScript and HTML websites.

## Objectives

- Examine major features in ES6 and implement those features to build applications
- Create promise and callback handlers to work with asynchronous processes
- Develop asynchronous flows using Promise chaining and async/await syntax
- Manipulate the DOM with JavaScript
- Handle JavaScript browser events

- Explore Test Driven Development and build code tests with JavaScript code testing frameworks.
- List the benefits and drawbacks of functional programming compared to other styles
- Construct applications with the Node.js backend framework and the React frontend framework

## Audience

This book is designed to target anyone who wants to write JavaScript in a professional environment. We expect the audience to have used JavaScript in some capacity and be familiar with the basic syntax. This book would be good for a tech enthusiast wondering when to use generators or how to use Promises and Callbacks effectively, or a novice developer who wants to deepen their knowledge on JavaScript and understand TDD.

## Approach

This book thoroughly explains the technology in an easy-to-understand way, while perfectly balancing theory and exercises. Each chapter is designed to build on what was learned in the previous chapter. The book contains multiple activities that use real-life business scenarios for you to practice and apply your new skills in a highly relevant context.

## Minimum Hardware Requirements

For the optimal student experience, we recommend the following hardware configuration:

- Processor: Intel Core i5 or equivalent
- Memory: 4 GB RAM
- Storage: 35 GB available space
- An internet connection

## Software Requirements

You'll also need the following software installed in advance:

- Operating system: Windows 7 SP1 64-bit, Windows 8.1 64-bit, or Windows 10 64-bit

- Google Chrome (https://www.google.com/chrome/)

- Atom IDE (https://atom.io/)

- Babel (https://www.npmjs.com/package/babel-install)

- Node.js and Node Package Manager (npm) (https://nodejs.org/en/)

Access to installation instructions can be provided separately to book material for large training centers and organizations. All source code is publicly available on GitHub and fully referenced within the training material.

## Installing the Code Bundle

Copy the code bundle for the class to the C:/Code folder.

## Additional Resources

The code bundle for this book is also hosted on GitHub at https://github.com/TrainingByPackt/Advanced-JavaScript.

We also have other code bundles from our rich catalog of books and videos available at https://github.com/PacktPublishing/. Check them out!

## Conventions

Code words in text, database table names, folder names, filenames, file extensions, pathnames, dummy URLs, user input, and Twitter handles are shown as follows: "The three ways to declare variables in JavaScript: var, let, and const."

A block of code is set as follows:

```
var example; // Declare variable
example = 5; // Assign value
console.log( example ); // Expect output: 5
```

Any command-line input or output is written as follows:

```
npm install babel --save-dev
```

New terms and important words are shown in bold. Words that you see on the screen, for example, in menus or dialog boxes, appear in the text like this: "This means that variables created with block scope are subject to the **Temporal Dead Zone (TDZ).**"

## Installing Atom IDE

1. To install Atom IDE, go to https://atom.io/ in your browser.

2. Click on **Download Windows Installer** for Windows to download the setup file called **AtomSetup-x64.exe**.

3. Run the executable file.

4. Add the `atom` and `apm` commands to your path.

5. Create shortcuts on the desktop and Start menu.

Babel is installed locally to each code project. To install Babel in a NodeJs project, complete the following steps:

1. Open a command, line interface and navigate to a project folder.

2. Run the command `npm init command`.

3. Fill in all the required questions. If you are unsure about the meaning of any of the prompts, you can press the 'enter' key to skip the question and use the default value.

4. Run the `npm install --save-dev babel-cli` command.

5. Run the command `install --save-dev babel-preset-es2015`.

6. Verify that the `devDependencies` field in `package.json` has `babel-cli` and `babel-presets-es2015`.

7. Create a file called `.babelrc`.

8. Open this file in a text editor and add the code `{ "presets": ["es2015"] }`.

## Installing Node.js and npm

1. To install Node.js, go to https://nodejs.org/en/ in your browser.

2. Click on **Download for Windows (x64)**, to download the LTS setup file recommended for most users called node-v10.14.1-x64.msi.

3. Run the executable file.

4. Ensure that you select the npm package manager bundle during the setup.

5. Accept the license and default installation settings.

6. Restart your computer for the changes to take effect.

# Introducing ECMAScript 6

**Learning Objectives**

By the end of this chapter, you will be able to:

- Define the different scopes in JavaScript and characterize variable declaration
- Simplify JavaScript object definitions
- Destructure objects and arrays, and build classes and modules
- Transpile JavaScript for compatibility
- Compose iterators and generators

In this chapter, you'll be learning how to use the new syntax and concepts of ECMAScript.

# Introduction

**JavaScript**, often abbreviated as JS, is a programming language designed to allow the programmer to build interactive web applications. JavaScript is one of the backbones of web development, along with HTML and CSS. Nearly every major website, including Google, Facebook, and Netflix, make heavy use of JavaScript. JS was first created for the Netscape web browser in 1995. The first prototype of JavaScript was written by Brendan Eich in just a mere 10 days. Since its creation, JavaScript has become one of the most common programming languages in use today.

In this book, we will deepen your understanding of the core of JavaScript and its advanced functionality. We will cover the new features that have been introduced in the ECMAScript standard, JavaScript's asynchronous programming nature, DOM and HTML event interaction with JavaScript, JavaScript's functional programming paradigms, testing JavaScript code, and the JavaScript development environment. With the knowledge gained from this book, you will be ready to begin using JavaScript in a professional setting to build powerful web applications.

## Beginning with ECMAScript

**ECMAScript** is a scripting language specification standardized by **ECMA International**. It was created to standardize JavaScript in an attempt to allow for independent and compatible implementations. **ECMAScript 6**, or **ES6**, was originally released in 2015 and has gone through several minor updates since then.

> **Note**
>
> You may refer to the following link for more information about ECMA specification:https://developer.mozilla.org/en-US/docs/Web/JavaScript/Language_Resources.

## Understanding Scope

In computer science, **scope** is the region of a computer program where the binding or association of a name to an entity, such as a variable or function, is valid. JavaScript has the following two distinct types of scope:

- **Function scope**
- **Block scope**

Until ES6, function scope was the only form of scope in JavaScript; all variable and function declarations followed function scope rules. Block scope was introduced in ES6 and is used only by the variables declared with the new variable declaration keywords let and const. These keywords are discussed in detail in the *Declaring Variables* section.

## Function Scope

**Function scope** in JavaScript is created inside functions. When a function is declared, a new scope block is created inside the body of that function. Variables that are declared inside the new function scope cannot be accessed from the parent scope; however, the function scope has access to variables in the parent scope.

To create a variable with function scope, we must declare the variable with the var keyword. For example:

```
var example = 5;
```

The following snippet provides an example of function scope:

```
var example = 5;
function test() {
  var testVariable = 10;
  console.log( example ); // Expect output: 5
  console.log( testVariable ); // Expect output: 10
}
test();
console.log( testVariable ); // Expect reference error
```

Snippet 1.1: Function Scope

**Parent scope** is simply the scope of the section of code that the function was defined in. This is usually the global scope; however, in some cases, it may be useful to define a function inside a function. In that case, the nested function's parent scope would be the function in which it is defined. In the preceding snippet, the function scope is the scope that was created inside the function test. The parent scope is the global scope, that is, where the function is defined.

> **Note**
>
> Parent scope is the block of code, which the function is defined in. It is not the block of code in which the function is called.

## Function Scope Hoisting

When a variable is created with function scope, it's declaration automatically gets hoisted to the top of the scope. **Hoisting** means that the interpreter moves the instantiation of an entity to the top of the scope it was declared in, regardless of where in the scope block it is defined. Functions and variables declared using var are hoisted in JavaScript; that is, a function or a variable can be used before it has been declared. The following code demonstrates this, as follows:

```
example = 5; // Assign value

console.log( example ); // Expect output: 5

var example; // Declare variable
```

Snippet 1.2: Function Scope Hoisting

> **Note**
>
> Since a hoisted variable that's been declared with var can be used before it is declared, we have to be careful to not use that variable before it has been assigned a value. If a variable is accessed before it has been assigned a value, it will return the value as undefined, which can cause problems, especially if variables are used in the global scope.

## Block Scope

A new block scope in JavaScript is created with curly braces ({}). A pair of **curly braces** can be placed anywhere in the code to define a new scope block. If statements, loops, functions, and any other curly brace pairs will have their own block scope. This includes floating curly brace pairs not associated with a keyword (if, for, etc). The code in the following snippet is an example of the block scope rules:

```
// Top level scope
function scopeExample() {
    // Scope block 1
    for ( let i = 0; i < 10; i++ ){ /* Scope block 2 */ }
    if ( true ) { /* Scope block 3 */ } else {  /* Scope block 4 */ }
    // Braces without keywords create scope blocks
    { /* Scope block 5 */ }
    // Scope block 1
```

```
}
// Top level scope
```

Snippet 1.3: Block Scope

Variables declared with the keywords let and const have **block scope**. When a variable is declared with block scope, it does NOT have the same variable hoisting as variables that are created in function scope. Block scoped variables are not hoisted to the top of the scope and therefore cannot be accessed until they are declared. This means that variables that are created with block scope are subject to the **Temporal Dead Zone** (**TDZ**). The TDZ is the period between when a scope is entered and when a variable is declared. It ends when the variable is declared rather than assigned. The following example demonstrates the TDZ:

```
// console.log( example ); // Would throw ReferenceError

let example;

console.log( example ); // Expected output: undefined

example = 5;

console.log( example ); // Expected output: 5
```

Snippet 1.4: Temporal Dead Zone

**Note**

If a variable is accessed inside the Temporal Dead Zone, then a runtime error will be thrown. This is important because it allows our code to be built more robustly with fewer semantic errors arising from variable declaration.

To get a better understanding of scope blocks, refer to the following table:

|  | Function Scope | Block Scope |
|---|---|---|
| **Scope Creation** | Block of scope for each function | Block pf scope for curly braces {} |
| **Variable Keyword** | Variables defined with var | Variables defined with let and const |
| **Hoisting and Instantiation** | Variable hoisting | Temporal Dead Zone |

Figure 1.1: Function Scope versus Block Scope

In summary, scope provides us with a way to separate variables and restrict access between blocks of code. Variable identifier names can be reused between blocks of scope. All new scope blocks that are created can access the parent scope, or the scope in which they were created or defined. JavaScript has two types of scope. A new function scope is created for each function defined. Variables can be added to function scope with the var keyword, and these variables are hoisted to the top of the scope. Block scope is a new ES6 feature. A new block scope is created for each set of curly braces. Variables are added to block scope with the let and const keywords. The variables that are added are not hoisted and are subject to the TDZ.

## Exercise 1: Implementing Block Scope

To implement block scope principles with variables, perform the following steps:

1. Create a function called fn1 as shown (function fn1()).

2. Log the string as scope 1.

3. Create a variable called scope with the value of 5.

4. Log the value of the variable called scope.

5. Create a new block scope inside of the function with curly braces ({}).

6. Inside the new scope block, log the string called scope 2.

7. Create a new variable called scope, inside the scope block and assign the value different scope.

8. Log the value variable scope inside our block scope (scope 2).

9. Outside of the block scope defined in step 5 (scope 2), create a new block scope (use curly braces).

10. Log the string called scope 3.

11. Create a variable inside the scope block (scope 3) with the same name as the variables (call it scope) and assign it the value a third scope.

12. Log the new variable's value.

13. Call fn1 and observe its output

## Code

index.js:

```
function fn1(){
  console.log('Scope 1');
```

```
let scope = 5;
console.log(scope);
{
   console.log('Scope 2');
   let scope = 'different scope';
   console.log(scope);
}
 {
   console.log('Scope 3');
   let scope = 'a third scope';
   console.log(scope);
 }
}
fn1();
```

https://bit.ly/2Ro0otW

Snippet 1.5: Block implementation output

**Outcome**

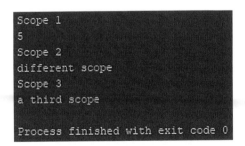

Figure 1.2: Scope outputs

You have successfully implemented block scope in JavaScript.

In this section, we covered the two types of JavaScript scope, function and block scope, and the differences between them. We demonstrated how a new instance of function scope was created inside each function and how block scope was created inside each set of curly braces. We discussed the variable declaration keywords for each type of scope, var for function scope and let/const for block scope. Finally, we covered the basics of hoisting with both function and block scope.

## Declaring Variables

Basic JavaScript uses the keyword var for **variable declaration**. ECMAScript 6 introduced two new keywords to declare variables; they are let and const. In the world of Professional JavaScript variable declaration, var is now the weakest link. In this topic, we will go over the new keywords, let and const, and explain why they are better than var.

The three ways to declare variables in JavaScript are by using var, let, and const. All function in slightly different ways. The key differences between the three variable declaration keywords are the way they handle variable reassignment, variable scope, and variable hoisting. These three features can be explained briefly as follows:

**Variable reassignment:** The ability to change or reassign the variable's value at any time.

**Variable scope:** The extent or area of the code from which the variable may be accessed.

**Variable hoisting**: The variable instantiation and assignment time in relation to the variable's declaration. Some variables can be used before they are declared.

The var keyword is the older variable declaration keyword that's used to declare variables in JavaScript. All variables created with var can be reassigned, have function scope, and have variable hoisting. This means that variables created with var are hoisted to the top of the scope block, where they are defined and can be accessed before declaration. The following snippet demonstrates this, as follows:

```
// Referenced before declaration
console.log( example ); // Expect output: undefined
var example = 'example';
```

Snippet 1.6: Variables created using var are hoisted

Since variables that are created with the keyword var are not constants, they can be created, assigned, and reassigned a value at will. The following code demonstrates this aspect of the functionality of var:

```
// Declared and assigned
var example = { prop1: 'test' };
console.log( 'example:', example );
// Expect output: example: {prop1: "test"}
// Value reassigned
example = 5;
```

```
console.log( example ); // Expect output: 5
```

Snippet 1.7: Variables created using var are not constant

Variables created with var can be reassigned at any time and once the variable is created, it can be accessed from anywhere in the function, even before the original declaration point.

The let keyword functions similar to the keyword var. As expected, the keyword let allows us to declare a variable that can be reassigned at any time. This is shown in the following code:

```
// Declared and initialized
let example = { prop1: 'test' };
console.log( 'example:', example );
// Expect output: example: {prop1: 'test"}
// Value reassigned
example = 5;
console.log( example ); // Expect output: 5
```

Snippet 1.8: Variables created with let are not constant

There are two significant differences between let and var. Where let and var differ is their scoping and variable hoisting properties. Variables declared with let are scoped at the block level; that is, they are only defined in the block of code contained within a matching pair of curly braces ({}).

Variables declared with let are not subject to variable hoisting. This means that accessing a variable declared with let before the assignment will throw a runtime error. As discussed earlier, this is the Temporal Dead Zone. An example of this is shown in the following code:

```
// Referenced before declaration
console.log( example );
// Expect ReferenceError because example is not defined
let example = 'example';
```

Snippet 1.9: Variables created with let are not hoisted

The last variable declaration keyword is `const`. The `const` keyword has the same scoping and variable hoisting rules as the `let` keyword; variables declared with `const` have block scoping and do not get hoisted to the top of the scope. This is shown in the following code:

```
// Referenced before declaration
console.log( example );
// Expect ReferenceError because example is not defined
const example = 'example';
```

Snippet 1.10: Variables created with const are not hoisted

The key difference between `const` and `let` is that `const` signifies that the identifier will not be reassigned. The `const` identifier signifies a read-only reference to a value. In other words, the value written in a `const` variable cannot be changed. If the value of a variable initialized with `const` is changed, a `TypeError` will be thrown.

Even though variables created with `const` cannot be reassigned, this does not mean that they are immutable. If an array or object is stored in a variable declared with `const`, the value of the variable cannot be overwritten. However, the array content or object properties can be changed. The contents of an array can be modified with functions such as `push()`, `pop()`, or `map()` and object properties can be added, removed, or updated. This is shown in the following code:

```
// Declared and initialized
const example = { prop1: 'test' };


// Variable reassigned
example = 5;
// Expect TypeError error because variable was declared with const


// Object property updated
example.prop1 = 5;
// Expect no error because subproperty was modified
```

Snippet 1.11: Variables created with const are constant but not immutable

To understand the different keywords in more detail, refer to the following table:

| | Var | Let | Const |
|---|---|---|---|
| **Scope Creation** | Function Scope | Block Scope | Block Scope |
| **Reassignment** | Can be reassigned | Can be reassigned | Cannot be reassigned |
| **Hoisting** | Hoisted | Not hoisted | Not hoisted |

Figure 1.3: Differences between var, let, and const

Now that we understand the nuances among var, let, and const, we can decide on which one to use. In the professional world, we should always use let and const, because they provide all the functionality of var and allow the programmer to be specific and restrictive with the variable scope and usage.

In summary, var, let, and const all function similarly. The key differences are in the nature of const, the scope, and the hoisting. var is function scoped, not constant, and hoisted to the top of the scope block. let and const are both block-scoped and not hoisted. let is not constant, while, const is constant but immutable.

## Exercise 2: Utilizing Variables

To utilize the var, const, and let variable declaration keywords for variable hoisting and reassignment properties, perform the following steps:

1. Log the string noisted before assignment: and the value of the hoisted variable.

2. Define a variable called hoisted with the keyword var and assign it the value this got hoisted.

3. Log the string hoisted after assignment: and the value of the hoisted variable.

4. Create a try-catch block.

5. Inside the try block, log the value of the variable called notnoisted1.

6. Inside the catch block, give the catch block the err parameter, then log the string not hoisted1 with error: and the value of err.message.

7. After the try-catch block, create the notnoisted1 variable with the let keyword and assign the value 5.

8. Log the string notnoisted1 after assignment and the value of notnoisted1.

9. Create another try-catch block.

10. Inside the try block, log the value of the notnoisted2 variable.

11. Inside the catch block, give the catch block the `err` parameter, then log the string `not hoisted2 with error:` and the value of `err.message`.

12. After the second try-catch block, create the `notnoisted2` variable with the keyword `const` and assign the value [1,2,3].

13. Log the string `notnoisted2 after assignment` and the value of `notnoisted2`.

14. Define a final try catch block.

15. Inside the `try` block, reassign `notnoisted2` to the `new value` string.

16. Inside the catch block, give the catch block the `err` parameter, then log the string `not hoisted 2 was not able to be changed`.

17. After the try-catch block, push the value 5 onto the array in `notnoisted2`.

18. Log the string `notnoisted2 updated. now is:` and the value of `notnoisted2`.

## Code

`index.js:`

```
var hoisted = 'this got hoisted';
try{
  console.log(notHoisted1);
} catch(err){}
let notHoisted1 = 5;
try{
  console.log(notHoisted2);
} catch(err){}
const notHoisted2 = [1,2,3];
try{
  notHoisted2 = 'new value';
} catch(err){}
notHoisted2.push(5);
```

Snippet 1.12: Updating the contents of the object

https://bit.ly/2RDEynv

**Outcome**

```
Hoisted before assignment: undefined
Hoisted after assignment: this got hoisted
Not hoisted1 with error: notHoisted1 is not defined
notHoisted1 after assignment 5
Not hoisted2 with error: notHoisted2 is not defined
notHoisted1 after assignment [ 1, 2, 3 ]
Not hoisted 2 was not able to be changed
notHoisted2 updated. Now is: [ 1, 2, 3, 5 ]


Process finished with exit code 0
```

Figure 1.4: Hoisting the variables

You have successfully utilized keywords to declare variables.

In this section, we discussed variable declaration in ES6 and the benefits of using the let and const variable declaration keywords over the var variable declaration keyword. We discussed each keywords variable reassignment properties, variable scoping, and variable hoisting properties. The keywords let and const are both create variables in the block scope where var creates a variable in the function scope. Variables created with var and let can be reassigned at will. However, variables created with const cannot be reassigned. Finally, variables created with the keyword var are hoisted to the top of the scope block in which they were defined. Variables created with let and const are not hoisted.

## Introducing Arrow Functions

**Arrow functions**, or **Fat arrow functions**, are a new way to create functions in ECMAScript 6. Arrow functions simplify function syntax. They are called **fat arrow functions** because they are denoted with the characters =>, which, when put together look like a fat arrow. Arrow functions in JavaScript are frequently used in callback chains, promise chains, array methods, in any situation where unregistered functions would be useful.

The key difference between arrow functions and normal functions in JavaScript is that arrow functions are **anonymous**. Arrow functions are not named and not bound to an identifier. This means that an arrow function is created dynamically and is not given a name like normal functions. Arrow functions can however be assigned to a variable to allow for reuse.

When creating an arrow function, all we need to do is remove the function keyword and place an arrow between the function arguments and function body. Arrow functions are denoted with the following syntax:

```
( arg1, arg2, ...., argn ) => { /* Do function stuff here */ }
```

Snippet 1.13: Arrow function syntax

As you can see from the preceding syntax, arrow functions are a more concise way of writing functions in JavaScript. They can make our code more concise and easier to read.

Arrow function syntax can also vary, depending on several factors. Syntax can vary slightly depending on the number of arguments passed in to the function, and the number of lines of code in the function body. The special syntax conditions are outlined briefly in the following list:

- Single input argument
- No input arguments
- Single line function body
- Single expression broken over multiple lines
- Object literal return value

## Exercise 3: Converting Arrow Functions

To demonstrate the simplified syntax by converting a standard function into an arrow function, perform the following steps:

1. Create a function that takes in parameters and returns the sum of the two parameters. Save the function into a variable called fn1.

2. Convert the function you just created to an arrow function and save into another variable called fn2.

   To convert the function, remove the function keyword. Next, place an arrow between the function arguments and the function body.

3. Call both functions and compare the output.

## Code

index.js:

```
const fn1 = function( a, b ) { return a + b; };
const fn2 = ( a, b ) => { return a + b; };
```

```
console.log( fn1( 3 ,5 ), fn2( 3, 5 ) );
```

**Snippet 1.14: Calling the functions**

```
https://bit.ly/2m6UKWN
```

## Outcome

**Figure 1.5: Comparing the function's output**

You have successfully converted normal functions into arrow functions.

## Arrow Function Syntax

If there are multiple arguments being passed in to the function, then we create the function with the parentheses around the arguments as normal. If we only have a single argument to pass to the function, we do not need to include the parentheses around the argument.

There is one exception to this rule, and that is if the parameter is anything other than a simple identifier. If we include a default value or perform operations in the function arguments, then we must include the parentheses. For example, if we include a default parameter, then we will need the parentheses around the arguments. These two rules are shown in the following code:

```
// Single argument arrow function
arg1 => { /* Do function stuff here */ }


// Non simple identifier function argument
( arg1 = 10 ) => { /* Do function stuff here */ }
```

**Snippet 1.15: Single argument arrow function**

If we create an arrow function with no arguments, then we need to include the parentheses, but they will be empty. This is shown in the following code:

```
// No arguments passed into the function
( ) => { /* Do function stuff here */ }
```

**Snippet 1.16: No argument**

Arrow functions can also have varied syntax, depending on the body of the function. As expected, if the body of the function is multiline, then we must surround it with curly braces. However, if the body of the function is a single line, then we do not need to include the curly braces around the body of the function. This is shown in the following code:

```
// Multiple line body arrow function
( arg1, arg2 ) => {
  console.log( `This is arg1: ${arg1}` );
  console.log( `This is arg2: ${arg2}` );
  /* Many more lines of code can go here */
}


// Single line body arrow function
( arg1, arg2 ) => console.log( `This is arg1: ${arg1}` )
```

**Snippet 1.17: Single line body**

When using arrow functions, we may also exclude the return keyword if the function is a single line. The arrow function automatically returns the resolved value of the expression on that line. This syntax is shown in the following code:

```
// With return keyword - not necessary
( num1, num2 ) => { return ( num1 + num2 ) }
// If called with arguments num1 = 5 and num2 = 5, expected output is 10


// Without return keyword or braces
( num1, num2 ) => num1 + num2
// If called with arguments num1 = 5 and num2 = 5, expected output is 10
```

**Snippet 1.18: Single line body when value is returned**

Since arrow functions with single expression bodies can be defined without the curly braces, we need special syntax to allow us to split the single expression over multiple lines. To do this, we can wrap the multi-line expression in parentheses. The JavaScript interpreter sees that the line are wrapped in parentheses and treats it as if it were a single line of code. This is shown in the following code:

```
// Arrow function with a single line body

// Assume numArray is an array of numbers

( numArray ) => numArray.filter( n => n > 5).map( n => n - 1 ).every( n => n
< 10 )


// Arrow function with a single line body broken into multiple lines

// Assume numArray is an array of numbers

( numArray ) => (
   numArray.filter( n => n > 5)
           .map( n => n - 1 )
           .every( n => n < 10 )
)
```

Snippet 1.19: Single line expression broken into multiple lines

If we have a single line arrow function returning an object literal, we will need special syntax. In ES6, scope blocks, function bodies, and object literals are all defined with curly braces. Since single line arrow functions do not need curly braces, we must use the special syntax to prevent the object literal's curly braces from being interpreted as either function body curly braces or scope block curly braces. To do this, we surround the returned object literal with parentheses. This instructs the JavaScript engine to interpret curly braces inside the parentheses as an expression instead of a function body or scope block declaration. This is shown in the following code:

```
// Arrow function with an object literal in the body

( num1, num2 ) => ( { prop1: num1, prop2: num2 } ) // Returns an object
```

Snippet 1.20: Object literal return value

When using arrow functions, we must be careful of the scope that these functions are called in. Arrow functions follow normal scoping rules in JavaScript, with the exception of the `this` scope. Recall that in basic JavaScript, each function is assigned a scope, that is, the `this` scope. Arrow functions are not assigned a `this` scope. They inherit their parent's `this` scope and cannot have a new `this` scope bound to them. This means that, as expected, arrow functions have access to the scope of the parent function, and subsequently, the variables in that scope, but the scope of `this` cannot be changed in an arrow function. Using the `.apply()`, `.call()`, or `.bind()` function modifiers will NOT change the scope of an arrow function's `this` property. If you are in a situation where you must bind `this` to another scope, then you must use a normal JavaScript function.

In summary, arrow functions provide us with a way to simplify the syntax of anonymous functions. To write an arrow function, simply omit the function keyword and add an arrow between the arguments and function body.

Special syntax can then be applied to the function arguments and body to simplify the arrow function even more. If the function has a single input argument, then we can omit the parentheses around it. If the function body has a single line, we can omit the `return` keyword and the curly braces around it. However, single-line functions that return an object literal must be surrounded with parentheses.

We can also use parentheses around the function body to break a single line body into multiple lines for readability.

## Exercise 4: Upgrading Arrow Functions

To utilize the ES6 arrow function syntax to write functions, perform the following steps:

1.  Refer to the `exercises/exercise4/exercise.js` file and perform the updates in this file.

2.  Convert `fn4` with basic ES6 syntax.

    Remove the function keyword before the function arguments. Add an arrow between the function arguments and function body.

3.  Convert `fn2` with single statement function body syntax.

    Remove the function keyword before the function arguments. Add an arrow between the function arguments and function body.

    Remove the curly braces (`{}`) around the function body. Remove the return keyword.

4.  Convert `fn3` with Single input argument syntax.

Remove the function keyword before the function arguments. Add an arrow between the function arguments and function body.

Remove the parentheses around the function input argument.

5. Convert fn4 with no input argument syntax.

Remove the function keyword before the function arguments. Add an arrow between the function arguments and function body.

6. Convert fn5 with object literal syntax.

Remove the function keyword before the function arguments. Add an arrow between the function arguments and function body.

Remove the curly braces ({}) around the function body. Remove the return keyword.

Surround the returned object with parentheses.

**Code**

index.js:

```
let fn1 = ( a, b ) => { ... };
let fn2 = ( a, b ) => a * b;
let fn3 = a => { ... };
let fn4 = () => { ... };
let fn5 = ( a ) => ( ... );
```

**Snippet 1.21: Arrow function conversion**

https://bit.ly/2m6qSfg

**Outcome**

**Figure 1.6: Converting the function's output**

You have successfully utilized the ES6 arrow function syntax to write functions.

In this section, we introduced arrow functions and demonstrated how they can be used to greatly simplify function declaration in JavaScript. First, we covered the basic syntax for arrow functions: `( arg1, arg2, argn ) => { /* function body */ }`. We proceeded to cover the five special syntax cases for advanced arrow functions, as outlined in the following list:

- Single input argument: `arg1 => { /* function body */ }`

- No input arguments: `( ) => { /* function body */ }`

- Single line function body: `( arg1, arg2, argn ) => /* single line */`

- Single expression broken over multiple lines: `( arg1, arg2, argn ) => ( /* multi line single expression */ )`

- Object literal return value: `( arg1, arg2, argn ) => ( { /* object literal */ } )`

## Learning Template Literals

**Template literals** are a new form of string that was introduced in ECMAScript 6. They are enclosed by the **backtick** symbol (`` ` ``) instead of the usual single or double quotes. Template literals allow you to embed expressions in the string that are evaluated at runtime. Thus, we can easily create dynamic strings from variables and variable expressions. These expressions are denoted with the dollar sign and curly braces (`${ expression }`). The template literal syntax is shown in the following code:

```
const example = "pretty";
console.log( `Template literals are ${ example } useful!!!` );
// Expected output: Template literals are pretty useful!!!
```

Snippet 1.22: Template literal basic syntax

Template literals are escaped like other strings in JavaScript. To escape a template literal, simply use a backslash (\) character. For example, the following equalities evaluate to true: `` `\`` `` `=== "`", `\t` === "\t"`, and `` `\n\r` `` `=== "\n\r"`.

Template literals allow for multiline strings. Any newline characters that are inserted into the source are part of the template literal and will result in a line break in the output. In simpler terms, inside a template literal, we can press the **Enter** key on the keyboard and split it on to two lines. This newline character in the source code will be parsed as part of the template literal and will result in a newline in the output. To replicate this with normal strings, we would have to use the \n character to generate a new line. With template literals, we can break the line in the template literal source and achieve the same expected output. An example of this is shown in the following code:

```
// Using normal strings
console.log( 'This is line 1\nThis is line 2' );
// Expected output: This is line 1
// This is line 2


// Using template literals
console.log( `This is line 1
This is line 2` );
// Expected output: This is line 1
// This is line 2
```

Snippet 1.23: Template literal multi-line syntax

## Exercise 5: Converting to Template Literals

To convert standard string objects to template literals to demonstrate the power of template literal expressions, perform the following steps:

1. Create two variables, a and b, and save numbers into them.

2. Log the sum of a and b in the format a + b is equal to <result> using normal strings.

3. Log the sum of a and b in the format a + b is equal to <result> using a single template literal.

## Code

index.js:

```
let a = 5, b = 10;
console.log( a + ' ' + ' ' + b + ' is equal to' ' + ( a + b ) );
console.log( `${a} + ${b} is equal to ${a + b}` );
```

Snippet 1.24: Template literal and string comparison

https://bit.ly/2RD5jbC

## Outcome

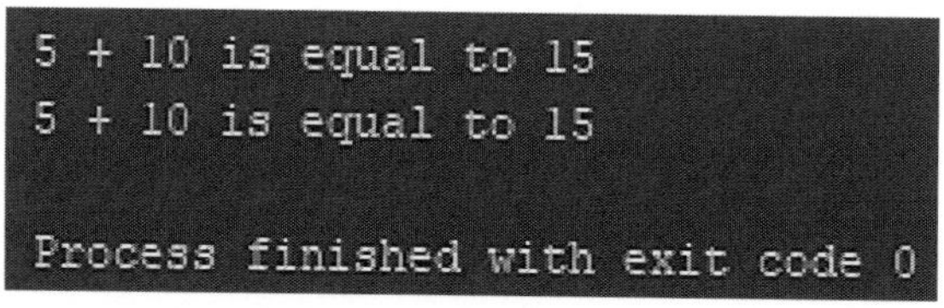

```
5 + 10 is equal to 15
5 + 10 is equal to 15

Process finished with exit code 0
```

Figure 1.7: Logging the sum of the variable's output

You have successfully converted standard string objects to template literals.

Template literals allow for expression nesting, that is, new template literals can be put inside the expression of a template literal. Since the nested template literal is part of the expression, it will be parsed as a new template literal and will not interfere with the external template literal. In some cases, nesting a template literal is the easiest and most readable way to create a string. An example of template literal nesting is shown in the following code:

```
function javascriptOrCPlusPlus() { return 'JavaScript'; }

const outputLiteral = `We are learning about ${ `Professional ${
javascriptOrCPlusPlus() }` }`
```

Snippet 1.25: Template literal nesting

A more advanced form of template literals are **tagged template literals**. Tagged template literals can be parsed with a special function called **tag functions**, and can return a manipulated string or any other value. The first input argument of a tag function is an array containing string values. The string values represent the parts of the input string, broken at each template expression. The remaining arguments are the values of the template expressions in the string. Tag functions are not called like normal functions. To call a tag function, we omit the parentheses and any whitespace around the template literal argument. This syntax is shown in the following code:

```
// Define the tag function
function tagFunction( strings, numExp, fruitExp ) {
    const str0 = strings[0]; // "We have"
    const str1 = strings[1]; // " of "
    const quantity = numExp < 10 ? 'very few' : 'a lot';
    return str0 + quantity + str1 + fruitExp + str2;
}
const fruit = 'apple', num = 8;
// Note: lack of parenthesis or whitespace when calling tag function
const output = tagFunction`We have +{num} of +{fruit}. Exciting!`
console.log( output )
// Expected output: We have very few of apples. Exciting!!
```

Snippet 1.26: Tagged template literal example

A special property named `raw` is available for the first argument of a tagged template. This property returns an array that contains the raw, unescaped, versions of each part of the split template literal. This is shown in the following code:

```
function tagFunction( strings ){ console.log( strings.raw[0] ); }
tagFunction`This is line 1. \n This is line 2.`
// Expected output: "This is line 1. \n This is line 2." The characters
//'\' and 'n' are not parsed into a newline character
```

Snippet 1.27: Tagged template raw property

In summary, template literals allow for the simplification of complicated string expressions. Template literals allow you to embed variables and complicated expressions into strings. Template literals can even be nested into the expression fields of other template literals. If a template literal is broken into multiple lines in the source code, the interpreter will interpret that as a new line in the string and insert one accordingly. Template literals also provide a new way to parse and manipulate strings with the tagged template function. These functions give you a way to perform complex string manipulation via a special function. The tagged template functions also give access to the raw strings as they were entered, ignoring any escape sequences.

## Exercise 6: Template Literal Conversion

You are building a website for a real estate company. You must build a function that takes in an object with property information and returns a formatted string that states the property owner, where the property is located (address), and how much they are selling it for (price). Consider the following object as input:

```
{
    address: '123 Main St. San Francisco CA. USA',
    floors: 2,
    price: 5000000,
    owner: 'John Doe'
}
```

Snippet 1.28: Object Input

To utilize a template literal to pretty-print an object, perform the following steps:

1.  Create a function called parseHouse that takes in an object.

2.  Return a template literal from the function. Using expressions, embed the owner, address, and price in the format <owner> is selling the property at <address> for <price>.

3.  Create a variable called house and save the following object into it: { address: "123 Main St. San Francisco CA. USA", floors: 2, price: 5000000, owner: "John Doe" }

4.  Call the parseHouse function and pass in the house variable.

5.  Log the output.

## Code

index.js:

```
function parseHouse( property ) {
  return `${property.owner} is selling the property at ${property.address}
for ${property.price} USD`
}
const house = {
  address: "123 Main St, San Francisco CA, USA",

  floors: 2,

  price: 5000000,

  owner: "John Doe"

};
console.log( parseHouse( house ) );
```

**Snippet 1.29: Template literal using expressions**

https://bit.ly/2RLlkkn

## Outcome

```
John Doe is selling the property at 123 Main St, San Francisco CA, USA for 5000000 USD

Process finished with exit code 0
```

**Figure 1.8: Template literal output**

You have successfully utilized a template literal to pretty-print an object.

In this section, we covered template literals. Template literals upgrade strings by allowing us to nest expressions inside them that are parsed at runtime. Expressions are inserted with the following syntax: `${ expression }`. We then showed you how to escape special characters in template literals and discussed how in-editor newline characters in template literals are parsed as newline characters in the output. Finally, we covered template literal tagging and tagging functions, which allow us to perform more complex template literal parsing and creation.

# Enhanced Object Properties

ECMAScript 6 added several enhancements to object literals as part of the **ES6 syntactic sugar**. ES6 added three ways to simplify the creation of object literals. These simplifications include a more concise syntax for initializing object properties from variables, a more concise syntax for defining function methods, and computed object property names.

> **Note**
>
> Syntactic sugar is a syntax that is designed to make expressions easier to read and express. It makes the syntax "sweeter" because code can be expressed concisely.

## Object Properties

The shorthand for initializing object properties allows you to make more concise objects. In ES5, we needed to define the object properties with a key name and a value, as shown in the following code:

```
function getPersionES5( name, age, height ) {

  return {

    name: name,

    age: age,

    height: height

  };

}
getPersionES5( 'Zachary', 23, 195 )
// Expected output: { name: 'Zachary', age: 23, height: 195 }
```

Snippet 1.30: ES5 object properties

Notice the repetition in the object literal returned by the function. We name the property in the object after variable name causing duplication (<code>name: name</code>). In ES6, we can shorthand each property and remove the repetition. In ES6, we can simply state the variable in the object literal declaration and it will create a property with a key that matches the variable name and a value that matches the variable value. This is shown in the following code:

```
function getPersionES6( name, age, height ) {

  return {
```

```
    name,

    age,

    height

  };

}

getPersionES6( 'Zachary', 23, 195 )

// Expected output: { name: 'Zachary', age: 23, height: 195 }
```

Snippet 1.31: ES6 object properties

As you can see, both the ES5 and ES6 examples output the exact same object. However, in a large object literal declaration, we can save a lot of space and repetition by using this new shorthand.

## Function Declarations

ES6 also added a shorthand for declaring function methods inside objects. In ES5, we had to state the property name, then define it as a function. This is shown in the following example:

```
function getPersonES5( name, age, height ) {

  return {

    name: name,

    height: height,


    getAge: function(){ return age; }

  };

}

getPersonES5( 'Zachary', 23, 195 ).getAge()

// Expected output: 23
```

Snippet 1.32: ES5 function properties

In ES6, we can define a function but with much less work. As with the property declaration, we don't need a key and value pair to create the function. The function name becomes the key name. This is shown in the following code:

```
function getPersionES6( name, age, height ) {
  return {
    name,
    height,

    getAge(){ return age; }
  };
}
getPersionES6( 'Zachary', 23, 195 ).getAge()
// Expected output: 23
```

Snippet 1.33: ES6 function properties

Notice the difference in the function declaration. We omit the function keyword and the colon after the property key name. Once again, this saves us a bit of space and simplifies things a little.

## Computed Properties

ES6 also added a new, efficient way to create property names from variables. This is through computed property notation. As we already know, in ES5, there is only one way to create a dynamic property whose name is specified by a variable; this is through bracket notation, that is, : `obj[ expression ] = 'value'` . In ES6, we can use this same type of notation during the object literal's declaration. This is shown in the following example:

```
const varName = 'firstName';
const person = {
  [ varName ] = 'John',
  lastName: 'Smith'
};
console.log( person.firstName ); // Expected output: John
```

Snippet 1.34: ES6 Computed property

As we can see from the preceding snippet, the property name of varName was computed to be firstName. When accessing the property, we simply reference it as person.firstName. When creating computed properties in object literals, the value that's computed in the brackets does not need to be a variable; it can be almost any expression, even a function. An example of this is shown in the following code:

```
const varName = 'first';

function computeNameType( type ) {

    return type + 'Name';

}


const person = {

    [ varName + 'Name' ] = 'John',

    [ computeNameType( 'last' ) ]: 'Smith'

};


console.log( person.firstName ); // Expected output: John

console.log( person.lastName ); // Expected output: Smith
```

**Snippet 1.35: Computed property from function**

In the example shown in the preceding snippet, we created two variables. The first contains the string first and the second contains a function that returns a string. We then created an object and used computed property notation to create dynamic object key names. The first key name is equal to firstName. When person.firstName is accessed, the value that was saved will be returned. The second key name is equal to lastName. When person.lastName is accessed, the value that was saved will be returned.

In summary, ES6 added three ways to simplify the declaration of object literals, that is, property notation, function notation, and computed properties. To simplify property creation in objects, when properties are created from variables, we can omit the key name and the colon. The name property that's created is set to the variable name and the value is set to the value of the variable. To add a function as a property to an object, we can omit the colon and function keyword. The name of the property that's created is set to the function name and the value of the property is the function itself. Finally, we can create property names from computed expressions during the declaration of the object literal. We simply replace the key name with the expression in brackets. These three simplifications can save us space in our code and make object literal creation easier to read.

## Exercise 7: Implementing Enhanced Object Properties

You are building a simple JavaScript math package to publish to **Node Package Manager (NPM)**. Your module will export an object that contains several constants and functions. Using ES6 syntax, create the export object with the following functions and values: the value of pi, the ratio to convert inches to feet, a function that sums two arguments, and a function that subtracts two arguments. Log the object after it has been created.

To create objects using ES6 enhanced object properties and demonstrate the simplified syntax, perform the following steps:

1.  Create an object and save it into the exportObject variable.

2.  Create a variable called PI that contains the value of pi (3.1415).

3.  Create a variable called INCHES_TO_FEET and save the value of the inches to feet conversion ratio (0.083333).

    Using ES6 enhanced property notation, add a property called PI from the variable PI. Add a property called INCHES_TO_FEET from the INCHES_TO_FEET variable, which contains the inches to feet conversion ratio.

    Add a function property called sum that takes in two input arguments and returns the sum of the two input arguments.

    Add a function property called subtract that takes in two input arguments and returns the subtraction of the two input arguments.

4.  Log the object exportObject.

## Code

index.js:

```
const PI = 3.1415;
const INCHES_TO_FEET = 0.083333;
const exportObject = {
 PI,
 INCHES_TO_FEET,
 sum( n1, n2 ) {
   return n1 + n2;
 },
 subtract( n1, n2 ) {
   return n1 - n2;
```

```
    }
  };
  console.log( exportObject );
```

Snippet 1.36: Enhanced object properties

https://bit.ly/2RLdnWk

**Outcome**

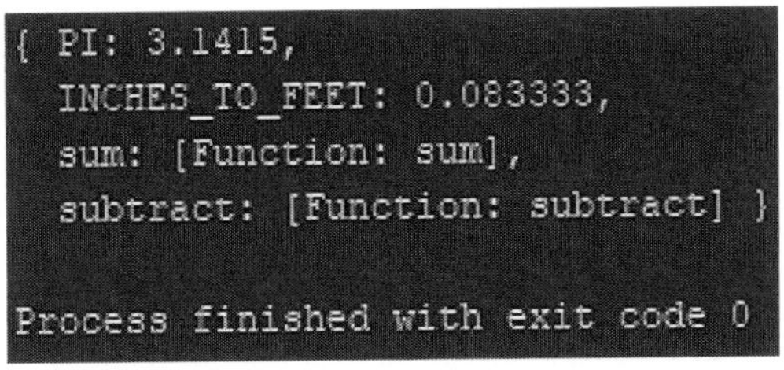

```
{ PI: 3.1415,
  INCHES_TO_FEET: 0.083333,
  sum: [Function: sum],
  subtract: [Function: subtract] }

Process finished with exit code 0
```

Figure 1.9: Enhanced object properties output

You have successfully created objects using ES6 enhanced object properties.

In this section, we showed you enhanced object properties, a syntactic sugar to help condense object property creation into fewer characters. We covered the shorthand for initializing object properties from variables and functions, and we covered the advanced features of computed object properties, that is, a way to create an object property name from a computed value, inline, while defining the object.

# Destructuring Assignment

**Destructuring assignment** is syntax in JavaScript that allows you to unpack values from arrays or properties from objects, and save them into variables. It is a very handy feature because we can extract data directly from arrays and objects to save into variables, all on a single line of code. It is powerful because it enables us to extract multiple array elements or object properties in the same expression.

## Array Destructuring

**Array destructuring** allows us to extract multiple array elements and save them into variables. In ES5, we do this by defining each variable with its array value, one variable at a time. This makes the code lengthy and increases the time required to write it.

In ES6, to destructure an array, we simply create an array containing the variable to assign data into, and set it equal to the data array being destructured. The values in the array are unpacked and assigned to the variables in the left-hand side array from left to right, one variable per array value. An example of basic array destructuring is shown in the following code:

```
let names = [ 'John', 'Michael' ];
let [ name1, name2 ] = names;


console.log( name1 ); // Expected output: 'John'
console.log( name2 ); // Expected output: 'Michael'
```

Snippet 1.37: Basic array destructuring

As can be seen in this example, we have an array of names and we want to destructure it into two variables, name1 and name2. We simply surround the variables name1 and name2 with brackets and set that expression equal to the data array names, and then JavaScript will destructure the names array, saving data into each of the variables.

The data is destructured from the input array into the variables from left to right, in the order of array items. The first index variable will always be assigned the first index array item. This leads to the question, what do we do if we have more array items than variables? If there are more array items than variables, then the remaining array items will be discarded and will not be destructured into variables. The destructuring is a one to one mapping in array order.

What about if there are more variables than array items? If we attempt to destructure an array into an array that contains more variables than the total number of array elements in the data array, some of the variables will be set to undefined. The array is destructured from left to right. Accessing a non-existent element in a JavaScript array results in an undefined value to be returned. This undefined value is saved to the leftover variables in the variable array. An example of this is shown in the following code:

```
let names = [ 'John', 'Michael' ];
let [ name1 ] = names
let [ name2, name3, name4 ] = names;
```

```
console.log( name1 ); // Expected output: 'John'
console.log( name2 ); // Expected output: 'John'
console.log( name3 ); // Expected output: 'Michael'
console.log( name4 ); // Expected output: undefined
```

**Snippet 1.38: Array destructuring with mismatched variable and array items**

> **Note**
>
> We must be careful when destructuring arrays to make sure that we don't unintentionally assume that a variable will contain a value. The value of the variable could be set to undefined if the array is not long enough.

ES6 array destructuring allows for skipping array elements. If we have an array of values and we only care about the first and third values, we can still destructure the array. To ignore a value, simply omit the variable identifier for that array index in the left-hand side of the expression. This syntax can be used to ignore a single item, multiple items, or even all the items in an array. Two examples of this are shown in the following snippet:

```
let names = [ 'John', 'Michael', 'Jessica', 'Susan' ];
let [ name1,, name3 ] = names;
// Note the missing variable name for the second array item
let [ ... ] = names; // Ignores all items in the array

console.log( name1 ); // Expected output: 'John'
console.log( name3 ); // Expected output: 'Jessica'
```

**Snippet 1.39: Array destructuring with skipped values**

Another very useful feature of array destructuring is the ability to set default values for variables that are created with destructuring. When we want to add a default value, we simply need to set the variable equal to the desired default value in the left-hand side of the destructuring expression. If what we are destructuring does not contain an index to assign to the variable, then the default value will be used instead. An example of this is shown in the following code:

```
let [ a = 1, b = 2, c = 3 ] = [ 'cat', null ];
console.log( a ); // Expected output: 'cat'
console.log( b ); // Expected output: null
console.log( c ); // Expected output: 3
```

Snippet 1.40: Array destructuring with skipped values

Finally, array destructuring can be used to easily swap values of variables. If we wish to swap the value of two variables, we can simply destructure an array into the reversed array. We can create an array containing the variables we want to reverse and set it equal to the same array, but with the variable order changed. This will cause the references to be swapped. This is shown in the following code:

```
let a = 10;
let b = 5;
[ a, b ] = [ b, a ];
console.log( a ); // Expected output: 5
console.log( b ); // Expected output: 10
```

Snippet 1.41: Array destructuring with skipped values

## Exercise 8: Array Destructuring

To extract values from an array using array destructuring assignment, perform the following steps:

1. Create an array with three values, 1, 2, and 3, and save it into a variable called data.

2. Destructure the array created with a single expression.

   Destructure the first array value into a variable called a. Skip the second value of the array.

   Destructure the third value into a variable called b. Attempt to destructure a fourth value into a variable called c and provide a default value of 4.

3.  Log the value of all of the variables.

**Code**

index.js:

```
const data = [ 1, 2, 3 ];
const [ a, , b, c = 4 ] = data;
console.log( a, b, c );
```

*Snippet 1.42: Array destructuring*

https://bit.ly/2D2nm5g

**Outcome**

*Figure 1.10: Destructured variable's output*

You have successfully applied an array destructuring assignment to extract values from an array.

In summary, array destructuring allows us to quickly extract values from arrays and save them into variables. Variables are assigned to array values, item by item, from left to right. If the number of variables exceeds the number of array items, then the variables are set to undefined, or the default value if specified. We can skip an array index in the destructuring by leaving a hole in the variables array. Finally, we can use destructuring assignment to quickly swap the values of two or more variables in a single line of code.

## Rest and Spread Operators

ES6 also introduces two new operators for arrays called **rest** and **spread**. The rest and spread operators are both denoted with three ellipses or periods before an identifier ( ...array ). The rest operator is used to represent an infinite number of arguments as an array. The spread operator is used to allow an iterable object to be expanded into multiple arguments. To identify which is being used, we must look at the item that the argument is being applied to. If the operator is applied to an iterable object (array, object, and so on), then it is the spread operator. If the operator is applied to function arguments, then it is the rest operator.

> **Note**
>
> In JavaScript, something considered iterable if something (generally values or key/value pairs) can be stepped through one at a time. For example, an array is iterable because the items in the array can be stepped through one at a time. Objects are considered iterable because the key/value pairs can be stepped through one at a time.

The **rest operator** is used to represent an indefinite number of arguments as an array. When the last parameter of a function is prefixed with the three ellipses, it becomes an array. The array elements are supplied by the actual arguments that are passed into the function, excluding the arguments that already have been given a separate name in the formal declaration of the function. An example of rest destructuring is shown in the following code:

```
function fn( num1, num2, ...args ) {
    // Destructures an indefinite number of function parameters into the
   //array args, excluding the first two arguments passed in.
    console.log( num1 );
    console.log( num2 );
    console.log( args );
}
```

```
fn( 1, 2, 3, 4, 5, 6 );
// Expected output
// 1
// 2
// [ 3, 4, 5, 6 ]
```

**Snippet 1.43: Array destructuring with skipped values**

Similar to the **arguments object** of a JavaScript function, the rest operator contains a list of function arguments. However, the rest operator has three distinct differences from the arguments object. As we already know, the arguments object is an array-like object that contains each argument that's passed into the function. The differences are as follows. First, the rest operator contains only the input parameters that have not been given a separate formal declaration in the function expression.

Second, the arguments object is not an instance of an **Array** object. The rest parameter is an instance of an array, which means that array functions like sort(), map(), and forEach() can be applied to them directly.

Lastly, the arguments object has special functionality that the rest parameter does not have. For example, the caller property exists on the arguments object.

The rest parameter can be destructured similar to how we destructure an array. Instead of putting a single variable name inside before the ellipses, we can replace it with an array of variables we want to fill. The arguments passed into the function will be destructured as expected for an array. This is shown in the following code:

```
function fn( ...[ n1, n2, n3 ] ) {
    // Destructures an indefinite number of function parameters into the
    // array args, which is destructured into 3 variables
    console.log( n1, n2, n3 );
}

fn( 1, 2 ); // Expected output: 1, 2, undefined
```

**Snippet 1.44: Destructured rest operator**

The spread operator allows an iterable object such as an array or string to be expanded into multiple arguments (for function calls), array elements (for array literals), or key-value pairs (for object expressions). This essentially means that we can expand an array into arguments for creating another array, object, or calling a function. An example of spread syntax is shown in the following code:

```
function fn( n1, n2, n3 ) {

  console.log( n1, n2, n3 );

}


const values = [ 1, 2, 3 ];
fn( ...values ); // Expected output: 1, 2, 3
```

Snippet 1.45: Spread operator

In the preceding example, we created a simple function that takes in three inputs and logs them to the console. We created an array with three values, then called the function using the **spread** operator to destructure the array of values into three input parameters for the function.

The rest operator can be used in destructuring objects and arrays. When destructuring an array, if we have more array elements than variables, we can use the rest operator to capture, or catch, all of the additional array elements during destructuring. When using the rest operator, it must be the last parameter in the array destructuring or function arguments list. This is shown in the following code:

```
const [ n1, n2, n3, ...remaining ] = [ 1, 2, 3, 4, 5, 6 ];
console.log( n1 ); // Expected output: 1
console.log( n2 ); // Expected output: 2
console.log( n3 ); // Expected output: 3
console.log( remaining ); // Expected output: [ 4, 5, 6 ]
```

Snippet 1.46: Spread operator

In the preceding snippet, we destructured the first three array elements into three variables, n1, n2, and n3. We then captured the remaining array elements with the rest operator and destructured them into the variable that remained.

In summary, the rest and spread operators allow iterable entities to be expanded into many arguments. They are denoted with three ellipses before the identifier name. This allows us to capture arrays of arguments in functions or unused items when destructuring entities. When we use the rest and spread operators, they must be the last arguments that are passed into the expression they are being used in.

## Object Destructuring

**Object destructuring** is used in a very similar way to array destructuring. Object destructuring is used to extract data from an object and assign the values to new variables. In ES6, we can do this in a single JavaScript expression. To destructure an object, we surround the variables we want to destructure with curly braces ({}), and set that expression equal to the object we are destructuring. A basic example of object destructuring is shown in the following code:

```
const obj = { firstName: 'Bob', lastName: 'Smith' };
const { firstName, lastName } = obj;


console.log( firstName ); // Expected output: 'Bob'
console.log( lastName ); // Expected output: 'Smith'
```

Snippet 1.47: Object destructuring

In the preceding example, we created an object with the keys firstName and lastName. We then destructured this object into the variables firstName and lastName. Notice that the names of the variables and the object parameters match. This is shown in the following example:

> **Note**
>
> When doing basic object destructuring, the name of the parameter in the object and the name of the variable we are assigning it to must match. If there is no matching parameter for a variable we are trying to destructure, then the variable will be set to undefined.

```
const obj = { firstName: 'Bob', lastName: 'Smith' };
const { firstName, middleName } = obj;


console.log( firstName ); // Expected output: 'Bob'
console.log( middleName ); // Expected output: undefined
```

**Snippet 1.48: Object destructuring with no defined key**

As we saw, the middleName key does not exist in the object. When we try to destructure the key and save it into the variable, it is unable to find a value and the variable is set to undefined.

With advanced object destructuring syntax, we can save the key that's extracted into a variable with a different name. This is done by adding a colon and the new variable name after the key name in the destructuring notation. This is shown in the following code:

```
const obj = { firstName: 'Bob', lastName: 'Smith' };
const { firstName: first, lastName } = obj;


console.log( first ); // Expected output: 'Bob'
console.log( lastName ); // Expected output: 'Smith'
```

**Snippet 1.49: Object destructuring into new variable**

In the preceding example, we could clearly see that we are destructuring the firstName key from the object and saving it into the new variable, called first. The lastName key is being destructured normally and is saved into a variable called lastName.

Much like with array destructuring, we can destructure an object and provide a default value. If a default value is provided and the key we are attempting to destructure does not exist in the object, then the variable will be set to the default value instead of undefined. This is shown in the following code:

```
const obj = { firstName: 'Bob', lastName: 'Smith' };
const { firstName = 'Samantha', middleName = 'Chris' } = obj;


console.log( firstName ); // Expected output: 'Bob'
console.log( middleName ); // Expected output: 'Chris'
```

**Snippet 1.50: Object destructuring with default values**

In the preceding example, we set the default values for both of the variables we are trying to destructure from the object. The default value for `firstName` is specified, but the `firstName` key exists in the object. This means that the value stored in the `firstName` key is destructured and the default value is ignored. The `middleName` key does not exist in the object and we have specified a default value to use when destructuring. Instead of using the undefined value of the `firstName` key, the destructuring assignment sets the destructured variable to the default value of `Chris`.

When we are providing a default value and assigning the key to a new variable name, we must put the default value assignment after the new variable name. This is shown in the following example:

```
const obj = { firstName: 'Bob', lastName: 'Smith' };

const { firstName: first = 'Samantha', middleName: middle = 'Chris' } = obj;


console.log( first ); // Expected output: 'Bob'

console.log( middle); // Expected output: 'Chris'
```

Snippet 1.51: Object destructuring into new variables with default values

The `firstName` key exists. The value of `obj.firstName` is saved into the new variable named `first`. The `middleName` key does not exist. This means that the new variable middle is created and set to the default value of `Chris`.

## Exercise 9: Object Destructuring

To extract data from an object by using object destructuring concepts, perform the following steps:

1. Create an object with the fields `f1`, `f2`, and `f3`. Set the values to `v1`, `v2`, and `v3`, respectively. Save the object into the `data` variable.

2. Destructure this object into variables with a single statement, as follows:

   Destructure the `f1` property into a variable named `f1`. Destructure the `f2` property into a variable named `field2`. Destructure the property `f4` into a variable named `f4` and provide a default value of `v4`.

3. Log the variables that are created.

## Code

index.js:

```
const data = { f1: 'v1', f2: '2', f3: 'v3' };
const { f1, f2: field2, f4 = 'v4' } = data;
console.log( f1, field2, f4 );
```

Snippet 1.52: Object destructuring

https://bit.ly/2SJuba9

## Outcome

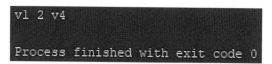

Figure 1.11: Created variable's output

You have successfully applied object destructuring concepts to extract data from an object.

JavaScript requires special syntax if we declare the variables before the object destructuring expression. We must surround the entire object destructuring expression with parentheses. This syntax is not required for array destructuring. This is shown in the following code:

```
const obj = { firstName: 'Bob', lastName: 'Smith' };
let firstName, lastName;


( { firstName: first, lastName } = obj );
// Note parentheses around expression
```

```
console.log( firstName ); // Expected output: 'Bob'
console.log( lastName ); // Expected output: 'Smith'
```

Snippet 1.53: Object destructuring into predefined variables

> **Note**
>
> Make sure that object destructuring done in this way is preceded by a semicolon on the same or previous line. This prevents the JavaScript interpreter from interpreting the parentheses as a function call.

The **rest operator** can also be used to destructure objects. Since object keys are iterable, we can use the rest operator to catch the remaining keys that were uncaught in the original destructuring expression. This is done similar to arrays. We destructure the keys that we want to capture, and then we can add the rest operator to a variable and catch the remaining key/value pairs that have not been destructured out of the object. This is shown in the following example:

```
const obj = { firstName: 'Bob', middleName: 'Chris', lastName: 'Smith' };
const { firstName, ...otherNames } = obj;
console.log( firstName ); // Expected output: 'Bob'
console.log( otherNames );
// Expected output: { middleName: 'Chris', lastName: 'Smith' }
```

Snippet 1.54: Object destructuring with the rest operator

In summary, object destructuring allows us to quickly extract values from objects and save them into variables. The key name must match the variable name in simple object destructuring, however we can use more advanced syntax to save the key's value into a new object. If a key is not defined in the object, then the variable will be set to `false`, that is, unless we provide it with a default value. We can save this into predefined variables, but we must surround the destructuring expression with parentheses. Finally, the rest operator can be used to capture the remaining key value pairs and save them in a new object.

Object and array destructuring support nesting. Nesting destructuring can be a little confusing, but it is a powerful tool because it allows us to condense several lines of destructuring code into a single line.

## Exercise 10: Nested Destructuring

To destructure values from an array that's nested inside an object using the concept of nested destructuring, perform the following steps:

1.  Create an object with a property, `arr`, that is, set to an array containing the values 1, 2, and 3. Save the object into the `data` variable.

2.  Destructure the second value of the array into a variable by doing the following:

    Destructure the `arr` property from the object and save it into a new variable called v2, which is the array. Replace v2 with array destructuring.

    In the array destructuring, skip the first element. Save the second element into a variable called v2.

3.  Log the variable.

### Code

`index.js`:

```
const data = { arr: [ 1, 2, 3 ] };
const { arr: [ , v2 ] } = data;
console.log( v2 );
```

Snippet 1.55: Nested array and object destructuring

https://bit.ly/2SJuba9

### Outcome

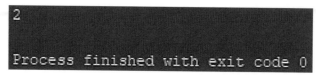

Figure 1.12: Nested destructuring output

You have successfully destructured values from an array inside an object.

In summary, object and array destructuring was introduced into ES6 to cut down code and allow for the quick creation of variables from objects and arrays. Array destructuring is denoted by setting an array of variables equal to an array of items. Object destructuring is denoted by setting an object of variables equal to an object of key value pairs. Destructuring statements can be nested for even greater effect.

## Exercise 11: Implementing Destructuring

You have registered for university courses and need to buy the texts required for the classes. You are building a program to scrape data from the book list and obtain the ISBN numbers for each text book that's required. Use object and array nested destructuring to obtain the ISBN value of the first text of the first book in the courses array. The courses array follows the following format:

```
[
  {
    title: 'Linear Algebra II',
    description: 'Advanced linear algebra.',
    texts: [ {
      author: 'James Smith',
      price: 120,
      ISBN: '912-6-44-578441-0'
    } ]
  },
  { ... },
  { ... }
]
```

**Snippet 1.56: Course array format**

To obtain data from complicated array and object nesting by using nested destructuring, perform the following steps:

1. Save the provided data structure into the courseCatalogMetadata variable.

2. Destructure the first array element into a variable called course:

```
[ course ] = [ ... ]
```

3. Replace the **course** variable with object destructuring to save the texts field into a variable called **textbooks**:

```
[ { texts: textbooks} ] = [ … ]
```

4. Replace the **textbooks** variable with array destructuring to get the first element of the texts array and save it into the variable called **textbook**:

```
[ { texts: [ textbook ] } ] = [ … ]
```

5. Replace the **textbook** variable with object destructuring to get the ISBN field and save it into the ISBN variable:

```
[ { texts: [ { ISBN } ] } ] = [ … ]
```

6. Log the value of the ISBN.

## Code

index.js:

```
const courseCatalogMetadata = [
  {
    title: 'Linear Algebra II',
    description: 'Advanced linear algebra.',
    texts: [ {
      author: 'James Smith',
      price: 120,
      ISBN: '912-6-44-572441-0'
    } ]
  }
];
const [ course ] = courseCatalogMetadata;
const [ { texts: textbooks } ] = courseCatalogMetadata;
const [ { texts: [ textbook ] } ] = courseCatalogMetadata;
const [ { texts: [ { ISBN } ] } ] = courseCatalogMetadata;
```

```
console.log( course );
console.log( textbooks );
console.log( textbook );
console.log( ISBN );
```

**Snippet 1.57: Implementing destructuring into code**

ʰttps://ᵇit.ly/2ᵀᴍlgtz

**Outcome**

```
912-6-44-578441-0

Process finished with exit code 0
```

**Figure 1.13: Array destructuring output**

You have successfully obtained data from arrays and objects using destructuring and nested destructuring.

In this section, we discussed destructuring assignment for arrays and objects. We demonstrated how array and object destructuring simplifies code and allows us to quickly extract values from objects and arrays. Destructuring assignment allows us to unpack values from objects and arrays, provide default values, and rename object properties as variables when destructuring. We also introduced two new operators– the rest and spread operators. The rest operator was used to represent an indefinite number of arguments as an array. The spread operator was used to break an iterable object into multiple arguments.

## Classes and Modules

Classes and Modules were added to ES6. Classes were introduced as a way to expand on prototype-based inheritance by adding some object oriented concepts. Modules were introduced as a way to organize multiple code files in JavaScript and expand on code reusability and scoping among files.

## Classes

**Classes** were added to ECMAScript 6 primarily as syntactic sugar to expand on the existing prototype-based inheritance structure. Class syntax does not introduce object oriented inheritance to JavaScript. Class inheritance in JavaScript do not work like classes in object oriented languages.

In JavaScript, a class can be defined with the keyword class. A class is created by calling the keyword class, followed by the class name and curly braces. Inside the curly braces, we define all of the functions and logic for the class. The syntax is as follows:

```
class name { /* class stuff goes here */ }
```

Snippet 1.58: Class syntax

A class can be created with the **optional function constructor**. The constructor, if not necessary for a JavaScript class, but there can only be one method with the name constructor in a class. The constructor is called when an instance of the class in initialized and can be used to set up all of the default internal values. An example of a class declaration is shown in the following code:

```
class House{
    constructor(address, floors = 1, garage = false) {
        this.address = address;
        this.floors = floors;
        this.garage = garage;
    }
}
```

Snippet 1.59: Basic class creation

In the example, we create a class called House. Our House class has a constructor method. When we instantiate the class, it calls the constructor. Our constructor method takes in three parameters, two of them with default values. The constructor saves these values to variables in the this scope.

The keyword this is mapped to each class instantiation. It is a global scope class object. It is used to scope all functions and variables globally inside a class. Every function that is added at the root of the class will be added to the this scope. All the variables that is added to the this scope will be accessible inside any function inside the class. Additionally, anything added to the this scope is accessible publicly outside of the class.

## Exercise 12: Creating Your Own Class

To create a simple class and demonstrate internal class variables, perform the following steps:

1. Declare a class called vehicle.

2. Add a constructor function to the class. Have the constructor take in two variables, wheels and **topSpeed**.

3. In the constructor, save the input variables to two variables in the this scope, that is, this.wheels and this.topSpeed.

4. Instantiate the class with wheels = 3 and **topSpeed** = 20 and save it into the tricycle variable.

5. Log the value for wheels and **topSpeed** from the class that was saved in tricycle.

### Code

index.js:

```
class Vehicle {
    constructor( wheels, topSpeed ) {
        this.wheels = wheels;
        this.topSpeed = topSpeed;
    }
}
const tricycle = new Vehicle( 3, 20 );
console.log( tricycle.wheels, tricycle.topSpeed );
```

**Snippet 1.60: Creating a class**

https://bit.ly/2Frpl8x

### Outcome

```
3 20

Process finished with exit code 0
```

**Figure 1.14: Creating classes output**

You have successfully created a simple class with values.

We instantiated a new instance of a class with the new keyword. To create a new class, simply declare a variable and set it equal to the expression new className(). When we instantiate a new class, the parameters that are passed into the class call are passed into the constructor function, if one exists. An example of a class instantiation is shown in the following code:

```
class House{
    constructor(address, floors = 1) {
        this.address = address;
        this.floors = floors;
    }
}
// Instantiate the class
let myHouse = new House( '1100 Fake St., San Francisco CA, USA', 2, false );
```

Snippet 1.61: Class instantiation

In this example, the class instantiation happens on the line with the new keyword. This line of code creates a new instance of the House class and saves it into the myHouse variable. When we instantiate the class, we are providing the parameters for address, floors, and garage. These value are passed into the constructor and then saved into the instantiated class object.

To add functions to a class, we declare them with the new ES6 object function declaration. As a quick reminder, when using the new ES6 object function declaration, we can omit the function keyword and object key name. When a function is added to an object, it is automatically attached to the this scope. Additionally, all functions that are added to the class have access to the this scope and will be able to call any function and access any variable attached to the this scope. An example of this is shown in the following code:

```
class House{
    constructor( address, floors = 1) {
        this.address = address;
        this.floors = floors;
    }
    getFloors() {
        return this.floors;
```

```
    }
  }
  let myHouse = new House( '1100 Fake St., San Francisco CA, USA', 2 );
  console.log( myHouse.getFloors() ); // Expected output: 2
```

**Snippet 1.62: Creating a class with functions**

As we can see from this example, the two functions getFloors and setFloors were added with the new ES6 enhanced object property syntax for function declarations. Both functions have access to the this scope. They can get and set variables in that scope, as well as call functions that have been attached to the this scope.

In ES6, we can also create subclasses using the extends keyword. **Subclasses** inherit properties and methods from the parent class. A subclass is defined by following the class name with the keyword extends and the name of the parent class. An example of a subclass declaration is shown in the following code:

```
class House {}
class Mansion extends House {}
```

**Snippet 1.63: Extending a class**

## Classes – Subclasses

In this example, we will create a class called House, and then we will create a subclass called Mansion that extends the class House. When we create a subclass, we need to take note of the behavior of the constructor method. If we provide a constructor method, then we must call the super() function. super is a function that calls the constructor of the parent object. If we try to access the this scope without a call to call super, then we will get a runtime error and our code will crash. Any parameters that are required by the parent constructor can be passed in through the super method. If we do not specify a constructor for the subclass, the default constructor behavior will automatically call the super constructor. An example of this is shown in the following code:

```
class House {
  constructor( address = 'somewhere' ) {
    this.address = address;
  }
}
class Mansion extends House {
  constructor( address, floors ) {
    super( address );
```

```
    this.floors = floors;
  }
}
let mansion = new Mansion( 'Hollywood CA, USA', 6, 'Brad Pitt' );
console.log( mansion.floors ); // Expected output: 6
```

**Snippet 1.64: Extending a class with and without a constructor**

In this example, we created a subclass that extended our `house` class. The `Mansion` subclass has a defined constructor, so we must call super before we can access the `this` scope. When we call `super`, we pass the address parameter to the parent constructor, which adds it to the `this` scope. The constructor for `Mansion` then continues execution and adds the floors variable to the `this` scope. As we can see from the output logging at the end of this example, the subclass's `this` scope also includes all variables and functions that were created in the parent class. If a variable or function is redefined in the subclass, it will overwrite the inherited value or function from the parent class.

In summary, classes allow us to expand on the prototype-based inheritance of JavaScript by introducing some object oriented concepts. Classes are defined with the keyword `class` and initialized with the keyword `new`. When a class is defined, a special scope called `this` is created for it. All items in the `this` scope are publicly accessible outside the class. We can add functions and variables to the `this` scope to give our class functionality. When a class is instantiated, the constructor is called. We can also extend classes to create subclasses with the `extends` keyword. If an extended class has a constructor, we must call the super function to call its parent-class constructor. Subclasses have access to the parent class methods and variables.

## Modules

Almost every coding language has a concept of modules. **Modules** are features that allow the programmer to break code into smaller independent parts that can be imported and reused. Modules are critical for the design of programs and are used to prevent code duplication and reduce file size. Modules did not exist in vanilla JavaScript until ES6. Moreover, not all JavaScript interpreters support this feature.

Modules are a way to reference other code files from the current file. Code can be broken into multiple parts, called **modules**. Modules allow us to keep unrelated code separate so that we can have smaller and simpler files in our large JavaScript projects.

Modules also allow the contained code to be quickly and easily shared without any code duplication. Modules in ES6 introduced two new keywords, export and import. These keywords allow us to make certain classes and variables publicly available when a file is loaded.

> **Note**
>
> JavaScript modules do not have full support across all platforms. At the time of writing this book, not all JavaScript frameworks could support modules. Make sure that the platforms you are releasing your code on can support the code you have written.

## Export Keyword

Modules use the export keyword to expose variables and functions contained in the file. Everything inside an ES6 module is private by default. The only way to make anything public is to use the export keyword. Modules can export properties in two ways, via **named exports** or **default exports**. Named exports allow for multiple exports per module. Multiple exports may be useful if you are building a math module that exports many functions and constants. Default exports allow for just a single export per model. A single export may be useful if you are building a module that contains a single class.

There are two ways to expose the named contents of a module with the export keyword. We can export each item individually by preceding the variable or function declaration with the export keyword, or we can export an object containing the key value pairs that reference each variable and function we want exported. These two export methods are shown in the following example:

```
// math-module-1.js
export const PI = 3.1415;
export const DEGREES_IN_CIRCLE = 360;
export function convertDegToRad( degrees ) {
    return degrees * PI / ( DEGREES_IN_CIRCLE /2 );
}


// math-module-2.js
const PI = 3.1415;
const DEGREES_IN_CIRCLE = 360;
function convertDegToRad( degrees ) {
```

```
    return degrees * PI / ( DEGREES_IN_CIRCLE /2 );
}
export { PI, DEGREES_IN_CIRCLE, convertDegToRad };
```

**Snippet 1.65: Named Exports**

Both of the modules outlined in the preceding example export three constant variables and one function. The first module, `math-module-1.js`, exports each item, one at a time. The second module, `math-module-2.js`, exports all of the exports at once via an object.

To export the contents of a module as a default export, we must use the **default keyword**. The `default` keyword comes after the `export` keyword. When we default export a module, we can also omit the identifier name of the class, function, or variable we are exporting. An example of this is shown in the following code:

```
// HouseClass.js
export default class() { /* Class body goes here */ }
```

```
// myFunction.js
export default function() { /* Function body goes here */ }
```

**Snippet 1.66: Default exports**

In the preceding example, we created two modules. One exports a class and the other exports a function. Notice how we include the `default` keyword after the `export` keyword, and how we omit the name of the class/function. When we export a default class, the `export` is not named. When we are importing default export modules, the name of the object we are importing is derived via the module's name. This will be shown in the next section, where we will talk about the `import` keyword.

## Import Keyword

The `import` keyword allows you to import a JavaScript module. Importing a module allows you to pull any items from that module into the current code file. When we import a module, we start the expression with the `import` keyword. Then, we identify what parts of the module we are going to import. Then, we follow that with the `from` keyword, and finally we finish with the path to the module file. The `from` keyword and file path tell the interpreter where to find the module we are importing.

> **Note**
>
> ES6 modules may not have full support from all browsers versions or versions of Node.js. You may have to make use of a transpiler such as Babel to run your code on certain platforms.

There are four ways we can use the `import` keyword, all of which are shown in the following code:

```
// math-module.js
export const PI = 3.1415;
export const DEGREES_IN_CIRCLE = 360;
// index1.js
import { PI } from 'math-module.js'
// index2.js
import { PI, DEGREES_IN_CIRCLE } from 'math-module.js'
// index3.js
import { PI as pi, DEGREES_IN_CIRCLE as degInCircle } from 'math-module.js'
// index4.js
import * as MathModule from 'math-module.js'
```

**Snippet 1.67: Different ways to import a module**

In the code shown in preceding snippet, we have created a simple module that exports a few constants and four import example files. In the first `import` example, we are importing a single value from the module exports and making it accessible in the variable API. In the second `import` example, we are importing multiple properties from the module. In the third example, we are importing properties and renaming them to new variable names. The properties can then be accessed from the new variables. In the fourth example, we are using a slightly different syntax. The asterisk signifies that we want to import all exported properties from the module. When we use the asterisk, we must also use the **as** keyword to give the imported object a variable name.

The process of importing and using modules is better explained through the following snippet:

```
// email-callback-api.js
export function authenticate( ... ){ ... }
export function sendEmail( ... ){ ... }
export function listEmails( ... ){ ... }


// app.js
import * as EmailAPI from 'email-callback-api.js';
const credentials = { password: '****', user: 'Zach' };
EmailAPI.authenticate( credentials, () => {
  EmailAPI.send( { to: 'ceo@google.com', subject: 'promotion', body: 'Please promote me' }, () => {} );'
} );
```

Snippet 1.68: Importing a module

To use an import in the browser, we must use the **script** tag. The module import can be done inline or via a source file. To import a module, we need to create a **script** tag and set the type property to **module**. If we are importing via a source file, we must set the **src** property to the file path. This is shown in the following syntax:

```
<script type="module" src="./path/to/module.js"></script>
```

Snippet 1.69: Browser import inline

> **Note**
>
> The script tag is an HTML tag that allows us to run JavaScript code in the browser.

We can also import modules inline. To do this, we must omit the src property and code the import directly in the body of the script tag. This is shown in the following code:

```
<script type="module">
  import * as ModuleExample from './path/to/module.js';
</script>
```

**Snippet 1.70: Browser import in script body**

> **Note**
>
> When importing modules in browsers, browser versions that do not support ES6 modules will not run scripts with type="module".

If the browser does not support ES6 modules, we can provide a fallback option with the nomodule attribute. Module compatible browsers will ignore script tags with the nomodule attribute so that we can use it to provide fallback support. This is shown in the following code:

```
<script type="module" src="es6-module-supported.js"></script>
<script nomodule src="es6-module-NOT-supported.js"></script>
```

**Snippet 1.71: Browser import with compatibility option**

In the preceding example, if the browser supports modules, then the first script tag will be run and the second will not. If the browser does not support modules, then the first script tag will be ignored, and the second will be run.

One final consideration for modules: be careful that any modules you build do not have circular dependencies. Because of the load order of modules, circular dependencies in JavaScript can cause lots of logic errors when ES6 is transpiled to ES5. If there is a circular dependency in your modules, you should restructure your dependency tree so that all dependencies are linear. For example, consider the dependency chain: Module A depends on B, module B depends on C, and module C depends on A. This is a circular module chain because through the dependency chain, A depends on C, which depends on A. The code should be restructured so that the circular dependency chain is broken.

## Exercise 13: Implementing Classes

You have been hired by a car sales company to design their sales website. You must create a vehicle class to store car information. The class must take in the car make, model, year, and color. The car should have a method to change the color. To test the class, create an instance that is a grey (color) 2005 (year) Subaru (make) Outback (model). Log the car's variables, change the car's color, and log the new color.

To build a functional class to demonstrate the capabilities of a class, perform the following steps:

1. Create a car class.

   Add a constructor that takes in the make, model, year, and color. Save the make, model, year, and color in internal variables (this scope) in the constructor function.

   Add a function called setColor that takes in a single parameter, color, and updates the internal variable color to the provided color.

2. Instantiate the class with the parameters Subaru, Outback, 2005, and Grey. Save the class into the Subaru variable.

3. Log the internal variables, that is, make, model, year, and color, of the class stored in Subaru.

4. Change the color with the setColor of the class stored in Subaru class method. Set the color to Red.

5. Log the new color.

### Code

index.js:

```
class Car {
  constructor( make, model, year, color ) {
    this.make = make;
    this.model = model;
    this.year = year;
    this.color = color;
  }
  setColor( color ) {
    this.color = color;
  }
}
```

```
}
let subaru = new Car( 'Subaru', 'Outback', 2005, 'Grey' );
subaru.setColor( 'Red' );
```

**Snippet 1.72: Full class implementation**

https://bit.ly/2FmavRS

**Outcome**

```
Make Subaru
Model Outback
Year 2005
Color Grey
New color: Red

Process finished with exit code 0
```

**Figure 1.15: Implementing classes output**

You have successfully built a functional class.

In this section, we introduced JavaScript classes and ES6 modules. We discussed the prototype-based inheritance structure and demonstrated the basics of class creation and JavaScript class inheritance. When discussing modules, we first showed how to create a module and export the functions and variables stored within them. Then, we showed you how to load a module and import the data contained within. We ended this topic by discussing browser compatibility and providing HTML script tag options for supporting browsers that do not yet support ES6 modules.

# Transpilation

**Transpilation** is defined as source-to-source compilation. Tools have been written to do this and they are called transpilers. **Transpilers** take the source code and convert it into another language. Transpilers are important for two reasons. First, not every browser supports every new syntax in ES6, and second, many developers use programming languages based off of JavaScript, such as CoffeeScript or TypeScript.

> **Note**
>
> The ES6 compatibility table can be found at https://kangax.github.io/compat-table/es6/.

Looking at the ES6 browser compatibility table clearly shows us that there are some holes in support. A transpiler allows us to write our code in ES6 and translate it into vanilla ES5, which works in every browser. It is critical to ensure that our code works on as many web platforms as possible. Transpilers can be an invaluable tool for ensuring compatibility.

Transpilers also allow us to develop web or server side applications in other programming languages. Languages such as TypeScript and CoffeeScript may not run natively in the browser; however, with a transpiler, we are able to build a full application in these languages and translate them into JavaScript for server or browser execution.

One of the most popular transpilers for JavaScript is **Babel**. Babel is a tool that was created to aid in the transpilation between different versions of JavaScript. Babel can be installed through the node package manager (npm). First, open your terminal and path to the folder containing your JavaScript project.

If there is no `package.json` file in this directory, we must create it. This can be done with the `npm init` command. The command-line interface will ask you for several entries so that you can fill out the defaults of the `package.json` file. You can enter the values or simply press the return key and accept the default values.

To install the Babel command-line interface, use the following command: npm install --save-dev babel-cli. After that has concluded, the babel-cli field will have been added to the devDependencies object in the package.json file:

```
{
  "devDependencies": {
    "babel-cli": "^6.26.0"
  }
}
```

Snippet 1.73: Adding the first dependency

This command only installed the base Babel with no plugins for transpiling between versions of JavaScript. To install the plugin to transpile to ECMAScript 2015, use the npm install --save-dev babel-preset-es2015 command. Once the command finishes running, our package.json file will contain another dependency:

```
"devDependencies": {
  "babel-cli": "^6.26.0",
  "babel-preset-es2015": "^6.24.1"
}
```

Snippet 1.74: Adding the second dependency

This installs the ES6 presets. To use these presets, we must tell Babel to configure itself with these presets. Create a file called .babelrc. Note the leading period in the name. The .babelrc file is Babel's configuration file. This is where we tell Babel what presets, plugins, and so on, we are going to use. Once created, add the following contents to the file:

```
{
  "presets": ["es2015"]
}
```

Snippet 1.75: Installing the ES6 presets

## Babel- Transpiling

Now that Babel has been configured, we must create the code file to transpile. In the root folder of your project, create a file called **app.js**. In this file, paste the following ES6 code:

```
const sum5 = inputNumber => inputNumber + 5;
console.log( `The sum of 5 and 5 is +{sum5(5)}!`);
```

**Snippet 1.76: Pasting the code**

Now that Babel has been configured and we have a file that we wish to transpile, we need to update our **package.json** file to add a transpile script for npm. Add the following lines to your **package.json** file:

```
"scripts": {
  "transpile": "babel app.js --out-file app.transpiled.js --source-maps"
}
```

**Snippet 1.77: Update the package.json file**

The scripts object allows us to run these commands from npm. We are going to name the npm script **transpile** and it will run the command chain **babel app.js --out-file app.transpiled.js --source-maps**. **app.js** is our input file. The **--out-file** command specifies the output file for compilation. **app.transpiled.js** is our output file. Lastly, **--source-maps** creates a source map file. This file tells the browser which line of transpiled code corresponds to which lines of the original source. This allows us to debug directly in the original source file, that is, **app.js**.

Now that we have everything set up, we can run our transpile script by typing **npm run transpile** into the terminal window. This will transpile our code from **app.js** into **app.transpiled.js**, creating or updating the file as needed. Upon examination, we can see that the code in **app.transpiled.js** has been converted into ES5 format. You can run the code in both files and see that the output is the same.

Babel has many plugins and presets for different modules and JavaScript releases. There are enough ways to set up and run Babel that we could write an entire book about it. This was just a small preview for converting ES6 code to ES5. For full documentation and information on Babel and the uses of each plugin, visit the documentation.

> **Note**
>
> Take a look at Babel's home page at https://babeljs.io.

In summary, transpilers allow you to do source to source compiling. This is very useful because it allows us to compile ES6 code to ES5 when we need to deploy on a platform that does not yet support ES6. The most popular and most powerful JavaScript transpiler is Babel. Babel can be set up on the command line to allow us to build entire projects in different versions of JavaScript.

## Exercise 14: Transpiling ES6 Code

Your office team has written your website code in ES6, but some devices that users are using do not support ES6. This means that you must either rewrite your entire code base in ES5 or use a transpiler to convert it to ES5. Take the ES6 code written in the *Upgrading Arrow Functions* section and transpile it into ES5 with Babel. Run the original and transpiled code and compare the output.

To demonstrate Babel's ability to transpile code from ES6 to ES5, perform the following steps:

Ensure that Node.js is already installed before you start.

1. Install Node.js if it is not already installed.

2. Set up a Node.js project with the command line command `npm init`.

3. Put the code from the *Upgrading Arrow Functions* section into the **app.js** file.

4. Install Babel and the Babel ES6 plugin with `npm install`.

5. Configure Babel by adding a `.babelrc` file with the es2015 preset.

6. Add a transpile script to **package.json** that calls Babel and transpiles from **app.js** to **app.transpiled.js**.

7. Run the transpile script.

8. Run the code in **app.transpiled.js**.

## Code

**package.json:**

```
// File 1: package.json
{
  "scripts": {
    "transpile": "babel ./app.js --out-file app.transpiled.js --source-maps"
  },
  "devDependencies": {
```

```
    "babel-cli": "^6.26.0",
    "babel-preset-es2015": "^6.24.1"
  }
}
```

**Snippet 1.78: Package.json config file**

https://bit.ly/2FsjzgD

.babelrc:

```
// File 2: .babelrc
{ "presets": ["es2015"] }
```

**Snippet 1.79: Babel config file**

https://bit.ly/2RMvWSW

app.transpiled.js:

```
// File 3: app.transpiled.js
var fn1 = function fn1(a, b) { ... };
var fn2 = function fn2(a, b) { ... };
var fn3 = function fn3(a) { ... };
var fn4 = function fn4() { ... };
var fn5 = function fn5(a) { ... };
```

**Snippet 1.80: Fully transpiled code**

https://bit.ly/2TLbuR7

**Outcome**

```
17
50
50
200
{ prop1: 5 }

Process finished with exit code 0
```

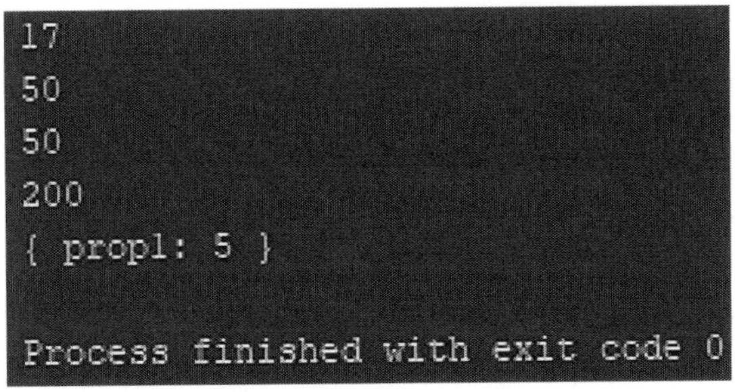

Figure 1.16: Transpiled script output

You have successfully implemented Babel's ability to transpile code from ES6 to ES5.

In this section, we discussed the concept of transpilation. We introduced the transpiler Babel and walked through how to install Babel. We discussed the basic steps to set up Babel to transpile ES6 into ES5 compatible code and, in the activity, built a simple Node. js project with ES6 code to test Babel.

## Iterators and Generators

In their simplest forms, **iterators** and **generators** are two ways to process a collection of data incrementally. They gain efficiency over loops by keeping track of the state of the collection instead of all of the items in the collection.

### Iterators

An **iterator** is a way to traverse through data in a collection. To iterate over a data structure means to step through each of its elements in order. For example, the `for/in` loop is a method that's used to iterate over the keys in a JavaScript object. An object is an iterator when it knows how to access its items from a collection one at a time, while tracking position and finality. An iterator can be used to traverse custom complicated data structure or for traversing chunks of large data that may not be practical to load all at once.

To create an iterator, we must define a function that takes a collection in as the parameter and returns an object. The return object must have a function property called next. When next is called, the iterator steps to the next value in the collection and returns an object with the value and the done status of the iteration. An example iterator is shown in the following code:

```
function createIterator( array ){
    let currentIndex = 0;
```

```
    return {
      next(){
        return currentIndex < array.length ?
          { value: array[ currentIndex++ ], done: false} :
          { done: true };
      }
    };
  }
```

Snippet 1.81: Iterator declaration

This iterator takes in an array and returns an object with the single function property next. Internally, the iterator keeps track of the array and the index we are currently looking at. To use the iterator, we simply call the next function. Calling next will cause the iterator to return an object and increment the internal index by one. The object returned by the iterator must have, at a minimum, the properties value and done. Value will contain the value at the index we are currently viewing. Done will contain a Boolean. If the Boolean equals true, then we have finished the **traversion on** the input collection. If it is **falsy**, then we can keep calling the next function:

```
// Using an iterator
let it = createIterator( [ 'Hello', 'World' ] );
console.log( it.next() );
// Expected output: { value: 'Hello', done: false }
console.log( it.next() );
// Expected output: { value: 'World' , done: false }
console.log( it.next() );
// Expected output: { value: undefined, done: true }
```

Snippet 1.82: Iterator use

**Note**

When an iterator's finality property is truthy, it should not return any new data. To demonstrate the use of iterator.next(), you can provide the example shown in the preceding snippet.

In summary, iterators provide us with a way to traverse potentially complex collections of data. An iterator tracks its current state and each time the next function is called, it provides an object with a value and a finality Boolean. When the iterator reaches the end of the collection, calls to `iterator.next()` will return a truthy finality parameter and no new values will be received.

## Generators

A **generator** provides an iterative way to build a collection of data. A generator can return values one at a time while pausing execution until the next value is requested. A generator keeps track of the internal state and each time it is requested, it returns a new number in the sequence.

To create a generator, we must define a function with an asterisk in front of the function name and the `yield` keyword in the body. For example, to create a generator called `testGenerator`, we would initialize it as follows:

```
function *testGen( data ) { yield 0; }.
```

The asterisk designates that this is a generator function. The `yield` keyword designates a break in the normal function flow until the generator function is called again. An example of a generator is shown in the following snippet:

```
function *gen() {
  let i = 0;
  while (true){
    yield i++;
  }
}
```

Snippet 1.83: Generator creation

This generator function that we created in the preceding snippet, called gen, has an internal state variable called i. When the generator is created, it is automatically initialized with an internal next function. When the next function is called for the first time, the execution starts, the loop begins, and when the `yield` keyword is reached, the execution of the function is stopped until the next function is called again. When the next function is called, the program returns an object containing a value and done.

## Exercise 15: Creating a Generator

To create a generator function that generates the values of the sequence of 2n to show how generators can build a set of sequential data, perform the following steps:

1. Create a generator called gen.

   Place an asterisk before the identifier name.

2. Inside the generator body, do the following:

   Create a variable called i and set the initial value to 1. Then, create an infinite while loop.

   In the body of the while loop, yield i and set i to i * 2.

3. Initialize gen and save it into a variable called generator

4. Call your generator several times and log the output to see the values change.

**Code**

index.js:

```
function *gen() {
  let i = 1;
  while (true){
    yield i;
    i = i * 2;
  }
}
const generator = gen();
console.log( generator.next(), generator.next(), generator.next() );
```

Snippet 1.84: Simple generator

https://bit.ly/2vK7M3d

### Outcome

```
{ value: 1, done: false } { value: 2, done: false } { value: 4, done: false }

Process finished with exit code 0
```

**Figure 1.17: Calling the generator output**

You have successfully created a generator function.

Similar to iterators, the **done** value contains the completion status of the generator. If the **done** value is set to **true**, then the generator has finished execution and will no longer return new values. The value parameter contains the result of the expression contained on the line with the **yield** keyword. In this case, it will return the current value of **i**, before the increment. This is shown in the following code:

```
let sequence = gen();
console.log(sequence.next());
//Expected output: { value: 0, done: false }
console.log(sequence.next());
//Expected output: { value: 1, done: false }
console.log(sequence.next());
//Expected output: { value: 2, done: false }
```

**Snippet 1.85: Generator use**

Generators pause execution when they reach the **yield** keyword. This means that loops will pause execution. Another powerful tool of a generator is the ability to pass in data via the next function and **yield** keyword. When a value is passed into the next function, the return value of the **yield** expression will be set to the value that's passed into next. An example of this is shown in the following code:

```
function *gen() {
 let i = 0;
 while (true){
   let inData = yield i++;
   console.log( inData );
 }
}
```

```
let sequence = gen();
sequence.next()
sequence.next( 'test1' )
sequence.next()
sequence.next( 'test2' )


// Expected output:
// 'test1'
// undefined
// 'test2'
```

**Snippet 1.86 Yield keyword**

In summary, generators are an iterative way of building a collection of data. They return values one at a time while tracking internal state. When the yield keyword is reached, internal execution is stopped and a value is returned. When the next function is called, execution resumes until a yield is reached. Data can be passed into a generator through the next function. Data that's passed in is returned through the yield expression. When a generator emits a value object with the done parameter set to true, calls to generator.next() should not yield any new values.

In the final topic, we introduced iterators and generators. Iterators traverse through data in a collection of data and return the value requested at each step. Once they have reached the end of the collection, a done flag is set to true and no new items will be iterated over. Generators are a way to generate a collection of data. At each step, the generator produces a new value based on its internal state. Iterators and generators both track their internal state as they progress through their life cycle.

## Activity 1: Implementing Generators

You have been tasked with building a simple app that generates numbers in the Fibonacci sequence upon request. The app generates the next number in the sequence for each request and resets the sequence it is given as input. Use a generator to generate the Fibonacci sequence. If a value is passed into the generator, reset the sequence.

To build a complex iterative dataset using a generator, perform the following steps:

1. Look up the Fibonacci sequence.

2. Create a generator that provides the values in the Fibonacci sequence.

3. If the generator's `yield` statement returns a value, reset the sequence

**Outcome**

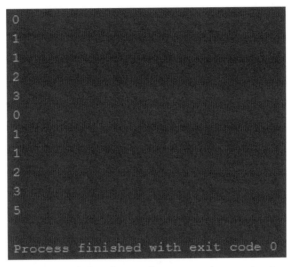

Figure 1.18: Implementing generators output

You have successfully created a generator that can be used to build an iterative dataset based on the Fibonacci sequence.

> **Note**
>
> The solution for this activity can be found on page 280.

## Summary

In this chapter, we saw how ECMAScript is a scripting language specification for modern JavaScript. ECMAScript 6, or ES6, was released in 2015. Through this chapter, we covered some of the various key points of ES6 and their differences from previous versions of JavaScript. We highlighted the rules of variable scoping, the keywords for declaring variables, fat arrow function syntax, template literals, enhanced object property notation, destructuring assignment, classes and modules, transpilation, and iterators and generators. You are ready to begin applying this knowledge to your professional JavaScript projects.

In the next chapter, we will learn what an asynchronous programming language is and how to write and understand asynchronous code.

# Asynchronous JavaScript

**Learning Objectives**

By the end of this chapter, you will be able to:

- Define asynchronous programming

- Characterize the JavaScript event loop

- Utilize callbacks and promises to write asynchronous code

- Simplify asynchronous code with async/await syntax

In this chapter, we shall learn Asynchronous JavaScript and its uses.

## Introduction

In the previous chapter, we covered many of the new and powerful features released in ES6. We discussed the evolution of JavaScript and highlighted the key additions in ES6. We discussed scope rules, variable declaration, arrow functions, template literals, enhanced object properties, destructuring assignment, classes and modules, transpiling, and iterators and generators.

In this chapter, we will learn what an asynchronous programming language is and how to write and understand asynchronous code. In the first topic, we will define asynchronous programming and show how JavaScript is an asynchronous, event driven programming language. Then, we will outline callbacks and show how to use callbacks to write asynchronous JavaScript. We will then define promises and demonstrate how to use promises to write asynchronous JavaScript. In the final topic, we will present the async/await syntax and simplify our asynchronous code using promises and this syntax.

## Asynchronous Programming

JavaScript is a single threaded, event driven, asynchronous programming language. What does this mean? This means that JavaScript runs on a single thread and delays/handles certain events or function calls through an event queue. We will break down the basics of how JavaScript does this through the following topic.

### Sync Versus Async

What does it mean for code to be synchronous or asynchronous? These two buzzwords get thrown around a lot in JavaScript. **Synchronous** is derived from the Greek root **syn**, meaning "with", and **chronos**, which means "time". Synchronous literally means "with time", or rather, code that is coordinated with time. Lines of code are run one at a time and are not started until the previous line has been handled. **Asynchronous**, or **async**, is derived from the Greek root *async*, meaning "not with", and chronos, hence asynchronous literally means "not with time" or rather, code that is not coordinated with time. The order code that is run is not coordinated with the time at which the interpreter first encounters the line of code.

### Synchronous versus Asynchronous Timing

There are two types of code – **synchronous** and **asynchronous**. We shall cover them in this section.

In asynchronous JavaScript, the JavaScript engine handles slow and fast code differently. We know what the words "fast" and "slow" mean, but how does this practically apply to our code? Asynchronous JavaScript allows the thread to execute new lines of code while waiting for the response from a slow time-dependent operation, such as file system I/O. To understand this, we must understand a little bit about computer operation speeds.

CPUs are very, very fast and can handle millions to billions of operations per second. Other parts of a computer or network run much slower than the CPU. For example, a hard drive can only perform hundreds to thousands of operations per second, and a computer network may only be able to perform one operation per second. A call to memory is many orders of magnitude slower than a CPU cycle.

Hard disk operations are several orders of magnitude slower than memory operations. Network calls are several orders of magnitude slower than hard-disk calls.

In **synchronous code**, we execute one line of code at a time. The next line of code does not execute until the previous line of code has finished running. Since synchronous code handles only execute one line of code at a time and wait for the operation to finish before starting a new line, if our code makes a request to a slower medium, such as memory, a hard disk, or a network, our program will not continue to the next line of code until the request to the slow medium (HDD, network, etc) is completed. The CPU will idle, wasting precious time, waiting for the operation to complete. In the case of a network call, this could be several seconds. When writing complex synchronous code, programmers generally write code that is multithreaded. The operating system then switches between threads while one is waiting for a slow operation. This helps reduce the CPU idle time.

In **asynchronous code**, we can execute lines of code out of chronological order. This means that we can start working on a new line of code before the previous line of code has finished its operation. JavaScript does this with the event loop, which will be covered later in the chapter.

In asynchronous code, when the JavaScript engine encounters a line of code that uses a slow, non-CPU-dependent operation, the operation is started, and instead of waiting for completion, the program moves on to the next line of code and continues running. When the slow operation has completed, the CPU jumps back to the operation, handles the response from the operation, and continues running the preceding code. This allows the CPU to not waste precious resources waiting for an operation that could potentially take several seconds. An example of a synchronous and asynchronous timing diagram is shown in the following diagram:

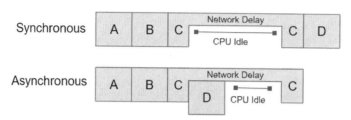

Figure 2.1: Sync versus async timing diagram

In the preceding diagram, we have four operations: A, B, C, and D. Operation C makes a call to the network and has a delay before completion, expressed by Network Delay. In the synchronous example, we run each operation sequentially. When we reach operation C, we must wait for the network delay before we can finish operation C. After operation C completes, we run operation D. During this wait, the CPU is idle and unable to do any other work.

In the asynchronous example, we run the first three operations in sequence. When we reach operation C, instead of waiting for the network delay, we run operation D. When the network delay ends, we finish operation C. In the asynchronous example, we can clearly see that the overall completion time for all the operations and the CPU idle time are shorter.

If this concept is still a little confusing, we can use a real-life situation to help explain it. Imagine synchronous code as a line of people waiting to buy tickets in a train station. Only one person cause use the ticket vending machine at a time. I cannot get a ticket from the machine until all the people in front of me have finished getting their tickets. Similarly, the person behind me cannot begin getting their ticket until I have finished getting mine. Even if the person in front of me decides to take five minutes to get their ticket, I am stuck waiting until my turn. Much like with the ticket line, synchronous code runes one step at a time, in order. No new code line is run until the previous has finished, no matter how long a single step might take.

Asynchronous code is more like eating at a restaurant. Each customer orders one at a time, and must wait while the kitchen cooks the orders. The orders are served as they finish cooking, but not the order that they were given the kitchen. Orders that take less time to cook may come out before orders that take a long time. This parallels asynchronous code quite neatly. Each asynchronous code operation, or food order in our example, is started in sequential order. While the operation is waiting for a response, the next operations can be started. The CPU can handle other operations while waiting for responses from previous operations. This clearly differs from synchronous code. If the kitchen ran in a synchronous format, you would not be able to order your food until the kitchen had finished cooking the previous order. Imagine how inefficient this would be!

## Introducing Event Loops

JavaScript is an event-driven, asynchronous, single-threaded language because of its asynchronous event loop feature. Asynchronous operations are handled in JavaScript in the form of events. When we make an asynchronous call, an event is fired as soon as the call is finished. The JavaScript Engine then handles that event by calling a callback function, and then moves on to whatever was next in the code.

**Event Loop** is the name we use for a four-part system that manages all operations in JavaScript. The parts of this system are the Stack, the Heap, the Event Queue, and the (main) Event Loop. The Stack, Heap, and Event Queue are all data structures that the JavaScript engine maintains. The main event loop is a process that runs behind the scenes and manages the three data structures. In its simplest form, this system is easy to understand. The stack tracks function calls. When a function makes an asynchronous operation, it puts an event handler into the heap. When the async operation completes, the event is pushed to the event queue. The event loop polls the queue for events, gets the associated handler off the heap, then calls the function and adds it to the stack. This is the absolute most basic form of the Event Loop. A visual representation of the event loop data structure is shown here:

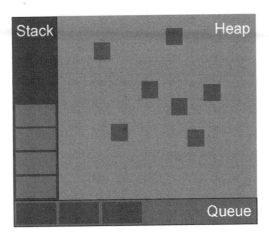

Figure 2.2: Event loop data structure visual model

This is the Event Loop in its simplest form—three data structures: one to track function calls, one to track event handlers, one to track event completions, and a loop to tie them all together. The individual parts will be discussed in more detail in the following subsections.

## Stack

The JavaScript engine has a single call stack, the event loop stack. The **event loop stack** is a traditional call stack—it keeps track of the currently executing function and what function is to be executed after that. The functions held in the stack are called frames. The event loop takes a first in last out approach. It is essentially an array-like data structure with special limitations. Function frames are added and removed only from the top of the stack, like a stack of plates in a kitchen. The first item placed onto the stack will always be at the bottom, and this will be the last one taken off.

The stack keeps track of the current executing function at the top of the stack and the chain of the function calls at the lower levels. When a function is executed, a frame gets created and added to the top of the stack. When a function finishes executing, its frame is removed from the top of the stack. These frames contain the function, the arguments, and the local variables.

If a function, function A, calls another function, function B, a new frame gets created for the newly executed function B. The new frame for function B gets put on the top of the stack, on top of the frame for function A, the function that called it. When function B finishes executing, its frame is removed from the stack and the frame for function A is now at the top. Function A resumes executing until it completes and when it completes, its frame is removed. An example of this is shown in the following code snippet and figure.

Consider the following code snippet:

```
function foo( x ) { return 2 * x; }
function bar( y ) { return foo( y + 5 ) - 10; }


console.log( bar( 15 ) ); // Expected output: 30
```

Snippet 2.1: Call stack example code

When the program starts, the first frame is created. This frame contains the global state. Then, a second frame is called when console.log is called. This frame is placed on top of the global frame. When the bar function is called, a third frame is created and added to the stack. The frame contains bar's arguments and local variables. When bar calls foo, a fourth frame is added to the stack, on top of the bar frame. The full call stack is shown in the following figure:

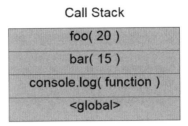

Figure 2.3: Call stack

When foo returns, its frame is removed from the stack. The stack now only contains a frame containing bar's arguments and variables, the console.log call, and the global frame.. When **bar** returns, its frame is removed from the stack and the stack contains only the last 2 frames..

## Heap and Event Queue

### Heap

The **heap** is a large, mostly unstructured, block of memory that is used to track what functions should be called when an event completes. When an asynchronous operation is started, it gets added to the heap. Items are removed from the heap once the asynchronous operation is complete. When the asynchronous operation completes, the heap pushes the necessary data to the event queue.

### Queue

The **queue** is a message queue used to track asynchronous event completions. It is a traditional first in, first out queue. This means that it is an array-like data structure where items are pushed to the back of the queue and removed from the front of the queue. The oldest items are removed and handled first.

Each message in the message queue has an associated function which gets called when the message is handled. To handle a message, it is removed from the queue and its corresponding function is called with the message's data as its input parameters. As expected, a new stack frame is created when the function is called.

Let's consider an example of two buttons in our web page, `button₁` and `button2`, set up to handle click events with the `clickhandler` handler function. The user clicks `button₁` and `button2` in quick succession. The event queue will contain the following simplified information:

```
Queue: { event: 'click', target: 'button1', handler: clickHandler }, {
event: 'click', target: 'button2', handler: clickHandler }
```

Snippet 2.2: Call stack example code

## Event Loops

The **event loop** is responsible for handling messages in the event queue. It does this through a constant polling cycle. At every "tick" of the event loop, the event queue does up to three things: check the stack, check the queue, and wait.

> **Note**
>
> An event queue "tick" is the synchronous calling of zero or more callback functions associated with a JavaScript event. It is the time it takes to handle an event and run the associated callback.

During every tick, the event loop first checks the call stack to see if it is empty and if we can do other work. If the call stack is not empty, the event queue will wait a bit, then check again. If the call stack is empty, the event loop will check the event queue for an event to handle. If the event queue is empty, then we have no work to do and the event loop will wait until the next tick and start the process over again. If there is an event to handle, the event loop will unqueue the event message from the event queue and call the function associated with the message. The called function has a frame created on the stack and the JavaScript Engine starts doing the work specified by the function. The event loop continues its polling cycle.

Looking at the event loop polling, we can notice that only one event can be processed at a time. If there is anything in the call stack, the event loop will not dequeue a message from the event queue. This functionality is called **run-to-completion**. Each message is processed completely before any other message starts processing.

**Run-to-completion** offers some benefits when writing applications. One such benefit is that functions cannot be pre-empted and will run before any other code runs, potentially modifying the data the function was manipulating.

The downside of this model, however, is that if an event callback or loop in the code takes a long time to complete, the application can delay other pending events. In a browser, a user interaction event like click or scroll could hang because another event callback was taking a long time to run. In server-side code, the result of a database query or HTTP request could hang because another event callback was taking a long time to complete.

It is good practice to make sure that the callback functions called by events are short. Long callback functions can be broken into several message with the **setTimeout** function. An example of the delay issue is shown in the following code snippet:

```
setTimeout( () => {
    // WARNING: this may take a long time to run on a slow computer
    // Try with smaller numbers first
    for( let i = 0; i < 2000000000; i++ ) {}
    console.log( 'done delaying' );
}, 0 );
setTimeout( () => { console.log( 'done!' ) }, 0 );
```

Snippet 2.3: Blocking loop example

In the preceding example, we created two asynchronous calls with **setTimeout**. The first one counts to two billion and then logs *done delaying*, the second just logs *done!*. When the first message is pulled off the event queue, the callback is put onto the call stack. Counting to two billion will cause a noticeable delay in most computers.

> **Note**
>
> If your computer is old, then this delay may be substantial. If you run this code, start with smaller numbers, such as 2,000,000.

While the computer is counting, the event loop will not pull the next message off of the event queue. The async call to log *done!* will not get handled until after the counting is finished. Be cautious, as making callback functions may take a long time. If the blocked **console.log( 'done!' )** callback were a user input event in a website, the website would be blocking user input and could lead to an upset user and potentially the loss of a valuable user.

## Things to Consider

When working with the event loop, we have three important things consider when writing our asynchronous code. The first thing to consider is that events may come out of sync. The second is that synchronous code is blocking. The third is that zero delay functions do not execute after 0 milliseconds. These three concepts are explained as follows:

### Events can occur out of order

- Events are added to the event queue in the order that they occur or are resolved.

- This may not be the order that asynchronous calls are started.

- If an asynchronous operation is slow, events that fire before it completes will be addressed first.

- We must account for program timing with callbacks and promises.

- We must make sure that we are careful about accessing data that is being filled in by an asynchronous call before the data is available.

### Synchronous code is blocking

- It is very bad practice to avoid asynchronous code by using synchronous modules that do the same or similar tasks.

- JavaScript is single threaded.

- Event message may not be handled in a prompt manner if a large amount of synchronous code is used.

- Events such as mouse clicks or scrolling could hang.

### Zero delay functions will not actually execute after 0 milliseconds

- A setTimeout adds an event to the event queue after the timeout has expired.

- If the event queue has a lot of messages to process, the timeout message may not be addressed for several milliseconds.

- The delay argument indicates a minimum time, not a guaranteed time.

The concepts of zero delay functions and the event loop states can be demonstrated in the following snippet:

```
setTimeout( () => { console.log( 'step1' ) }. 0 );

setTimeout( () => { console.log( 'done!' ) }. 0 );

console.log( 'step0' );

//Expected output:

// step0

// step1

// done!
```

Snippet 2.4: Handling Asynchronous code

In the preceding snippet, we saw that there is work to be done in the main code file. The main program body is run, and a frame is added to the call stack. The first line of code is then interpreted and the setTimeout function adds its callback to the heap and schedules an event to fire after 0 milliseconds. The event then fires, and a message is added to the event queue. The JavaScript engine interprets the next line of code, the second setTimeout call. The callback is added to the heap, and the event is registered to fire after 0 ms. The second timeout event immediately fires, and a second message is added to the event queue. The JavaScript engine handles the console.log call and step0 is logged to the console. The main program body has no more synchronous work to do and the call stack is empty. The event loop now begins to handle the events in the event queue. The event queue contains two messages, one for the first timeout event and one for the second timeout event. The event loop then takes the first message and adds the associated callback function to the call stack. The JavaScript engine handles that call stack frame and logs step1. The JavaScript engine then handles the second message that was in the event queue. The event queue message is removed from the queue and a frame is added to the call stack. The JS engine handles the frame in the stack and logs done!. No more work can be done. All events have fired, and the stack and queue are both empty.

**Conclusion**

Unlike most programming languages, JavaScript is an asynchronous programming language. More specifically, it is a single threaded, event driven, asynchronous programming language. This means that JavaScript does not idle when waiting for the results of a long-running operation. It runs other code blocks while waiting. JavaScript manages this with the Event Loop. The event loop is composed of four parts, a function stack, a memory heap, an event queue, and the event loop. These four parts work together to handle events fired from operation completion.

## Exercise 16: Handling the Stack with an Event Loop

To better understand why events in your program are being fired and handled in the expected order, look at the program provided next, and without running the program, write out the expected output of the program.

For the first 10 steps of the program, write the expected stack, queue, and heap at each step. A step is any time an event fires, the event loop dequeues an event, or the JS Engine handles a function call:

```
step 0

stack: <global>

queue: <empty>

heap: <empty>
```

Snippet 2.5: Call stack example code (starting step)

The program is displayed in the following snippet:

```javascript
function f1() { console.log( 'f1' ); }
function f2() { console.log( 'f2' ); }
function f3() {
  console.log( 'f3' );
  setTimeout( f5, 90 );
}
function f4() { console.log( 'f4' ); }
function f5() { console.log( 'f5' ); }
setTimeout( f1, 105 );
setTimeout( f2, 15 );
setTimeout( f3, 10 );
setTimeout( f4, 100 );
```

Snippet 2.6: Call stack example code (program)

To demonstrate a simplified form of how the Event Loop handles the stack, queue, and heap while handling JavaScript events, perform the following steps:

1.  Add an event loop stack frame to the stack if a function is called and being handled.

    Process the function and add the necessary event and handler info to the heap. Remove the event and handler in the next step.

2. Push to the event queue if an event completes.

3. Pull from the event queue and call the handler function.

4. Repeat this for the rest of the steps (first 10 only).

## Code

https://bit.ly/2R5vGPA

## Outcome

```
step 0
stack: <gobal>
queue: <empty>
heap: <empty>

step 1
stack: <gobal>, setTimeout( f1, 105 );
queue: <empty>
heap: <empty>

step 2
stack: <gobal>, setTimeout( f2, 15 );
queue: <empty>
heap: setTimeout( f1, 105 )

step 3
stack: <gobal>, setTimeout( f3, 10 );
queue: <empty>
heap: setTimeout( f1, 105 ), setTimeout( f2, 15 )

step 4
stack: <gobal>, setTimeout( f4, 100 );
queue: <empty>
heap: setTimeout( f1, 105 ), setTimeout( f2, 15 ), setTimeout( f3, 10 )

step 5
stack: <gobal>
queue: { event: timeout, handler: f3 }
heap: setTimeout( f1, 105 ), setTimeout( f2, 15 ), setTimeout( f4, 100 )
```

Figure 2.4: Scope outputs

```
step 6
stack: <gobal>, f3
queue: <empty>
heap: setTimeout( f1, 105 ), setTimeout( f2, 15 ), setTimeout( f4, 100 )

step 7
stack: <gobal>, f3, console.log( 'f3' )
queue: <empty>
heap: setTimeout( f1, 105 ), setTimeout( f2, 15 ), setTimeout( f4, 100 )

step 8
stack: <gobal>, f3, setTimeout( f5, 90)
queue: <empty>
heap: setTimeout( f1, 105 ), setTimeout( f2, 15 ), setTimeout( f4, 100 )

step 9
stack: <gobal>, f3
queue: <empty>
heap: setTimeout( f1, 105 ), setTimeout( f2, 15 ), setTimeout( f4, 100 ), setTimeout( f5, 90)
```

Figure 2.5: Scope outputs

```
f3
f2
f4
f5
f1

Process finished with exit code 0
```

Figure 2.6: Scope outputs

You have successfully demonstrated a simplified form of how the Event Loop handles the stack.

## Callbacks

**Callbacks** are the most basic form of JavaScript asynchronous programming. In the simplest terms, a callback is a function that gets called after another function completes. Callbacks are used to handle the response of an asynchronous function call.

In JavaScript, functions are treated like objects. They can be passed around as arguments, returned by functions, and saved into variables. A callback is a function object that is passed as an argument into a higher order function. A higher order function is simply a mathematics and computer science term for a function that takes one or more functions as arguments (callbacks) or returns a function. In JavaScript, a higher order function will take a callback as a parameter. Once the higher order finishes doing some form of work, such as an HTTP request or database call, it calls the callback function with the error or return values.

As mentioned in the Event Loop section in *Asynchronous Programming*, JavaScript is an event driven language. Since JavaScript is single threaded, any long-running operations are blocking. JavaScript handles this blocking effect by using events. When an operation completes and event fires, the event has an attached handler function that gets called to handle the result. These functions are **callbacks**. Callbacks are the key that allow JavaScript events to perform work when handling asynchronous events.

## Building Callbacks

Callbacks in JavaScript follow a simple unofficial convention. A callback function should take in at least two arguments: **error** and **result**. When building callback APIs or writing callback functions, we recommend that you follow this convention so that your code can seamlessly integrate with other libraries. An example of a callback function is shown in the following snippet:

```
TwitterAPI.listFollowers( { user_id: "example_user" }, (err, result) => {
    console.log( err, result );
} );
```

Snippet 2.7: Basic callback example

In the preceding example, we used a fake Twitter API. Our fake API has a higher order function, listFollowers, that accepts an object and a callback function as parameters. Once listFollowers completes its internal work, in this case an HTTP request to the Twitter API, our callback function will be called.

A callback may take in as many arguments as needed or specified by the higher order function, but the first argument must be the error object. This convention is followed by nearly every API in existence. Breaking from this convention when writing APIs will make your code much more difficult to integrate with any third-party APIs or applications.

A callback's error argument will only be set if the higher order function encounters an error while running. The contents of the error argument may be any legal JavaScript value. In most cases, it is an instance of the Error class; however, there is no convention for the contents of the error object. Some APIs may return an object, string, or number instead of an Error instance. Be sure to read the documentation of any third-party API to ensure that your code can handle the error format being returned.

If the higher order function does NOT encounter an error, the error parameter should be set to null. When building your own APIs, it is recommended that you also follow this convention. Some third-party APIs may return a falsy value that is not null, but this is discouraged because it can make error handling logic more complicated.

> **Note**
>
> **Falsy** is a term used in JavaScript type comparison and conversion. Falsy values in JavaScript translate to the Boolean false when used in type comparisons. Examples of falsy values are null, undefined, 0, and the Boolean false.

The result argument of a callback function contains the evaluated result of the higher order function. This may be the result of an HTTP request, database query, or any other asynchronous operation. Some APIs also may provide more detailed error information in the result field when an error is returned. It is important to not assume a function completed successfully if the result object is present. You must check the error field.

When handling errors in callback functions, we must check the error argument. If the error argument is not null or undefined, then we must handle the error in some way. An example error handler is shown in the following snippet:

```
TwitterAPI.listFollowers( { user_id: "example_user" }, (err, result) => {
  if ( err ) {
    // HANDLE ERROR
  }
  console.log( err, result );
} );
```

Snippet 2.8: Basic callback error handling

Most developers check to see if the error value is a truthy value. If err is truthy then error handling code is executed. This is a general practice; however, it is the lazy way of coding. In some cases, the error object could be the Boolean false, the number 0, the empty string, and so on. These all evaluate to falsy, even though the value is not null or undefined. If you are using an API, be sure to check that it will not return an error that evaluates to falsy. If you are building an API, we do not recommend ever returning an error that could evaluate to falsy.

## Callback Pitfalls

Callbacks are easy to use and serve their purpose very well, but there are a few pitfalls to consider when using callbacks. The two most common pitfalls are callback hell and callback existence assumption. Both of these pitfalls are easily avoided if the code is written with foresight.

The most common callback pitfall is **callback hell**. After asynchronous work completes and a callback is called, the callback function can call another asynchronous function to do more asynchronous work. When it calls the new asynchronous function, another callback will be provided. The new callback will be nested inside of the old callback. An example of callback nesting is shown in the following snippet:

```
TwitterAPI.listFollowers( { user_id: "example_user" }, (err, result) => {
  if ( err ) { throw err; }
  TwitterAPI.unfollow( { user_id: result[ 0 ].id }, ( err, result ) => {
    if ( err ) { throw err; }
    console.log( "Unfollowed someone!" );
  } );
} );
```

Snippet 2.9: Callback nesting

In the preceding snippet, we have nested callbacks. The callback of the first asynchronous operation, listFollowers calls a second asynchronous operation. The unfollow operation also has a callback that simply handles an error or logs text. Since callbacks can be nested, after several nesting layers the code can become quite hard to read. This is callback hell. An example of callback hell is shown in the following snippet:

```
TwitterAPI.listFollowers( { user_id: "example_user" }, (err, result) => {
  const [ id1, id2, id3 ] = [ result[ 0 ].id, result[ 1 ].id, result[ 2 ].id
  ];
  TwitterAPI.unfollow( { user_id: id1 }, ( err, result ) => {
    TwitterAPI.block( { user_id: id1 }, ( err, result ) => {
```

```
TwitterAPI.unfollow( { user_id: id2 }, ( err, result ) => {
  TwitterAPI.block( { user_id: id2 }, ( err, result ) => {
    TwitterAPI.unfollow( { user_id: id3 }, ( err, result ) => {
      TwitterAPI.block( { user_id: id3 }, ( err, result ) => {
        console.log( "Unfollowed and blocked 3 users!" );
```

**Snippet 2.10: Callback hell**

In the preceding snippet, we listed our followers, then unfollow and block the first three followers. It is very simple code, but because the callbacks are nested, the code becomes messier. This is callback hell.

> **Note**
>
> Callback hell is about untidy code presentation, not the logic behind it. Callback nesting can lead to code that runs without errors but is very hard to read. Code that is very difficult to read can be very difficult to explain to new developers or debug when an error occurs.

## Fixing Callback Hell

Callback hell can easily be avoided with two tricks: **named functions** and **modules**. A named function is very simple; define the callback and assign it to an identifier (variable). The defined callback functions can be kept in the same file or put into a module and imported. Using named functions in callbacks will help prevent callback nesting from cluttering your code. This is shown in the following snippet:

```
function listHandler( err, result ) {
  TwitterAPI.unfollow( { user_id: result[ 0 ].id }, unfollowHandler );
}


function unfollowHandler( err, result) {
  TwitterAPI.block( { user_id: result.id }, blockHandler );
}


function blockHandler( err, result ) {
  console.log( "User unfollowed and blocked!" );
}
```

```
TwitterAPI.listFollowers( { user_id: "example_user" }, listHandler);
```

**Snippet 2.11: Fixing callback hell**

As we can see from the preceding snippet, the code without nesting is much cleaner. If we had a callback nesting depth of 30, the only way to make the code readable would be to break the callbacks into named functions.

Another potential pitfall is the non-existence of a callback function. If we are writing an API, we must consider the possibility that the user of the API might not pass a valid callback function into the API. If the intended callback is not a function or does not exist, then trying to call it will cause a runtime error. It is a good practice to validate that a callback exists and that it is a function before attempting to call it. If the user passes in an invalid callback, then we can fail gracefully. An example of this is shown in the following snippet:

```
Function apiFunction( args, callback ){
    if ( !callback || !( typeof callback === "function" ) ){
        throw new Error( "Invalid callback. Provide a function." );
    }
    let result = {};
    let err = null;
    // Do work
    // Set err and result
    callback( err, result );
}
```

**Snippet 2.12: Checking callback existence**

In the preceding code snippet, we checked to make sure that the callback argument exists and is truthy, and that it is of type function. If the callback does not exist or is not a function, we throw an error to let the user know exactly what went wrong. If the callback is a function, we proceed.

## Conclusion

A callback is simply a function passed as an argument into another function, called a **higher order** function. JavaScript uses callbacks to handle events. Callbacks are defined with an error argument and a result argument. If there is an error in the higher order function, the callback error field will be set. If the higher order function completes with results, the result field will contain the result of the completed operation.

When using callbacks, we should be cautious of two pitfalls. We must be careful of nesting too many callbacks together and creating callback hell. We must make sure that we validate the arguments passed into our higher order functions to ensure that the callback is a function.

## Exercise 17: Working with Callbacks

Your team is building an API that is based around callbacks. To prevent runtime errors, you need to validate that the callback arguments passed into the callback API functions are valid callable functions. Create a function for your API. In the body of that function, validate that the callback argument is a function. If it is not a function, throw an error. After a delay, log the data passed into the API function and call the callback.

To build a callback API with callbacks function, perform the following steps:

1. Write a function called `higherOrder` that takes in two arguments; an object called `data` and a callback function called `cb`.

2. In the function, check that the callback is a function argument (`cb`) is a function.

   If `cb` does not exist or it is not of type `function`, then throw an error.

3. In the function, log the `data` object.

4. In the function, call the `callback` function after a timeout of 10 ms.

5. Outside the function, create a `try-catch` block.

6. Inside the try section, call the `higherOrder` function with a data object and no callback function.

7. Inside the catch section, catch the error and log the error message we got.

8. After the `try-catch` block, call the `higherorder` function with a data object and a `callback` function. The callback function should log the string `Callback Called!`

## Code

```
Index.js

function higherOrder( data, cb ) {
  if ( !cb || !( typeof cb === 'function' ) ) {
    throw new Error( 'Invalid callback. Please provide a function.' );
  }
  console.log( data );
  setTimeout( cb, 10 );
}


try {
  higherOrder( 1, null );
} catch ( err ) {
  console.log( 'Got error: ${err.message}' );
}


higherOrder( 1, () => {
  console.log( 'Callback Called!' )
} );
```

**Snippet 2.13: Implementing callbacks**

https://bit.ly/2vTGG9L

## Outcome

```
Got error: Invalid callback. Please provide a function.
1
Callback Called!

Process finished with exit code 0
```

**Figure 2.7: Callback output**

You have successfully built a callback API with callback functions.

# Promises

In JavaScript, a **promise** is an object that wraps an asynchronous operation and notifies the program when the asynchronous operation completes. The promise object represents the eventual completion or failure of the wrapped operation. A promise is a proxy for a value not necessarily known. Instead of providing the value immediately, like a synchronous program, it promises to provide a value at some point in the future. Promises allow you to associate success and error handlers with an asynchronous action. These handlers are called at the completion or failure of the wrapped asynchronous process.

## Promises States

Every promise has a state. A promise can only succeed with a value or fail with an error once. The state of a promise defines where the promise is in its work towards the resolution of a value.

A promise comes in three states: **pending**, **fulfilled**, or **rejected**. A promise starts in the pending state. This means that the async operation being done inside the promise is not complete. Once the asynchronous operation completes, the promise is considered settled and will enter either the fulfilled or rejected state.

When a promise enters the fulfilled state, it means that the async operation has completed without an error. The promise is fulfilled and a value is available. The value generated by the async operation has been returned and can be used.

When a promise enters the rejected state, it means that the async operation has completed with an error. When a promise is rejected, no future work will be done and no value will be provided. The error from the asynchronous operation has been returned and can be referenced from the promise object.

## Resolving or Rejecting a Promise

A promise is created by instantiating a new object of the `Promise` class. The promise constructor accepts a single argument, a function. This function must have two arguments: **resolve** and **reject**. An example of promise creation is shown in the following snippet:

```
const myPromise = new Promise( ( resolve, reject ) => {
    // Do asynchronous work here and call resolve or reject
} );
```

**Snippet 2.14: Promise creation syntax**

The main asynchronous work of the promise will be done in the body of the function passed into the constructor. The two arguments, `resolve` and `reject`, are functions that can be used to complete the promise.. To complete the promise with an error, call the reject function with the error as its argument. To mark the promise as successful, call the `resolve` function and pass in the result in to resolve as a parameter. Examples of promise rejection and resolution are shown in the following two snippets:

```
// Reject promise with an error
const myPromise = new Promise( ( resolve, reject ) => {
  // Do asynchronous work here
  reject( new Error( 'Oh no! Promise was rejected' ) );
} );
```

**Snippet 2.15: Rejecting a promise**

```
// Resolve the promise with a value
const myPromise = new Promise( ( resolve, reject ) => {
  // Do asynchronous work here
  resolve( { key1: 'value1' } );
} );
```

**Snippet 2.16: Resolving a promise**

An example of resolving a promise that performs asynchronous work, is shown in the following snippet:

```
const myPromise = new Promise( ( resolve, reject ) => {
  setTimeout( () => { resolve( 'Done!' ) }, 1000 )
} );
```

**Snippet 2.17: Resolving a promise**

## Using Promises

The promise class has three member functions that can be used to handle promise fulfillment and rejection. These functions are called promise handlers. These functions are `then()`, `catch()`, and `finally()`. When a promise completes, one of the handler functions is called. If the promise fulfills, the `then()` function is called. If the promise is rejected, either the `catch()` function is called, or the `then()` function with a rejection handler is called.

The then() member function is designed to handle and get the promise fulfillment or rejection result. The then function takes in two function arguments, a fulfillment callback and a rejection callback. This is shown in the following example:

```
// Resolve the promise with a value or reject with an error

myPromise.then(

    ( result ) => { /* handle result */ }, // Promise fulfilled handler

    ( err ) => { /* handle error here */ } // Promise rejected handler

) ;
```

Snippet 2.18: Promise.then() syntax

The first argument in the then() function is the promise fulfillment handler. If the promise is fulfilled with a value, the promise fulfillment handler callback is called. The promise fulfillment handler takes one argument. The value of this argument will be the value passed in to the fulfilled callback in the promise function body. An example of this is shown in the following snippet:

```
// Resolve the promise with a value

const myPromise = new Promise( ( resolve, reject ) => {

    // Do asynchronous work here

    resolve( 'Promise was resolved!' );

} );

myPromse.then( value => console.log( value ) );

// Expected output: 'Promise was resolved'
```

Snippet 2.19: Promise.then() with resolved promise

The second argument in the then() function is the promise rejection handler. If the promise is rejected with an error, the promise rejection handler callback is called. The promise rejection handler takes one argument. The value of this argument is the value passed in to the reject callback in the promise function body. An example of this is shown in the following snippet:

```
// Reject the promise with a value

const myPromise = new Promise( ( resolve, reject ) => {

    // Do asynchronous work here

    reject( new Error ( 'Promise was rejected!' ) );

} );

myPromse.then( () => {}, error => console.log( error) );
```

```
// Expected output: Error: Promise was rejected!
// ** output stack trace omitted
```

Snippet 2.20: Promise rejection with Promise.then()

## Exercise 18: Creating and Resolving Your First Promise

To build our first asynchronous promise, perform the following steps:

1. Create a promise and save it into a variable called myPromise.

2. Inside the body of the promise, log Starting asynchronous work!

3. Inside the body of the promise, do asynchronous work with a timeout.

   Have the timeout callback fire after 1000 ms. Inside the timeout callback function, call the promise resolution function and pass in the value Done!

4. Attach a then handler to the promise saved in myPromise.

5. Pass a function into the then handler that takes in one parameter and logs the value of the parameter.

### Code

Index.js

```
const myPromise = new Promise( ( resolve, reject ) => {
    console.log( 'Starting asynchronous work!' );
    setTimeout( () => { resolve( 'Done!' ); }, 1000 );
} );
myPromise.then( value => console.log( value ) );
```

Snippet 2.21: Promise rejection with Promise.then()

https://bit.ly/2TvQNcz

### Outcome

```
Starting asynchronous work!
Done!

Process finished with exit code 0
```

Figure 2.8: Scope outputs

You have successfully utilized the syntax you just learned to build our first asynchronous promise.

## Handling Promises

When `Promise.then()` is called, it returns a new promise in the pending state. After the promise handler for fulfilled or rejected has been called, the handlers in `Promise.then()` get called asynchronously. When the handler called from `Promise.then()` returns a value, that value is used to resolve or reject the promise returned by `promise.then()`. The following table provides the action taken if the handler function returns a value, an error, or a promise at any stage:

| Handler Return Value | Action Taken |
|---|---|
| Returns a value | The promise returned by promise.then() is resolved with the value returned by the handler function. |
| Throws an error | The promise returned by promise.then() gets rejected, with the thrown error as its value. |
| Returns a resolved promise | The promise returned by promise.then() gets resolved with the handler function's returned promise's resolution value. |
| Returns a rejected promise | The promise returned by promise.then() gets rejected with the handler function's returned promise's rejection value. |
| Returns a pending promise | The resolution or rejection of the promise returned by promise.then() will be subsequent to the rejection or resolution of the promise returned by the handler function. |

Figure 2.9: Returning a promise

`Promise.catch` takes in one argument, a handler function, to handle the promise rejection value. When `Promise.catch` is called, internally it calls `Promise.then( undefined, rejecthandler )`. This means that internally, the `Promise.then()` handler is called with only the promise rejection callback, `rejecthandler`, and no promise fulfillment callback. `Promise.catch()` returns the value of the internal `Promise.then()` call:

```
const myPromise = new Promise( ( resolve, reject ) => {
    reject( new Error 'Promise was resolved!' );
} );
myPromise.catch( err => console.log( err ) );
```

Snippet 2.22: Promise rejection with Promise.then()

The promise member function, `Promise.finally()`, is a promise handler that is used to catch all promise completion cases. A `Promise.finally()` handler will be called for both promise rejections and resolutions. It takes in a single function argument that is called when the promise is rejected or fulfilled. `Promise.finally()` will catch both rejected and resolved promises, and run the specified function. It provides us with a catch all handler to handle either fulfillment case. `Promise.finally()` should be used to prevent duplication of code between the then and catch handlers. The function passed in to `Promise.finally()` does not take in any arguments, so any value passed in to a promise's resolution or rejection will be ignored. Because there is no way to reliably distinguish between a rejection and a fulfillment when using `Promise.finally()`, `Promise.finally()` should only be used when we do not care if the promise has been rejected or fulfilled. An example of this is shown in the following snippet:

```
// Resolve the promise with a value
const myPromise = new Promise( ( resolve, reject ) => {
    resolve( 'Promise was resolved!' );
} );
myPromse.finally( value => {
    console.log( 'Finally!' );
} );
// Expected output:
// Finally!
```

Snippet 2.23: Promise.then()

When using promises, there are times when we may want to create a promise that is already in the fulfilled state. The Promise class has two static member functions that allow us to do this. These functions are `Promise.reject()` and `Promise.resolve()`. `Promise.reject()` takes a single argument and returns a promise that has been rejected with the value passed in to the reject function. `Promise.resolve()` takes in a single argument and returns a promise that has been resolved with the value passed in to resolve:

```
Promise.resolve( 'Resolve value!' ).then( console.log );

Promise.reject( 'Reject value!' ).catch( console.log );

//Expected output:

// Resolve value!

// Reject value!
```

**Snippet 2.24: Promise.then()**

## Promise Chaining

When using promises, we can run into **promise hell**. This is very similar to callback hell. When a promise body needs to do more async work after the value is obtained, another promise can be nested. The nested promise calls can get difficult to follow when the nesting chain gets very deep. To avoid promise hell, we can chain promises together. `Promise.then()`, `Promise.catch()`, and `Promise.finally()` all return promises that get fulfilled or rejected with the result of the handler functions. This means we can tack on another then handler to this promise and make a promise chain to handle the newly returned promise. This is shown in the following snippet:

```
function apiCall1( result ) { // Function that returns a promise

  return new Promise( ( resolve, reject ) => {

    resolve( 'value1' );

  } );

}
```

```
function apiCall2( result ) {// Function that returns a promise
  return new Promise( ( resolve, reject ) => {
    resolve( 'value2' );
  } );
}
myPromse.then( apiCall1 ).then( apiCall2 ).then( result => console.log(
'done!') ) ;
```

Snippet 2.25: Promise chaining example

In the preceding example, we created two functions, apiCall1() and apiCall2(). These functions returned a promise that does more asynchronous work. The async work has been omitted from this example for brevity. When the original promise, myPromise, completes, the Promise.then() handler calls apiCall1(), which returns another promise. The second Promise.then() handler is applied to this newly returned promise. When the promise returned by apiCall1() is resolved, the handler function calls apiCall2(), which also returns a promise. When the promise returned by apiCall2() is returned, the final Promise.then() handler is called. If these handler functions with asynchronous work were nested, it could get very difficult to follow the program. With callback chaining, it becomes very easy to follow the program flow.

When chaining promises, it is possible for the promise handler to return a value instead of a new promise. If a value is returned, the value gets passed as an input to the next Promise.then() handler in the chain.

For example, the first promise completes and calls the Promise.then() handler. This handler does synchronous work and returns the number 10. The next promise.then() handler will have the input parameter set to 10 and can continue doing the asynchronous work. This allows you to embed synchronous steps into the promise chain.

When chaining promises, we must be careful with catch handlers. When a promise is rejected, it jumps to the next promise rejection handler. This can be the second argument in a `then` handler or a `catch` handler. All fulfillment handlers between where the promise is rejected, and the next rejection handlers, will be ignored. When the catch handler completes, the promise returned by `catch()` will be fulfilled with the returned value of the rejection handler. This means that the following promise fulfillment handler will be given a value to run with. If the `catch` handler is not the last handler in the promise chain, the promise chain will continue to run with the returned value of the `catch` handler. This can be a tricky error to debug; however, it allows us to catch a promise rejection, handle the error in a specific way, and continue with the promise chain. It allows the promise chain to handle a reject or accept in different ways, then continue with the async work. This is shown in the following snippet:

```
// Promise chain handles rejection and continues

// apiCall1 is a function that returns a rejected promise

// apiCall2 is a function that returns a resolved promise

// apiCall3 is a function that returns a resolved promise

// errorHandler1 is a function that returns a resolved promise

myPromse.then( apiCall1 ).then( apiCall2, errorHandler1 ).then( apiCall3
).catch( errorHandler2 );
```

Snippet 2.26: Handle error and continue

In the preceding snippet, we have a promise chain with three asynchronous API calls in a row, after the resolution of `myPromise`. The first API call will reject the promise with an error. The rejected promise is handled by the second then handler. Since the promise is rejected, it ignores `apiCall2()` and routes to the `errorHandler1()` function. `errorHandler1()` will do some work and return a value or promise. That value or promise is passed to the next handler, which calls `apiCall3()`, which returns a resolved promise. Since the promise is resolved and there are no more `then` handlers, the promise chain ends. The final catch is ignored.

To skip from one rejection handler to the next rejection handler, we need to throw an error inside the rejection `handler` function. This will cause the returned promise to be rejected with the error thrown and skip to the next `catch` handler.

If we wish to exit the promise chain early and not continue when a promise is rejected, you should only include a single catch handler at the end of the chain. When a promise is rejected, the rejection is handled by the first handler found. If this handler is the last handler in the promise chain, the chain ends. This is shown in the following snippet:

```
// Promise chain handles rejection and continues

// apiCall1 returns a rejected promise

myPromse.then( apiCall1 ).then( apiCall2 ).then( apiCall3 ).catch(
errorHandler1 );
```

**Snippet 2.27: Handle error at end of chain to abort**

In the promise chain shown in the preceding snippet, when myPromise is resolved with a value, and the first then handler is called. apiCall1() is called and it returns a rejected promise. Since the next two then handlers do not have an argument to handle promise rejection, the rejection is passed to the catch handler. The catch handler calls errornandler1 and then the promise chain ends.

Chaining promises is used to ensure that all promises complete in the order of the chain. If promises need not be completed in order, we can use the Promise.all() static member function. The Promise.all() function is not created on instances of the promise class. It is a static class function. Promise.all() takes in an array of promises and when all of the promises have been resolved, the then handler will be called. The then handler function's parameter will be an array with the resolve value of each promise in the original Promise.all() call. The array of the resolution values will match the order of the array of the input to Promise.all(). This is shown in the following snippet:

```
// Create promises

let promise1 = new Promise( ( resolve, reject ) => setTimeout( () =>
resolve( 10 ), 100 ) );

let promise2 = new Promise( ( resolve, reject ) => setTimeout( () =>
resolve( 20 ), 200 ) );

let promise3 = new Promise( ( resolve, reject ) => setTimeout( () =>
resolve( 30 ), 10 ) );

Promise.all( [ promise1, promise2, promise3 ] ).then( results => console.
log( results ) );

//Expected output: [ 10, 20, 30 ]
```

**Snippet 2.28: Promise.all() example**

In the preceding example, we created three promises that resolve after 100ms, 200ms, and 10ms respectively. We then pass these promises into the `Promise.all()` function. Once all of the promises have resolved, the then handler attached to the function `Promise.all()` is called. This handler logs the results of the promises. Notice that the order of the result array matches the order of the promise array, not the completion order of the promises.

If one or many of the promises in the `Promise.all()` call are rejected, the reject handler will be called with the rejection value of the first promise. All of the other promises will run to completion but rejections or resolutions of these promises will not call any of the `then` or `catch` handlers of the `Promise.all()` promise chain. This is shown in the following snippet:

```
// Create promises
let promise1 = new Promise( ( resolve, reject ) => {
    setTimeout( () => { reject( 'Error 1' ); }, 100 );
} );

let promise2 = new Promise( ( resolve, reject ) => {
    setTimeout( () => { reject( 'Error 2' ); }, 200 );
} );

let promise3 = new Promise( ( resolve, reject ) => {
    setTimeout( () => { reject( 'Error 3' ); }, 10 );
} );

Promise.all( [ promise1, promise2, promise3 ] ).then( console.log ).catch(
console.log );

// Expected output:

// Error: Error 3
```

Snippet 2.29: Promise.all() rejection

In this example, we create three promises that log the promise number and then are all rejected with various errors. We pass these promises into a `Promise.all` call. `Promise3` has the shortest timeout and therefore is the first promise to be rejected. When `Promise3` is rejected, the promise rejection is passed to the nearest error handler (`.catch()`) which logs the promise rejection. Promises 1 and 2 complete running shortly thereafter and are both rejected. The rejection handler is not called again for these promises.

A last function that exists to handle multiple promises is the `Promise.race()` function. The `Promise.race()` function is designed to handle only the first promise fulfilled or rejected.

> **Note**
>
> If for some reason, your program has an intentional race condition or multiple code paths that should only cause a successful response handler to be called once, `Promise.race()` is the perfect solution.

Like `Promise.all()`, `Promise.race()` is passed an array of promises; however, `Promise.race()` only calls the promise fulfillment handler for the first promise completed. It then proceeds with the promise chain as normal. The results from the other promises are discarded, whether they are rejected or resolved. Promise rejection handling with `Promise.race()` works the same way as `Promise.all()`. Only the first rejected promise is handled. The other promises are ignored, regardless of the fulfillment state. An example of `Promise.race()` is shown in the following snippet:

```
// Create promises
let promise1 = new Promise( ( resolve, reject ) => setTimeout( resolve( 10
), 100 ) );

let promise2 = new Promise( ( resolve, reject ) => setTimeout( resolve( 20
), 200 ) );

let promise3 = new Promise( ( resolve, reject ) => setTimeout( resolve( 30
), 10 ) );

Promise.race( [ promise1, promise2, promise3 ] ).then( result => console.
log( result ) );

//Expected output: 30
```

Snippet 2.30: Promise.race() example

In the preceding example, we created three promises. These promises all resolve after various timeouts. `Promise3` resolves first because it has the shortest timeout. When `promise3` resolves, the then handler is called and the result of `promise3` is logged. When `promise1` and `promise2` resolve, their results are ignored.

## Promises and Callbacks

Promises and callbacks should never be mixed together. Writing code that utilizes both callbacks and promises to do asynchronous work can get very complicated and lead to errors that are extremely difficult to debug. To prevent mixing callback logic and promise logic, we must add shims in our code to handle callbacks as promises and promises as callbacks. There are two ways to do this: promises can be wrapped in callbacks or callbacks can be wrapped in promises.

> **Note**
>
> A shim is a code file used to add missing functionality to a code base. Shims are usually used to ensure cross-browser compatibility for web applications.

## Wrapping Promises in Callbacks

To wrap a promise function in a callback, we simply create a wrapper function that takes the **promise** function, the arguments, and a **callback**. Inside the **wrapper** function, we call the **promise** function and pass in the provided arguments. We attach **then** and **catch** handlers. When these handlers resolve, we call the **callback** function with the result or the error returned by the promise. This is shown in the following snippet:

```
// Promise function to be wrapped
function promiseFn( args ){
  return new Promise( ( resolve, reject ) => {
    /* do work */
    /* resolve or reject */
  } );
}
// Wrapper function
function wrapper( promiseFn, args, callback ){
  promiseFn( args ).then( value => callback( null, value )
       .catch( err => callback( err, null );
}
```

Snippet 2.31: Wrap promise in a callback

In the preceding example, we called the callback with the result of the promise. If the promise is resolved with a value, we pass that value into the callback with the error field set to null. If the promise is rejected, we pass the error into the callback with a null result field.

To wrap a callback-based function in a promise, we simply create a wrapper function that takes the function to wrap and the function arguments. Inside the wrapper function, we call the function being wrapped inside a new promise. When the callback returns a result or error, we reject the promise if there is an error, or we resolve the promise if there is no error. This is shown in the following snippet:

```
// Callback function to be wrapped
function wrappedFn( args, cb ){
  /* do work */
  /* call cb with error or result */
}
// Wrapper function
function wrapper( wrappedFn, args ){
  return new Promise( ( resolve, reject ) => {
    wrappedFn( args, ( err, result ) => {
      if( err ) {
        return reject( err );
      }
      resolve( result );
    } );
  } );
}
```

**Snippet 2.32: Wrap callback in a promise**

In the preceding example, we created a wrapper function that takes in a function and that function's arguments. We return a promise that calls this function and depending on the result, rejects or resolves the promise. Since this function returns a promise, it can be embedded in a promise chain or can have a then or catch handler attached to it.

## Conclusion

Promises are another way to handle asynchronous programming in JavaScript. When created, a promise starts in the pending state and enters the fulfilled or the rejected state depending on the result of the asynchronous work. To handle the result of a promise, we use the .then(), .catch(), and .finally() member functions. The .then() function takes in two handler functions, one for promise fulfillment and one for promise rejection. The .catch() function takes in only one function and handles promise rejection. Promise.finally() takes in one function and is called for either a promise fulfillment or rejection.

When multiple promises need to be run but order does not matter, we can use the Promise.all() and Promise.race() static functions. The Promise.all() resolution handler is called when all of the promises have finished running. The Promise.race() resolution handler is called when the first promise has finished running.

Promises and callback are not compatible and should never be mixed in the body of a program. To allow for compatibility between functions and modules using promises or callback functions, we can write a wrapper function. We can wrap a callback in a promise or a promise in a callback. This allows us to shim third-party modules to be compatible with our code.

## Exercise 19: Working with Promises

You are building a promise-based API. In your API, you must validate user input to ensure data passed into your database models is of the right type. Write a function that returns a promise. This promise should validate that the data value passed into the API function is not a number. If the user passes a number into the function, reject the promise with an error. If the user passes a non-number into the API function, resolve the promise with the word Success!.

To build a function that uses promises for real scenarios, perform the following steps:

1.  Write a function called promiseFunction that takes in one data argument and returns a promise.

2.  Pass a function that takes in two arguments, resolve and reject, into the constructor of the promise.

3.  In the promise, start doing asynchronous work by creating a timeout that runs after 10ms.

4.  In the timeout callback function, log the input data that was provided to promiseFunction.

5.  In the timeout callback, check that the type of data is a number. If it is, reject the promise with an error, otherwise resolve the promise with the string Success!.

6. Run promiseFunction and provide a number as the parameter. Attach a then()
   handler and a catch() handler to the promise returned by the function.

> **Note**
>
> The then handler should log the promise resolution value. The catch handler
> should log the error's message property.

## Code

Index.js

```javascript
function promiseFunction( data ) {
  return new Promise( ( resolve, reject ) => {
    setTimeout( () => {
      console.log( data );
      if ( typeof data === 'number' ) {
        return reject( new Error( 'Data cannot be of type \'number\'.' ) );
      }
      resolve( 'Success!' );
    }, 10 );
  } );
}
promiseFunction( 1 ).then( console.log ).catch( err => console.log( `Error:
${err.message}` ) );
promiseFunction( 'test' ).then( console.log ).catch( err => console.log(
`Error: ${err.message}` ) );
```

Snippet 2.33: Implementing promises

**Outcome**

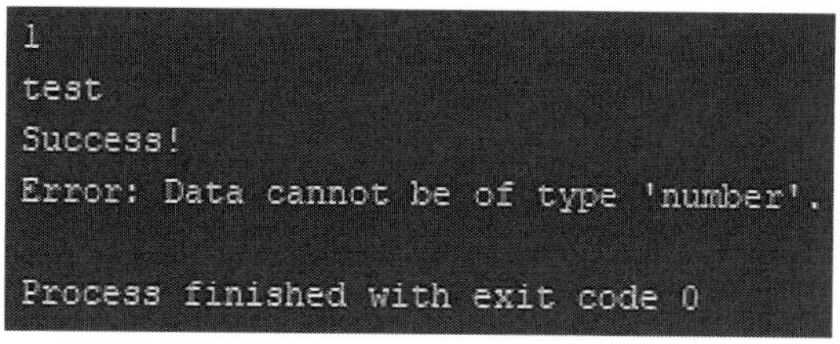

Figure 2.10: Scope outputs

# Async/Await

**Async/await** is a new syntax form added to simplify code that uses promises. Async/await introduces two new keywords: **async** and **await**. Async is added to function declarations and await is used inside an **async** function. It is surprisingly easy to understand and use. In its simplest form, async/await allows us to write promise-based asynchronous code that looks almost identical to the synchronous code that does the same task. We will use async/await to simplify code using promises and make it even easier to read and understand.

## Async/Await Syntax

The **async** keyword is added to function declarations; it must precede the function keyword. An **async** function declaration defines an asynchronous function. An example declaration of an **async** function is shown in the following snippet:

```
async function asyncExample( /* arguments */  ){ /* do work */ }
```

Snippet 2.34: Implementing promises

An **async** function implicitly returns a promise, no matter what the return value is specified to be. If the return value is specified as a non-promise type, JavaScript automatically creates a promise and resolves that promise with the returned value. This means that all async functions can have the **Promise.then()** and **Promise.catch()** handlers applied to the return value. This allows for very easy integration with existing promise-based code. This is shown in the following snippet:

```
async function example1( ){ return 'Hello'; }
async function example2( ){ return Promise.resolve( 'World' ); }
example1().then( console.log ); // Expected output: Hello
example2().then( console.log ); // Expected output: World
```

Snippet 2.35: Async function output

The await keyword can only be used inside of an **async** function. Await tells JavaScript to wait until the associated promise settles and returns its result. This means that JavaScript pauses execution of that block of code, waits for the promise to be resolved while doing other async work, then resumes that block of code once the promise settles. This makes the awaited block of code run like a synchronous function, but it does not cost any resources because the JavaScript engine can still do other work, such as run scripts or handle events, while the asynchronous code is being awaited. An example of the await keyword is shown in the following snippet.

> **Note**
>
> Even though async/await functionality makes JavaScript code look and act as if it were synchronous, JavaScript is still running the code asynchronously with the event loop.

```javascript
async function awaitExample( /* arguments */ ){
  let promise = new Promise( ( resolve, reject ) => {
    setTimeout( () => resolve( 'done!'), 100 );
  });
  const result = await promise;
  console.log( result ); // Expected output: done!
}
awaitExample( /* arguments */ );
```

Snippet 2.36: Await keyword

In the preceding example, we defined an **async** function, awaitExample(). Since it is an **async** function, we can use the await keyword. Inside the function, we create a promise that does asynchronous work. In this case, it simply waits 100 milliseconds and then resolves the promise with the string done!. We then await the created promise. When the promise is resolved with a value, the await takes that value and returns it, and the value is saved in the variable result. We then log the value of result to the console. Instead of using a then handler on the promise to get the resolution value, we simply await the value. The await block of this code looks similar to a synchronous code block.

## Asnyc/Await Promise Rejection

Now that we know how to handle promise fulfillment with async/await, how can we handle promise rejection? Error rejection with async/await is very simple and works fantastically with the standard JavaScript error handling. If a promise is rejected, the await statement waiting for that promise resolution throws an error. When an error is thrown inside an **async** function, it is caught automatically by the JavaScript engine and the promise returned by the **async** function is rejected with that error. This sounds slightly complicated, but it is very simple. These relations are shown in the following snippet:

```
async function errorExample1( /* arguments */ ){
  return Promise.reject( 'Rejected!' );
}
async function errorExample2( /* arguments */ ){
  throw 'Rejected!';
}
async function errorExample3( /* arguments */ ){
  await Promise.reject( 'Rejected!' );
}
errorExample1().catch( console.log ); // Expected output: Rejected!
errorExample2().catch( console.log ); // Expected output: Rejected!
errorExample3().catch( console.log ); // Expected output: Rejected!
```

Snippet 2.37: Async/await promise rejection

In the preceding snippet, we created three async functions. In the first function, errorExample1(), we return a promise that is rejected with the string Rejected!. In the second function, errorExample2(), we throw the string Rejected!. Since this is an error thrown inside an **async** function, the **async** function wraps it in a promise and returns a promise rejected with the thrown value. In this case, it returns a promise rejected with the string Rejected!. In the third function, errorExmaple3, we await a rejected promise. Awaiting rejected promises causes JavaScript to throw the promise rejection value, which is Rejected!. The **async** function then catches the error thrown with this value,, wraps it in a promise, rejects the promise with that value, and returns the rejected promise. All three example functions return a promise rejected with the same value.

Since await throws an error if the awaited promise is rejected, we can simply use the standard try/catch error handling mechanism in JavaScript to handle the async errors. This is very useful because it allows us to handle all errors in the same manner, whether asynchronous or synchronous. This is shown in the following example:

```javascript
async function tryCatchExample() {

    // Try to do asynchronous work

    try{

        const value1 = await Promise.resolve( 'Success 1' );

        const value2 = await Promise.resolve( 'Success 2' );

        const value3 = await Promise.reject( 'Oh no!' );

    }


    // Catch errors

    catch( err ){

        console.log( err ); // Expected output: Oh no!

    }

}

tryCatchExample()
```

**Snippet 2.38: Error handling**

In the preceding example, we created an async function that tries to do asynchronous work. The function tries to await three promises in a row. The final one is rejected, which causes an error to be thrown. This error is caught and handled by the catch block.

Since errors are wrapped in promises and rejected by async functions, and await throws errors when a promise is rejected, async/await function error propagate upwards to the highest level await call. This means that unless an error needs to be handled in a special manner at various nesting levels, we can simply use a single try catch block for the outermost error. The error will propagate up the async/await function stack through rejected promises, and only needs to be caught by the top-level await block. This is shown in the following snippet:

```
async function nested1() { return await Promise.reject( 'Error!' ); }

async function nested2() { return await nested1; }

async function nested3() { return await nested2; }

async function nestedErrorExample() {

  try{ const value1 = await nested3; }

  catch( err ){ console.log( err ); } // Expected output: Oh no!

}

nestedErrorExample();
```

Snippet 2.39: Nested error handling

In the preceding example, we created several async functions that await the result of another async function. They are called in the order nestedErrorExample() -> nested3() -> nested2() -> nested1(). The body of nested1() awaits a rejected promise, which throws an error. nested1() catches this error and returns a promise rejected with that error. The body of nested2() awaits the promise returned by nested1(). The promise returned by nested1() was rejected with the original error, so the await in nested2() throws an error, which is wrapped in a promise by nested2(). This propagates down until the await in nestedErrorExample(). The await in the nested error example throws an error, which is caught and handled. Since we only need to handle the error at the highest level, we put the try/catch block at the outermost await call and allow the error to propagate upward until it hits that try/catch block.

## Using Async Await

Now that we know how to use async/await, we need to integrate it into our promise code. To convert our promise code to use async/await, we simply need to break the promise chains into async functions and await each step. The chain of promise handlers is separated at each handler function (then(), catch(), and so on). The value returned by the promise is caught with an await statement and saved into a variable. This value is then passed into the callback function of the first promise then() promise handler, and the result of the function should be caught with an await statement and saved into a new variable. This is done for each then() handler in the promise chain.

To handle the errors and promise rejections, we surround the entire block with a try catch block. An example of this is shown in the following snippet:

```
// Promise chain - API functions return a promise
myPromse.then( apiCall1 ).then( apiCall2 ).then( apiCall3 ).catch(
errorHandler );
async function asyncAwaitUse( myPromise ) {
  try{
    const value1 = await myPromise;
    const value2 = await apiCall1( value1 );
    const value3 = await apiCall2( value2 );
    const value4 = await apiCall3( value3 );
  } catch( err ){
    errorHandler( err );
  }
}
asyncAwaitUse( myPromise );
```

Snippet 2.40: Integrating async/await

As we can see in the promise chain, we chain three API calls and an error handler on to the resolution of `myPromise`. At each promise chain step, a promise is returned and a new `Promise.then()` handler is attached. If one of the promise chain steps is rejected, the catch handler is called.

In the async/await example, we break the promise chain at each `Promise.then()` handler. We then convert the `then` handlers into functions that return promises. In this case, `apiCall1()`, `apiCall2()`, and `apiCall3()` already return promises. We then await each API call step. To handle a promise rejection, we must surround the entire block with a try catch statement.

Much like with promise chains with multiple chained then handlers, an `async` function with multiple await calls will run each await call one at a time, not starting the next await call until the previous await call has received a value from the associated promise. This can slow down asynchronous work if we are trying to complete several asynchronous tasks at the same time. We must wait for each step to complete before starting the next step. To avoid this, we can use `Promise.all` with `await`.

As we learned earlier, Promise.all runs all the child promises at the same time and returns a pending promise that is not fulfilled until all of the child promises have been resolved with a value. We can await a Promise.all much like we would attach a then handler to a Promise.all. The value returned by an await Promise.all call will only be available when all the child promises have completed. This is shown in the following snippet:

```
async function awaitPromiseAll(){

    let promise1 = new Promise( ( resolve, reject ) => setTimeout( () =>
resolve( 10 ), 100 ) );

    let promise2 = new Promise( ( resolve, reject ) => setTimeout( () =>
resolve( 20 ), 200 ) );

    let promise3 = new Promise( ( resolve, reject ) => setTimeout( () =>
resolve( 30 ), 10 ) );

    const result = await Promise.all( [ promise1, promise2, promise3 ] );

    console.log( result ); //Expected output: [ 10, 20, 30 ]

}
awaitPromiseAll();
```

**Snippet 2.41: Parallel await promises**

As we can see from the preceding example, we created several promises, pass those promises into a Promise.all call, then await the resolution of the promise returned by Promise.all. This follows the rules of async/await just as we would expect it to. This same logic can be applied to Promise.race as well.

An example of a promise race is shown in the following snippet:

```
async function awaitPromiseAll(){

    let promise1 = new Promise( ( resolve, reject ) => setTimeout( () =>
resolve( 10 ), 100 ) );

    let promise2 = new Promise( ( resolve, reject ) => setTimeout( () =>
resolve( 20 ), 200 ) );

    const result = await Promise.race( [ promise1, promise2 ] );

    console.log( result ); //Expected output: 10]

}
awaitPromiseAll();
```

**Snippet 2.42: Promise race example**

## Conclusion

Async/await is an amazing new syntax format that helps us simplify promise-based code. It allows us to write code that looks like synchronous code. Async/await introduces two keywords, **async** and **await**. Async is used to denote an **async** function. It prepends the function keyword when declaring functions. Async functions always return a promise. The await keyword can only be used inside async functions on promises. It tells the JavaScript engine to wait on a promise resolution, and on rejection or fulfillment, throws an error or returns the value. Async/await error handling is done through thrown errors and rejected promises. An **async** function automatically catches thrown errors and returns a promise rejected with that error. Awaited promises throw errors on rejection. This allows error handling to be coupled easily with the standard JavaScript try/catch error handling. Async/await is very easy to integrate into your promise-based code and can make it very easy to read.

## Activity 2: Using Async/Await

You have been tasked to build a server that interfaces with a database. You must write code to create and look up basic user objects in the database. Import the `simple_db.js` file. Using the `get` and `insert` commands, write the following program using async/await syntax:

1. Look up the `john` key and if it exists, log the age field of the result object.

2. Look up the `sam` key and if it exists, log the age of the result object.

3. Look up your name. If it does not exist, insert your name. If you must add an object, look up the new object and log the age.

For any `db.get` operation that fails, save the key into an array. At the end of the program, print the keys that failed.

DB API:

`db.get( index ):`

This takes in an index and returns a promise. A promise is fulfilled with the `db` entry associated with that index. If the index does not exist, the lookup fails, or the key is not specified, the promise is rejected with an error.

`db.insert( index, insertData )`:

This takes in an index and data, and returns a promise. The promise is fulfilled with the key inserted if the operation completes. If the operation fails, or there is no key or insert data specified, the promise is rejected with an error.

To utilize promises and async/await syntax to build a program, perform the following steps:

1. Write an **async** function called **main**. All operations will go in here.

2. Create an array to keep track of keys that cause db errors.

3. Catch all errors and log them.

4. Outside all of the try-catch blocks, at the end of the **main** function, return the array.

5. Call the main function and attach a **then()** and **catch()** handler to the returned promise.

**Outcome**

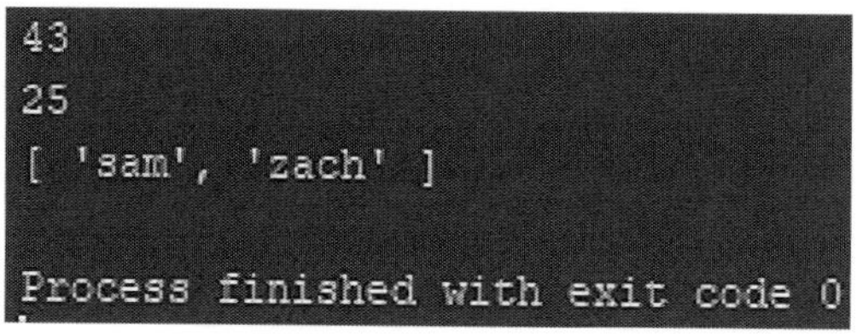

```
43
25
[ 'sam', 'zach' ]

Process finished with exit code 0
```

Figure 2.11: Scope outputs

You successfully used promises and async/await syntax to build a program that accesses a database.

> **Note**
>
> The solution for this activity can be found on page 282.

## Summary

JavaScript is an asynchronous, event-driven, single-threaded language. Instead of hanging during a long-running operation to another resource, JavaScript does work on other operations if any work is pending. JavaScript accomplishes this with the event loop. The event loop is composed of the call stack, heap, event queue, and main event loop. These four components work together to schedule when JavaScript runs different parts of the code. To leverage JavaScript's asynchronous nature, we use callbacks or promises. Callbacks are simply functions passed as arguments into other functions. Promises are special classes with event handler functions. When an asynchronous operation finishes, the JavaScript engine runs the callback or calls the promise handler attached to that operation's complete event. This is asynchronous JavaScript in its simplest form.

In the next chapter, we will learn about the **Document Object Model** (DOM), the **JavaScript event object**, and the **jQuery library**.

# 3

# DOM Manipulation and Event Handling

**Learning Objectives**

By the end of this chapter, you will be able to do the following:

- Explain DOM traversal and manipulation
- Create the event object and browser events
- Organize event propagation and bubbling
- Delegate events efficiently
- Utilize JQuery to handle events and DOM manipulation

This chapter will cover working with document nodes, event objects, and the process of chaining, navigation, and handling events.

## Introduction

In the first chapter, we covered many of the new and powerful features that were released in ES6. We discussed the evolution of JavaScript and highlighted the key additions in ES6. We discussed scope rules, variable declaration, arrow functions, template literals, enhanced object properties, destructuring assignment, classes and modules, transpiling, and iterators and generators.

In the second chapter, we covered JavaScript's asynchronous programming paradigms. We discussed the JavaScript event loop, callbacks, promises, and the async/await syntax. This chapter prepared us to apply the material from *Chapter 1, Introducing ECMAScript 6* and write powerful asynchronous programs.

In this chapter, we will learn about the **Document Object Model (DOM)** and the **JavaScript Event object**. In the first topic, we will define the Document Object Model and explain DOM chaining, navigation, and manipulation. Then, we will explain the JavaScript event object and show how to interact with and handle DOM events. In this chapter, we will cover jQuery and use it to traverse the DOM and handle events.

## DOM Chaining, Navigation, and Manipulation

The **Document Object Model (DOM)** is an interface for HTML documents. The DOM represents a web page in such a way that programs can change the document structure, style, and content. The DOM is the object-oriented representation of a web page.

There are two standards for the DOM: the **World Wide Web Consortium (W3C)** standard and the **Web Hypertext Application Technology Working Group (WHATWG)** standard. WHATWG was developed in response to the slow development of the W3C standard. Both standards define HTML elements as objects that can be accessed by JavaScript code, and properties, accessor methods, and events for all HTML elements. DOM object methods are actions you can perform on HTML elements and DOM object properties are values you can get or set. The DOM standard provides a way for JavaScript to add, get, change, or delete HTML elements programmatically.

> **Note**
>
> The W3C DOM standard and WHATWG DOM standard are implemented by most modern browsers (Chrome, Firefox, and Edge), and many browsers extend the standard. When interfacing with the DOM, we must make sure that all of the functions we use are compatible with the browsers our users may have.

The DOM for a web page is constructed as a tree of objects, called **nodes**. The object at the head of the tree is a **document node**. The **document** is the interface that serves as an entry point for the web page's content, the DOM tree. HTML elements in the page are added to the DOM tree under the document. They are called **element nodes**.

Elements in the DOM tree can have three types of relationships with the elements around them: **parent**, **sibling**, and **child**. An element's parent element is the element that it is contained by. An element's sibling nodes are elements that are also contained by the element's parent. An element's child nodes are the elements that it contains. An example DOM tree is shown in the following diagram:

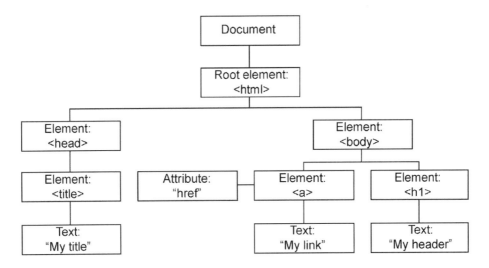

Figure 3.1: DOM tree structure

In the preceding diagram, we can see that the global parent is the **document object**. The document object has one child node, the <html> element. The <html> element's parent node is the document and it has two child nodes, the <head> and <body> elements. The <head> and <body> elements are sibling nodes to each other because they both have the same parent.

## Exercise 20: Building the HTML Document from a DOM Tree Structure

The aim here is to create a web page, "My title", which displays the header "My header" and the link "My link". Reference the preceding diagram for the DOM tree structure.

To build an HTML document from a DOM tree structure, perform the following steps:

1.  Create an HTML file.

2.  Add an <html> tag to the file.

3.  Add a <head> tag inside the <html> tag.

4.  Add a <title> tag after the <head> tag.

5.  Add the text **My title** in the <title> tag.

6.  Add a <body> tag below the <head> tag.

7.  Add the elements <a> and <h4> under the <body> tag.

8.  Add the href attribute to the <a> tag and set its internal text to **My link**.

9.  Add the text **My header** inside the <h4> tag.

10. Close the body and html tags and fetch the output.

## Code

index.js

```
<html>
  <head>
    <title>My title</title>
  </head>
  <body>
    <a href>My link</a>
    <h4>My header</h4>
  </body>
</html>
```

https://bit.ly/2FiLgcE

Snippet 3.1: Simple site to demonstrate a DOM tree

**Outcome**

My link

# My header

Figure 3.2: My header link output

You have successfully built an HTML document from a DOM tree structure.

## DOM Navigation

Now that we understand the basic structure of the DOM, we are ready to start interfacing with it in our applications. Before we can begin to modify the DOM with JavaScript, we have to navigate the DOM tree to find the specific element nodes that we want to modify. We can find a specific node in one of two ways: **finding it by identifier** or **navigating the DOM tree**. The fastest look up method is looking up an element by identifier. DOM elements can be looked up in one of four ways:

- ID
- Tag name
- Class
- CSS query selector

## Finding a DOM Node

Getting an element by ID is done with the `document.getElementById( id )` method. This method takes in a parameter id, which represents the id of the element to look up, and returns an element object. The object that's returned will be the element object that describes the DOM node of the specified id. If no element matches the id provided, the function will return null. An example of the `getElementById` function is shown in the following snippet:

```
<div id="exampleDiv">Some text here</div>

<script>
  const elem = document.getElementById( 'exampleDiv' );
</script>
```

Snippet 3.2: Getting an element by its id

Getting an element by tag name is done with the `document.getElementsByTagName( name )` method. The function takes in a single argument that represents the HTML tag name to search for. `getElementsByTagName` returns a live `HTMLCollection` of elements that match the given tag name. The returned list is live, which means that it updates itself with the DOM tree automatically. There is no need to call the function several times with the same element and arguments. An example of `getElementsByTagName` is shown in the following snippet:

```
<div id="exampleDiv1">Some text here</div>
<div id="exampleDiv2">Some text here</div>
<div id="exampleDiv3">Some text here</div>
<script>
  const elems = document.getElementsByTagName( 'div' );
</script>
```

Snippet 3.3: Getting elements by tag name

> **Note**
>
> An `HTMLCollection` is an interface that represents a collection (array-like object) of element nodes. It can be iterated over and offers methods and properties for selecting from the list.

To get an element by class name, we use the `document.getElementsByClassName( name )` method. The function takes in a single argument that represents the HTML class name to search for and returns a live `HTMLCollection` of elements that match the given `classname`. An example of `getElementsByClassName` is shown in the following snippet:

```
<div class="example">Some text here</div>
<img class="example"></img>
<style class="example"></style>
<script>
  const elems = document.getElementsByClassName( 'example' );
</script>
```

Snippet 3.4: Getting elements by class name

The two functions, **querySelector()** and **querySelectorAll()**, are used to get HTML elements by CSS query selector. They both take in a single string parameter that represents a CSS selector string. **querySelector** will return a single element. **querySelectorAll** will return a static (non-live) **NodeList** of the elements that match the query. Multiple query selectors can be passed into the function by creating a comma-separated string that contains each selector. If multiple selectors are passed into the query selector functions, the function will match and return elements that meet any of the selector's requirements. The functionality for **querySelector** and **querySelectorAll** is shown in the following snippet:

```
<div id="id1">Some text here</div>

<img class="class"></img>

<script>

  const elem = document.querySelector( 'img.class' );

  const elems = document.querySelectorAll( 'img.class, #id1' );

</script>
```

Snippet 3.5: Getting elements by using the CSS selector

> **Note**
>
> A **NodeList** is similar to an **HTMLCollection**. It is an array-like collection of HTML nodes that can be iterated over.

Each of the methods covered previously and their function syntax are shown in the following table:

| | Id | Tag Name | Class | Query |
|---|---|---|---|---|
| **Syntax** | getElementById() | getElementsByTagName() | getElementsByClassName() | querySelector() querySelectorAll() |
| **Description** | Get an element by its id attribute. Returns null or an element object. | Get an element by the HTML tag name. Returns a live HTMLCollection of the matching elements. | Get an element by the class attribute. Returns a live HTMLCollection of the matching elements. | Get elements by CSS selector. querySelector returns an element object and querySelectorAll returns a static NodeList. |

Figure 3.3: Methods and syntax

The getElementsByTagName, getElementsByClassName, querySelector, and querySelectorAll functions are not limited to only the document object; they can also be called on element nodes. If they are called on an element node, the resulting elements collection returned by the function will be limited to only the children of the element, which the function was called on. This is shown in the following example.

**Example**: We get the element object for the div with the id div1 and save it in the elem variable. We then use getElementsByTagName to get other div elements. The function is called on the element object saved in elem, so the search space is limited to child nodes of div1. getElementsByTagName will return an HTMLCollection with the divs div2 and div3 because they are descendants of div1:

```
<div id="div1">
  <div id="div2">
    <div> id="div3"> Some text here </div>
  </div>
</div>
<div> Some other text here </div>
<script>
  const elem = document.getElementById( 'div1' );
  const elems = elem.getElementsByTagName( 'div' );
</script>
```

*Snippet 3.6: Returning an HTMLCollection*

The second way to find DOM elements is by navigating the DOM tree through the element relationships. Once we have found a DOM element to work with, we can use several properties to get that element's child, parent, and sibling nodes. We can traverse the DOM tree by going from node to node with the properties parentNode, childNodes, firstChild, lastChild, previousSibling, and nextSibling.

The parentNode property returns a node's parent node. The parent node is a node in the DOM tree that the node is a descendent of. The parent node will always exist unless parentNode is called on the document node. Since the document node is at the top of the DOM tree, it has no parent, and the call to parentNode will return null. The DOM tree can be climbed with the parentNode property. An example of parentNode is shown in the following example:

```
<div id="div1">
  <div id="div2">
```

```
    <div id="div3"> Some text here </div>
  </div>
</div>
<script>
  const div3 = document.getElementById( 'div3' );
  const div2 = div3.parentNode;
  const div1 = div2.parentNode;
</script>
```

**Snippet 3.7: Parent node**

The nextSibling and previousSibling properties are to get a node's siblings in the DOM tree. previousSibling will return the previous sibling in the DOM tree (the sibling added to the parent node before the current node) and nextSibling will return the next sibling in the DOM tree (the sibling node added to the parent node after the current node). When DOM trees are drawn, the node's previous sibling is usually shown to the left and the next sibling is usually shown on the right. The DOM tree can be traversed laterally with the nextSibling and previousSibling functions. These properties are shown in the following example:

```
<div id="div0">
  <div id="div1"> Some text here </div>
  <div id="div2"> Some text here </div>
  <div id="div3"> Some text here </div>
</div>
<script>
  const div2 = document.getElementById( 'div2' );
  const sibling1 = div2.previousSibling; //div1
  const sibling2 = div2.nextSibling; // div3
</script>
```

**Snippet 3.8: Traversing sibling nodes**

The three last properties are for navigating to a node's child node; they are childNodes, firstChild, and lastChild. The childNodes property returns a live NodeList of the child nodes of an element. The firstChild and lastChild properties return the first or last node from the child NodeList respectively. The use of these properties is shown in the following snippet:

```html
<div id="div0">
  <div id="div1"> Some text here </div>
  <div id="div2"> Some text here </div>
  <div id="div3"> Some text here </div>
</div>
<script>
  const div0 = document.getElementById( 'div0' );
  const child1 = div0.firstChild; //div1
  const child2 = div0.childNodes[1]; // div2
  const child3 = div0.lastChild; // div3
</script>
```

**Snippet 3.9: Traversing sibling nodes**

## Traversing the DOM

The DOM tree navigation properties are summarized in the following table:

| Property | Description |
| --- | --- |
| parentNode | Returns the node's parent node. Returns null if there is no parent node. |
| nextSibling | Returns the node's next sibling in the DOM tree. Returns null if there is no sibling. |
| previousSibling | Returns the node's previous sibling in the DOM tree. Returns null if there is no sibling. |
| childNodes | Returns a NodeList of the node's children. |
| firstChild | Returns the first node's child. Returns null if the node has no children. |
| lastChild | Returns the last node's child. Returns null if the node has no children. |

Figure 3.4: DOM tree navigation properties

## DOM Manipulation

When you write an app or web page, one of the most powerful tools you have is manipulating the document structure in some way. This is done through DOM manipulation functions, for controlling the HTML and styling the app or page. Being able to manipulate the HTML document while the user uses an app or website allows us to dynamically change parts of the page without fully reloading the content. For example, when you use a messaging app on your cell phone, the app's code is manipulating the document you're looking at. Every time you send a message, it updates the document to append the elements and styling that makes up the message. There are three basic ways we can manipulate the DOM. We can add elements or nodes, remove elements or nodes, and update elements or nodes.

Adding new elements to the DOM tree is a must-have for interactive applications. There are many examples in most of the web applications you use. Both Google's Gmail and Microsoft's Skype actively add elements to the DOM as you use the application. There are two steps to adding a new element to the DOM. First, we must create a node for the element we want to add, and then we must add the new node to the DOM tree.

To create a new element or node, we can use the `document.createElement()`, `node.cloneNode()`, and `document.createTextNode()` functions. `createElement` is called on the global document object and takes in two arguments. The first is `tagName`. **tagName** is a string that specifies the type of element to be created. If we want to create a new div element, we would pass the `div` string in through `tagName`. The second argument is an optional argument called options. Options is an `ElementCreationObject` that contains a single property, named 'is'. This property allows us to specify if the element being added is a custom element. We will not be using this property, but it is important to know what it is used for. `createElement` returns a newly created Element object. The syntax and usage of `document.createElement()` are shown in the following snippet:

```
<script>
  const newElem = document.createElement( 'div' );
</script>
```

Snippet 3.10: Using document.createElement

A new element node can also be created with the `cloneNode` function. `cloneNode` is called on a DOM node object and duplicates the node that it is called on. It takes in one argument, a Boolean called `deep`, and returns a copy of the node to clone. If `deep` is set to `false`, `cloneNode` will do a shallow clone and only clone the node that it was called on. If `deep` is set to `true`, `cloneNode` will do a deep copy and copy the node and all of its child nodes (the node's full DOM tree). Cloning a node copies all of its attributes and their values. This includes event listeners that are added inline in the HTML, but not listeners added through JavaScript with `addEventListener`, or those assigned with element properties.

The following is an example of `cloneNode`:

```
<div id="div1">
  <div id="div2"> Text </div>
</div>
<script>
  const div1 = document.getElementById( 'div1' );
  const div1Clone = div1.cloneNode( false );
  const div1Div2Clone = div1.cloneNode( true )
</script>
```

Snippet 3.11: Cloning a node

In the preceding example, we created a document with two divs, div1 and div2. div2 is nested inside of div1. In the preceding code, we selected div1 by its id and cloned it into div1Clone by doing a shallow nodeClone. We then did a deep nodeClone and cloned div1 and its nested child, div2, into div1Div2Clone.

> **Note**
>
> cloneNode may lead to duplicate element ids in a document. If you copy a node with an id, you should update that node's id property to something unique.
>
> The spec for DOM has been updated recently. In the DOM4 specification, deep was an optional parameter for cloneNode. If omitted, the method would default the value to true, using deep cloning as the default behavior. To create a shallow clone, deep must be set to false. In the latest DOM spec, this behavior has been changed. Deep is still an optional parameter; however, it defaults to false. We recommend always providing the deep parameter for backward and forward compatibility.

CreateTextNode is used to create text-only nodes. Text-only DOM nodes are used when filling the page with text. We use createTextNode to place new text in an element like a div. CreateTextNode takes in one argument, a string called data, and returns a text node. An example of createTextNode is shown in the following snippet:

```
<script>
  const textNode = document.createTextNode( 'Text goes here' );
</script>
```

*Snippet 3.12: Creating a text node*

Now that we know how to create new DOM nodes, we must add the new nodes to the DOM tree to see changes in our application. We can add new nodes with two functions: Node.appendChild() and Node.insertBefore(). Both functions are called on a DOM node object.

Node.appendChild adds a node to the end of the child list of the node it is called on.
Node.appendChild takes in one argument, aChild, and returns the appended child.
The aChild argument is the node that we want to append to the parent node's child
list. If appendChild is passed in a node that already exists in the DOM tree, the node
is moved from its current position to the new position in the DOM, as a child of the
specified parent node. If appendChild is passed a DocumentFragment, the entire content
of the DocumentFragment is moved into the child list of the parent node, and an empty
Document Fragment is returned. The syntax and use of appendChild are shown in the
following snippet:

```
<div id="div1"></div>
<script>
  const div1 = document.getElementById( 'div1' );
  const aChild = document.createElement( 'div' );
  parent.appendChild( aChild );
</script>
```

**Snippet 3.13: Inserting a node with appendChild**

> **Note**
>
> A DocumentFragment is simply a DOM tree that does not have a parent.

In the preceding example, we created an HTML document with a div, div1. We then
created a new div, div2, and then appended it to the div1 child list with the appendChild
function.

A node can also be inserted into the DOM with the Node.insertBefore() function. The
insertBefore function inserts a node into the child list of the node it is called on, in
front of a specified reference node. The insertBefore function takes in two parameters,
newNode and referenceNode, and returns the inserted node. The newNode parameter
represents the node that we are inserting. The referenceNode parameter is a node
from the parent's child node list or the value null. If referenceNode is a node from the
parent's child list, newNode will be inserted in front of that node, but if referenceNode is
the value null, newNode will be inserted at the end of the parent's child node list. Much
like Node.appendChild(), if the function is given a node to insert that is already in the
DOM tree, the node will be removed from its old position in the DOM tree and placed
in its new position as a child of the parent node. InsertBefore can also insert an entire
DocumentFragment. If newNode is a DocumentFragment, the function will return an empty
DocumentFragment.

An example of **appendChild** is shown in the following snippet:

```
<div id="div1">
  <div id="div2"></div>
</div>
<script>
  const div1 = document.getElementById( 'div1' );
  const div2 = document.getElementById( 'div2' );
  const div3 = document.createElement( 'div' );
  const div4 = document.createElement( 'div' );
  div1.insertBefore( div3, div2 );
  div1.insertBefore( div4, null );
</script>
```

**Snippet 3.14: Inserting a node with insertBefore**

In the preceding example, we created a div, div1, with a nested child div, div2. In the script, we got div1 and div2 by element id. We then created two new divs, div3 and div4. We inserted div3 into div1's child list. We passed div2 as the reference node, so div3 is inserted in front of div2 in div1's child list. We then inserted div4 into the div1 child list. We passed in null as the reference node. This causes div4 to be appended to the end of the div1 child list.

> **Note**
>
> The referenceNode parameter is not an optional parameter. You must explicitly pass in a node or the value null. Different browsers and browser versions interpret invalid values differently and app functionality may be compromised.

Another key functionality of manipulating the DOM is the ability to remove DOM nodes from the DOM tree. This functionality can be seen in Gmail and Facebook. When you delete an email in Gmail or remove a Facebook post, the DOM element associated with that email or post is being removed from the DOM tree. DOM node removal is done with the `Node.removeChild()` function. `RemoveChild` removes the specified child from the parent node it is called from. It takes in one argument, child, and returns the child DOM node removed. The child argument must be a child in the parent node's child list. If the child element is not a child of the parent node, an exception will be thrown.

An example of the `removeChild` functionality is shown in the following snippet:

```
<div id="div1">
  <div id="div2"></div>
</div>
<script>
  const div1 = document.getElementById( 'div1' );
  const div2 = document.getElementById( 'div2' );
  div1.removeChild( div2 );
</script>
```

Snippet 3.15: Removing a node from the DOM

In the preceding example, we created a div, `div1`, with a nested child div, `div2`. In the script, we get both divs by element id, then remove `div2` from the `div1` child list.

Now that we can add and remove nodes from the DOM, it would be very useful to be able to modify nodes that already exist. Nodes can be updated in the following ways:

- Replacing the node
- Changing the inner HTML
- Changing attributes
- Changing the class
- Changing the style

## Updating Nodes in the DOM

The first way to modify a DOM node is by replacing it entirely with a new DOM node. A DOM node can have any of its children replaced with the `node.replaceChild()` function. `ReplaceChild` replaces one child of the parent node and it is called on with a new specified node. It takes in two arguments, `newChild` and `oldChild`, and returns the replaced node (`oldChild`). The `oldChild` parameter is the node in the parent's child list that will be replaced and the `newChild` parameter is the node that will replace `oldChild`.

An example of this is shown in the following snippet:

```
<div id="div1">
  <div id="div2"></div>
</div>
<div id="div3"></div>
<script>
  const div1 = document.getElementById( 'div1' );
  const div2 = document.getElementById( 'div2' );
  const div3 = document.getElementById( 'div3' );
  div1.replaceChild( div3, div2 );
</script>
```

Snippet 3.16: Replacing nodes in the DOM

In the preceding example, we created two divs, `div1` and `div2`. `Div1` is created with a nested child div, `div2`. In the script, we get each div by its element id. We then replace the `div1` child, `div2`, with `div3`.

The second way to manipulate a DOM node is by changing the node's inner HTML. The node's innerhTML property can be used to get or set the HTML or XML markup contained in the element. The property can be used to change the current HTML code of the element's children. It can be used to update or overwrite anything below the element in the DOM tree. To insert HTML into the node, set the innerhTML parameter equal to a string containing the HTML, elements you want to add. The string passed into the parameter is parsed as HTML and new DOM nodes are created; they're then added as children to the parent node the property was referenced from. An example of the innerhTML property is shown in the following snippet:

```
<div id="div1"></div>

<script>
  const div1 = document.getElementById( 'div1' );
  div1.innerHTML = '<p>Paragraph1</p><p>Paragraph2</p>';
</script>
```

**Snippet 3.17: Replacing the innerHTML of a node**

> ### Note
>
> Setting the value of innerhTML completely overwrites the old value. DOM nodes will be removed and replaced with the new nodes that have been parsed from the HTML string.
>
> For security reasons, innerhTML will not parse and execute script contained in <script> tags inside of the HTML string. There are, however, other ways to execute JavaScript through the innerhTML property. You should never use innerhTML to append string data you have no control over.

The third way to manipulate an element node is by changing the node's attributes. Element node attributes can be interacted with through three functions: `Element.getAttribute()`, `Element.setAttribute()`, and `Element.removeAttribute()`. All three of these functions must be called on an element node.

> **Note**
>
> Some attributes applied to element nodes have special meanings. Be careful when adding or removing attributes. A list of HTML attributes is shown here: https://developer.mozilla.org/en-US/docs/Web/HTML/Attributes.

The `getAttribute` function takes in one parameter, the name of the attribute, and returns the value of the specified attribute. If the attribute does not exist, the function will return null or the empty string (""). Modern DOM specifications state that the function should return the value null and most browsers follow this specification, but some browsers still follow the old DOM3 specification, which states that the correct return value should be the empty string. It is important to handle both cases.

The `setAttribute` function is used to set or update the value of the specified attribute. It takes in two parameters, **name** and **value**, and does not return any value. The `name` parameter is the name of the attribute that will be set. The `value` parameter is the string value that the attribute will be set to. If the value passed in is not a string, it will be converted in to a string before being set. Since the value is converted in to a string, setting an attribute to an object or null will not have the expected value. The attribute will get set to the stringified version of the value that's passed in.

The `removeAttribute` function removes the specified attribute from the node. It takes in a single parameter, `attrName`, and returns no value. The `attrName` parameter is the name of the attribute to be removed. You can use `removeAttribute` instead of attempting to set an attribute's value to null with `setAttribute`. An example of `getAttribute`, `setAttribute`, and `removeAttribute` is shown in the following snippet:

```
<div id="div1"></div>
<script>
  const div1 = document.getElementById( 'div1' );
  div1.setAttribute( 'testName', 'testValue' );
  div1.getAttribute( 'testName' );
  div1.removeAttribute( 'testName' );
</script>
```

Snippet 3.18: Getting, setting, and removing attributes

In the preceding example, we create a div called ᵈiᵛ₄. We then get that div by its id, add the testₙₐᵐe attribute, and set its value to testvalᵘe. We then get the value of testₙₐᵐe and remove it.

The fourth way to manipulate a node is by changing its class information. Element class information is used to associate similar HTML elements for styling and grouping purposes. An element's class can be accessed in two ways, the classₙₐᵐe property or the classₗist property. The classₙₐᵐe property returns a string containing all of the element's class information. This property can be used to get or set the class value. The classₗist property returns a live DOₘᵀoᵏeₙₗist object. This object is simply a live list of the current class information with special methods for getting and updating class information.

## Updating Nodes in the DOM

The classₗist object has six helper functions. They are detailed in the following table:

| Function | Input Parameters | Description |
| --- | --- | --- |
| .add() | Any number of string arguments. | Adds the specified class values. If the class already exists it is ignored. |
| .remove() | Any number of string arguments. | Removes the specified class values. Class values that do not exist are ignored. |
| .item() | A number. | Returns the class value by index in the list. |
| .toggle() | A string and an optional force Boolean. | Toggles the class value (removes or adds). If the force Boolean is truthy then the class is added. If the Boolean value is falsey the class is removed. |
| .contains() | A string. | Checks if the class value exists. Returns a Boolean. |
| .replace() | An old class string with a new class string. | Replaces an existing class with a new class. |

Figure 3.5: Helper functions

These helper functions are used in the following snippet:

```
<div id="div1" class="testClass"></div>
<script>
  const classes = document.getElementById( 'div1' ).classList;
  classes.add( 'class1', 'class2' ); // adds class1 and class2
  classes.remove( 'testClass' ); // removes testClass
  classes.item( 1 ); // gets class at index 1: class2
  classes.toggle( 'class2' ); // removes class2 because it exists
  classes.contains( 'class2' ); // checks for class2: false
  classes.replace( 'class1', 'class0' ) // replaces class1 with class3
</script>
```

**Snippet 3.19: Using the classList object**

The fifth and final way we typically modify a node is through the style object. The style object reflects the node's CSS styling, and every element node has a style object. The style object can be obtained through `Element.style`. The style object contains properties for each CSS style that can be assigned to the object. This object is meant to be read-only, so element style should not be set directly by overwriting the style object. Instead, we should change the individual properties of the style object:

```
<div id="div1" style="color:blue">Hello World!</div>
<script>
  const style = document.getElementById( 'div1' ).style;
  style[ 'color' ]; // Returns blue
  style[ 'background-color' ] = 'red'; // Sets background-color to red
</script>
```

**Snippet 3.20: Using the classList object**

> **Note**
>
> A list of all of the available style properties can be found online at https://www.w3schools.com/jsref/dom_obj_style.asp.

DOM manipulation is one of the most important parts of a web page. The DOM can be manipulated by finding, adding, removing, and updating the nodes in the tree. We can find a DOM node in several ways—by unique id, by class, or by CSS query selector. Once we have found a DOM node, we can traverse the DOM tree by stepping to that element's child, sibling, or parent nodes. To add new elements to the DOM tree, we must first create a new element node, then append that element somewhere in the DOM. To remove an element, we simply get the node for the element we want to remove and then call the node remove function. To update a node, we can change any of its properties, attributes, or flat out replace the node. DOM manipulation allows us to build dynamic web pages and it is important to master it.

### Conclusion

Web documents built from HTML code are represented by the Document Object Model, or DOM. The DOM is a tree-like structure built from nodes. Each node corresponds to an element in the HTML source. As programmers, we can interact with the DOM to dynamically updated web pages. We can interact with the DOM by finding, creating, removing, and updating element nodes. Combining all of these concepts allows us to create dynamic web pages that can update the view based on user interaction. This kind of functionality can be seen on nearly every website, including Amazon, Facebook, and Google.

### Exercise 21: DOM Manipulation

Your team is building an email website. The site needs to load the user's email data from a JSON file and dynamically populate a table with the email data that's loaded. The emails are provided in the example code file. The email table should show the **From**, **To**, and **Subject** fields and have a row for each email. Use the emails object to build the email table in the DOM through the DOM manipulation you learned about in this chapter.

To build an email list with JavaScript using DOM manipulation techniques, perform the following steps:

1. Open the file called **exercise** from **/exercises/exercise21/exercise.html**.

2. In the `script` tag, at the bottom of the file, write the JavaScript code (under *Code*, at the end of this exercise).

3. Make a new table element (`<table>`) and save it into a variable called `table`.

4. Create a new scope block with curly braces (`{}`).

   Create an array to hold the header types **To**, **From**, and **Subject**. Save the array into the variable headers.

Create a table row element (<tr>) and save it into the variable row. Loop through the headers array with a forEach function.

5.  Inside the callback of forEach, do the following:

Create the table header element (<th>) and save it into the header variable. Using appendChild(), append a new text node to header. The text node should contain the header name.

Append the header element stored in header as a child to the table row stored in row.

6.  Append the table row stored in row as a child to the table stored in table. The output is shown in the following figure:

## To From Subject

Figure 3.6: Step 4 output

7.  Create a new scope block with curly braces ({}).

8.  Loop over the data array, data, with a forEach loop and do the following:

Create a new table row element (<tr>) and save it in the row variable. Create another new table data element (<td>) and save it in the to variable.

Next, create two more table data elements (<td> and <td>) and save them as variables (subject and from).

Append a text node to the table data element stored in to that contains the forEach loop's data object's to value. Append another text node to the table data element stored in from that contains the forEach loop's data object's from value.

Append a text node to the table data element stored in subject that contains the forEach loop's data object's subject value.

Append the element stored in to to the table row stored in row. Append the element stored in from to the table row stored in row.

Append the element stored in subject to the table row stored in row. Append the row stored in row to the table stored in table.

9. Get the `emailTableHolder` DOM node and append the table stored in the `table` variable as a child node.

10. Load the HTML file in a web browser to view the results:

| To | From | Subject |
|----|------|---------|
| Tim | Zach | Hello |
| Tim | Kirsten | Car for sale |
| Tim | Jessica | Code review |
| Tim | Walter | Donations |
| Tim | Tristain | Birthday party |

Figure 3.7: Final output

## Code

solution.html

```
const table = document.createElement( 'table' );
const row = document.createElement( 'tr' );
[ 'to', 'from', 'subject' ].forEach( h => {
  const header = document.createElement( 'th' );
  header.appendChild( document.createTextNode( h ) );
  row.appendChild( header );
} );
table.appendChild( row );
data.forEach( email => {
  const row = document.createElement( 'tr' );
  /* code omitted for brevity */
  table.appendChild( row );
} );
document.getElementById( 'emailTableHolder' ).appendChild( table );
```

Snippet 3.21: DOM manipulation to create an email list

https://bit.ly/2Fmvdk4

## Outcome

You have successfully analyzed DOM manipulation techniques.

# DOM Events and Event Objects

DOM events are the backbone of functional and responsive web applications. Events are used in any website that has any form of user interaction. Websites such as Facebook, Google, and Skype all heavily make use of events. An event is a signal that tells the programmer that something has happened to a DOM node. An event can be fired for nearly any reason. We can use JavaScript to listen for events and run functions when an event occurs.

## DOM Event

A **DOM event** is a notification sent by a DOM node to let the programmer know that something has happened to the DOM node. This can be anything from a user clicking on an element or pressing a key on the keyboard to video playback ending. There are a lot of events that can be fired. Every event that can be fired can have an event listener attached to it. An event listener is an interface that waits for an event to fire and then calls an event handler. An event handler is code that is run in response to an event. Event handlers are JavaScript functions that we, as programmers, assign to an event. This is called registering an event handler.

> **Note**
>
> A complete list of events can be found here: https://developer.mozilla.org/en-US/docs/Web/Events.

The best way to add an event handler is with the `addEventListener` function. The `addEventListener` function sets up the specified event handler to be called when an event of the specified type fires. The function takes in three parameters, **type**, **listener**, and either **options** or **useCapture**. The first argument, type, is the case-sensitive event type to listen for. The second argument, listener, is the object that can receive a notification, usually a JavaScript function. The options and **useCapture** parameters are optional and you may only provide one of them. The options argument specifies an options objects with the **capture**, **once**, and **passive** properties. In the options argument, the property named 'capture' is a Boolean indicating that events will be dispatched to the event handler before they are pushed to the DOM tree. The property named 'once' is a Boolean that indicates whether the event handler should be removed after it has been called once. The property named 'passive' is a Boolean that indicates that event handler will never call the `preventDefault` function (discussed in the handling events subtopic). The useCapture parameter functions the same way as the `options.capture` property.

## Event Listeners

**Event listeners** can be attached to any DOM node. To attach an event listener, we must select the node that needs to listen to the event, and then we can call the `addEventListener` function on that node. This is shown in the following snippet:

```
<button id="button1">Click me!</button>
<script>
  const button1 = document.getElementById( 'button1' );
  button1.addEventListener( 'click', () => {
    console.log( 'Clicked' );
  }, false );
</script>
```

Snippet 3.22: Getting, setting, and removing attributes

In the preceding example, we created a button with the id `button1`. In the script, we selected that button and added an event listener. The event listener listens for click events. When a click event happens, it calls the handler function, which logs to the console.

> **Note**
>
> You may see inline event handlers in HTML code, for example, `<button onclick="alert( 'Hello!' )">Press me</button>`. You should not do this. It is best practice to keep JavaScript and HTML separate. When you mix HTML and JavaScript, the code can quickly become unmanageable, inefficient, and harder to parse and interpret.

At a later time, if we decide we no longer want an event listener, we can remove it with the `removeEventListener` function. The `removeEventListener` function removes the specified handler function from the specified event type. It takes the same parameters as `addEventListener`. To properly remove an event listener, `removeEventListener` must match it with a listener that's been added. `RemoveEventListener` looks for a listener that has the same type, listener function, and capture option. If a match is found, then the event listener is removed. An example of `removeEventListener` is shown in the following snippet:

```
<button id="button1">Click me!</button>
<script>
  const button1 = document.getElementById( 'button1' );
```

```
function eventHandler() { console.log( 'clicked!' }
button1.addEventListener( 'click', eventHandler, true );
button1.removeEventListener( 'click', eventHandler, true );
</script>
```

Snippet 3.23: Getting, setting, and removing attributes

In the preceding example, we created a button with the id button1. In the script, we get that button by its id by adding add an event listener for the click event. We then remove that same listener, providing the exact same parameters we provided to the addEventListener function, so that removeEventListener can properly match the listener that we want to remove.

## Event Objects and Handling Events

Every event handler function takes in a single parameter. This is the event object. You will often see this parameter defined as event, evt, or simply e. It is automatically passed to the event handler to provide information about the event. The event handler can leverage the information in the event object to manipulate the DOM and allow the user to interact with the page:

```
<div id="div1">Click me!</div>
<script>
  const div1 = document.getElementById( 'div1' );
  button1.addEventListener( 'click', ( e ) => {
    e.target.style.backgroundColor = 'red';
  }, false);
</script>
```

Snippet 3.24: Using an event handler to manipulate the DOM

A new instance of an event object can be created by calling a new instance of the event class (new Event()). The constructor takes in two arguments: **type** and **options**. Type is the type of the event and options is an optional object containing the following fields: **bubbles**, **cancelable**, and **composed**. All three of these fields are also optional. The bubbles property indicates whether the event should bubble. The cancelable property indicates whether the event can be canceled. The composed property indicates whether the event should trigger listeners outside of a shadow root. All three default to false.

The event object has many useful properties and functions. These properties can be leveraged to gain additional information about the event. For example, we can use the `Event.target` property to obtain the DOM node that the event was originally fired from, or we can use `Event.type` to see the name of the event. `Event.target` is very useful when you want to use the same handler for multiple elements. Instead of having a new handler function for each event, we can reuse a handler and simply use `Event.target` to check which element fired the event.

When an event is fired from a DOM element, it notifies the event listeners attached to the DOM node. The event then propagates, or bubbles, up the DOM tree to each parent node, until it reaches the top of the tree. This effect is called event propagation or event bubbling. It allows us make our code more efficient by reducing the number of event listeners required in the page. If we have an element with many child elements that all require the same user interaction, we could add a single event listener to the parent element and catch any event that bubbles up from the child nodes. This is called event delegation. Instead of attaching a listener to each child node, we delegate the event handing to the parent node.

## Event Propagation

Event propagation can be controlled with the `stopPropagation` function. This function is one of the many functions in the event object. `StopPropagation` takes in no arguments. When it is called, it prevents further propagation of the current event. This means that it fully captures the event and prevents it from bubbling upwards to any other parent nodes. Stopping an event's propagation can be very useful if we are using delegation, or if we have event listeners on child and parent nodes that listen to the same event but do different tasks.

## Firing Events

Standard DOM events are fired automatically by the browser. JavaScript gives us two very powerful tools that allow us to have even more control over how events in our page are fired. The first tool is firing events through JavaScript. The second is custom events.

We learned earlier in this chapter that we can create new instances of the event object. A lone event is not very useful if we cannot fire the event and have the DOM tree be notified that something happened. DOM nodes have a member function, dispatchEvent(), that allows us to fire, or dispatch, instances of the event object. DispatchEvent() should be called on the DOM node that you want the event node to be fired from. It takes in a single argument and returns a Boolean value. This argument is the event object that will be fired on the target DOM node. The DispatchEvent() boolean return value will be false if the event is cancelable and one of the event handlers that handled the event was called Event.preventDefault(). Otherwise, dispatchEvent() will return true. An example of dispatchEvent() is shown in the following snippet:

```
const event = new MouseEvent( 'click' , {
  bubbles: true,
  cancelable: true
} );
const element = document.getElementById( 'button' );
const canceled = element.dispatchEvent(event);
```

Snippet 3.26: Firing an event

The dispatchEvent method will throw an UNSPECIFIED_EVENT_TYPE_ERR error if the event's type is not specified properly. This means that if an event's type is null or an empty string, or the event was not initialized before dispatchEvent() is called, a runtime error will be thrown.

It is important to note that events fired with dispatchEvent() do not get called asynchronously via the event loop. Normal events that are fired by DOM nodes call the event handlers asynchronously via the event loop. When dispatchEvent() is used, the event handlers get invoked synchronously. All applicable event handlers are executed and return before the code continues with the code after the dispatchEvent call. Other events could be blocked if there are many event handlers for that event, or if one of the event handlers does a lot of synchronous work.

> **Note**
>
> Some browsers implement the fireEvent() function for firing events on DOM nodes. This function is a non-standard function that will not work on most browsers. Do not use this method in production code.

## Exercise 22: Handling Your First Event

To set up an event listener and catch an event fired, perform the following steps:

1. Create an HTML file with a `body` tag.

2. Inside the `body` tag, create a button with the text `Click me!` in it and the id `button1`.

3. Add a `script` tag after the button.

4. In the `script` tag, select the button by id and save it into the `button1` variable.

5. Add an event listener for the `click` event to the element stored in `button1`.

> **Note**
>
> The callback should call the alert function and alert the browser with the `clicked!` string.

### Code

index.html

```html
<html>
<body>
  <button id="button1">Click me!</button>
  <script>
    const button1 = document.getElementById( 'button1' );
    button1.addEventListener( 'click', ( e ) => {
      alert('clicked!');
    }, false );
  </script>
</body>
</html>
```

Snippet 3.25: DOM event handling

https://bit.ly/2M0Bcp5

## Outcome

Click me!

Figure 3.8: Step 2 Click me! button

localhost:63342 says

clicked!

OK

Figure 3.9: Output view

You have successfully set up an event listener and caught an event that fired.

## Custom Events

JavaScript also allows for the creation of custom events. Custom events are a way to fire events and listen for events with a custom type. The type of the event can be any non-empty string. The most basic way to create a custom event is by initializing a new instance of the event object with the event type as the custom event name. This is done with the following syntax: `const event = new Event( 'myCustomEvent' )`. Creating an event like this does not allow you to add any custom information or properties to the event. To create a custom event with additional information, we can use the `CustomEvent` class. The `CustomEvent` class constructor takes in two arguments. The first argument is a string that represents the type name of the custom event we want to create. The second argument is an object that represents the custom event initialization options. It accepts the same fields as the options passed into the event class initializer, with the addition of a field called `detail`. The detail field defaults to null and is an event-dependent value associated with the event. Any information we want passed in to our custom event can be passed in through the detail parameter. The data in this parameter is also passed to all of the handlers that listen for the custom event.

> **Note**
>
> The event constructor works will all modern browsers except for Internet Explorer. For full compatibility with IE, you must use the `createEvent()` and `initEvent()` methods discussed later, or use a `polyfill` to simulate the `CustomEvent` class.

To maximize code browser compatibility, we must also discuss the initEvent() and createEvent() methods for creating custom events. These methods are deprecated and have been removed from the web standard. Some browsers, however, still support these functions. To create a custom event in an older browser, you must first create the event with var event = document.createEvent( 'Event' ) (we must use var instead of const in old browsers) and then initialize the new event with event.initEvent(). CreateEvent() takes in a single argument, type. This is the type of event object that will be created. This type must be one of the standard JavaScript event types, such as Event, MouseEvent, and so on. InitEvent() takes in three arguments. The first argument is a string that represents the type name of the event. For example, a click event's type is **click**. The second argument is a Boolean that represents the event's bubble behavior. The third argument is a Boolean that represents the event's cancelable behavior. These two behaviors were discussed in the *Event Objects and Handling Events* section of this topic.

To catch and handle custom events, we can use the standard event listener behaviors. All we need to do is attach an event listener with addEventListener() that listens for the custom event type that's been added. For example, if we create a CustomEvent with the event type myEvent, all we need to do to listen for that event is add an event listener on that type with addEventListener( 'myEvent'. e => {} ). Whenever an event with the type myEvent is fired, the added event listener callback will be called.

When the event listener callback is called, the event parameter in the callback will have an additional field, detail. This field will contain the information passed in to the custom event through the detail field of the custom event options object. Any information that's relevant to the custom event should be passed through the detail object. An example of the detail object is shown in the following snippet:

```
const element = document.getElementById( 'button' );
element.addEventListener( 'myClick'. e => {
  console.log( e.detail );
} );
const event = new CustomEvent( 'myClick' . { detail: 'Hello!' } );
const canceled = element.dispatchEvent( event );
```

**Snippet 3.27: Firing a custom event with data in the detail**

## Exercise 23: Handling and Delegating Events

You are building a shopping list page to help busy shoppers manage shopping lists without pencil and paper. Our shopping list application will be a page with a table, a text input, and an add row button. The add row button will add a new row to the shopping list table. The rows that are added have the shopping list item (text from the text input) and a remove button. The remove button will remove that row from the shopping list table.

The following steps will build the app:

1.  Open the starter file at **exercises/exercise23/exercise.html**.

2.  In the HTML `body`, in the `userInteractionHolder div`, add a text input and a button.

    Give the button the id `addButton`.

    Add a table element with the id `shoppingList` to the `div` with the id `shoppingListHolder`.

    Add a row to the table created in the previous step (`id = "shoppingList"`).

    Add two header items to the table, one with the text `Item` and one with the text `Remove`.

# Shopping List

Item to add: [        ]  Add!
**Item Remove**

Figure 3.10: Output After step 2

3.  In the `script` tag, select the button by its id and add a click listener that calls the `_addRow` function. Create the `_addRow` function with the following functionality:

    Take in one parameter, e, which is the event object. Get the text input with DOM traversal using the `previousSibling` property on the event target. Save the text input element node to a variable, `inputBox`.

    Save the value of the text in the `inputBox` to the `value` variable.

    Clear the value of the text area by setting it to the empty string (`""`).

Create a table row element and save it in the `row` variable.

Use DOM manipulation and chaining to append a table data element to the table row. Append a text node to the table data element.

> **Note**
>
> The text node should contain the value that's stored in `value`.

4. Use DOM manipulation and chaining to append table data to the table row.

5. Append a button to the table data element.

6. Append the text `remove` to the button.

7. Navigate back up to the button element.

8. Add a listener to the button and have it call the `_removeRow` function.

9. Select the `shopingList` table and append the row to it.

10. Create the `_removeRow` function with the following functionality:

    Take in an argument, **e** that will contain the event object.

    Get the row element, that the button click occurred in with DOM traversal, and the `parentNode` property. Log the row element.

    Using DOM traversal and chaining, get the table that contains the row, and then remove the row from the table:

Figure 3.11: Final output

## Code

solution.html

```
<body>
<h4>Shopping List</h4>
<div id="userInteractionHolder">
   <!-- add a text input and an add button -->
</div>
 <div id="shoppingListHolder">
   <!-- add a table with a row for column headers -->
</div>
<script>
   /* add event listener to add button */
   function _addRow( e ) { /* get input data and add row with it */ }
   function _removeRow( e ) { /* get row from event and it */ }
</script>
```

Snippet 3.28: DOM manipulation and event handling to build a shopping list app

https://bit.ly/2D4c3rC

## Outcome

You have successfully applied event handling concepts to build a useful web app.

# JQuery

**jQuery** is a lightweight JavaScript library that's designed to simplify DOM interaction. It is one of the most popular libraries used in web development. jQuery is designed to simplify calls to the DOM and to make code more streamlined. In this topic, we will outline what jQuery is, how to install jQuery in a project, jQuery basics, using jQuery for DOM manipulation, and handling events with jQuery.

jQuery is a library that's designed to make DOM traversal, manipulation, event handling, animation, and AJAX requests simpler to use and to make code that uses those elements more streamlined. jQuery is an extensive JavaScript library. A strong grasp of JavaScript is essential for harnessing all of the power of jQuery.

jQuery provides an easy to use API that has extensive cross browser compatibility. jQuery implements what they call "current " browser support. This simply means that JQuery will run and is supported on a browser's current release version and previous release (v23.x and 22.x, but not v21.x). Code may run successfully on older browser versions, but bug fixes to jQuery will not be pushed for any bugs that appear with older browser versions. jQuery browser compatibility also extends to stock mobile browsers on Android and IOS devices.

> **Note**
>
> The full documentation can be found on the official JQuery web page: https:// jquery.com/.

The first way to install jQuery is to download the source JavaScript files directly. The files can be found at http://code.jquery.com. The JavaScript files can be added directly to a project's file structure. You should use the minified version in production code due to the smaller file size.

> **Note**
>
> **Code minification** is the process of removing unnecessary characters from source code without changing its functionality. Minification is done to reduce the size of the code file. This is important for JavaScript, HTML, and CSS files as it reduces the resources required to send and load web pages.

The second way to install JQuery is by using a package manager. The most popular command-line package managers for this are NPM, Yarn, and Bower. NPM will be discussed in more detail in the final chapter of this book. To install jQuery with one of these CLI (Command-Line Interface) package managers, first install and configure the relevant package manager. To install with NPM, run the following line: `npm install jquery`. This will place the jQuery files in the `node_modules` folder under `node_modules/jquery/dist/`. To install with Yarn, use the following command: `yarn add jquery`. To install with Bower, use the following command: `bower install jquery`. Installing with Bower will place the files in the `bower_components` folder under `bower_components/jquery/dist/`.

Once JQuery has been installed, we are ready to start load jQuery into our project. This is as simple as adding a script tag to the HTML file. In the main HTML file, simply add a script tag with the source being the jQuery library file (`<script src="path/to/jquey.js"></script>`). JQuery is now installed and ready to be used in the project!

## jQuery Basics

JQuery is a library built around selecting and working with DOM nodes. All of the JQuery operations, by default, are available under both the library name `jQuery` and the shortcut variable `$`. We will call all JQuery functions by referencing the shortcut variable.

When creating or selecting DOM nodes, jQuery always returns an instance of the JQuery object. The JQuery object is an array-like collection that contains a zero indexed sequence of DOM elements, some familiar array functions and properties, and all the built-in JQuery methods. It is important to note two things about the JQuery object. First, JQuery objects are not live objects. The contents of the JQuery object will not update as the DOM tree changes. If the DOM has changed, the JQuery object can be updated by rerunning the same JQuery selector. Second, JQuery objects are also not equal. An equality comparison between two JQuery objects that are built with the same query will not be truthy. To compare JQuery objects, you must inspect the elements contained inside the collection.

> **Note**
>
> Zero indexed means that the object has numeric properties that can be used to reference the items from the items sequence (0, 1, 2, ..., n).
>
> The JQuery object is not an array. Built-in array properties and functions may not exist on the JQuery object.

## jQuery Selector

The core functionality of JQuery revolves around selecting and manipulating DOM elements. This is done with the jQuery core selector. To select DOM elements, we call the jQuery selector function `jQuery( selector )`, or `$( selector )` for short. The selector passed in to the jQuery function can take nearly any valid CSS selector, a callback function, or an HTML string. If a CSS selector is passed in to the JQuery selector, a collection of matched elements will be returned in a JQuery object. If the selector passed in is a HTML string, a collection of nodes will be created from the provided HTML string. If a callback function is passed in to the selector function, the callback will be run when the DOM has finished loading. jQuery can also accept a DOM node and create a JQuery object from that. If a DOM node is passed into the jQuery selector function, that node will be automatically selected and returned in a JQuery collection. An example of the JQuery selector function is shown in the following snippet:

```
const divs = $( "div" ); // JQuery select all divs

const div1 = document.getElementById( 'div1' ); // DOM select a div

const jqueryDiv1 = $( div1 ); // Create a JQuery object from div
```

*Snippet 3.29: Selecting DOM nodes*

Most jQuery functions operate on a selection of DOM nodes (`$()`); however, JQuery also offers a set of functions that do not. These are referenced directly through the `$` variable. The distinction between the two can be confusing for new jQuery users. The easiest way to remember this difference is to note that functions in the `$` namespace are generally utility methods and do not work with selections. There are cases where the selector methods and the core utility methods have the same name, for example, `$.each()` and `$().each()`. When reading the jQuery documentation and learning new functions, be sure that you are exploring the correct function.

An HTML page's DOM cannot be safely manipulated until the base DOM structure has been created. JQuery offers a way to safely wait until the DOM is ready before running any code. This is done with the `ready()` JQuery object function. This function should be called on a jQuery object containing the HTML document (`$( document ).ready()`). The `ready()` function take in a single argument, a callback function. This function is run once the DOM is ready. Code that manipulates the DOM should be put in this callback function.

When working with multiple libraries in JavaScript, namespace conflicts can always be a concern. jQuery and all of its plugins and functionality are contained within the `jQuery` namespace. Because of this, there should not be a conflict between jQuery and any other library. There is one caveat, however, jQuery, by default, uses the `$` as a shortcut for the jQuery namespace. If you are using another library that uses the `$` variable, there could be conflicts with jQuery. To avoid this, you can put JQuery in no-conflict mode. To do this, call the `noConflict()` function on the jQuery namespace (`jQuery.noConflict()`). This will turn on no-conflict mode and allow you to assign the jQuery library a new shortcut variable name. The variable name can be anything you like, from `$` to `mySuperAwesomeJQuery`. A full example of enabling no-conflict mode and changing the jQuery shortcut variable name is shown in the following snippet:

```
<script src="jquery.js"></script>
<script>
   // Set the jQuery alias to $j instead of $
   const $j = jQuery.noConflict();
</script>
```

**Snippet 3.30: Enabling no-conflict mode**

## jQuery DOM Manipulation

JQuery is built around DOM manipulation. Here, we will cover the very basics of JQuery DOM manipulation. We will start by selecting elements, then move on to traversing and manipulating the DOM, and we will end with chaining.

## Selecting Elements

The first step in DOM manipulation is always selecting the DOM nodes you're going to work with. JQuery's most basic concept is "select some elements and do something with them." jQuery makes selecting elements very easy with the selector function: `$()`. selector. jQuery supports most CSS3 selectors for selecting nodes. The simplest ways to select elements are by id, by class name, by attribute, and by CSS.

Selecting an element by id is done by passing the CSS element id selector into the jQuery selector function: `$( '#elementId' )`. This will return a JQuery object that contains an element matching that id. Selecting by class name is done just like selecting by id. Pass the CSS class name selector into the jQuery selector function: `$( '.className' )`. This will return a jQuery object that contains all of the elements that match that class name. Selecting elements by attribute is done by passing the attribute CSS selector into the jQuery selector function: `$( "div[attribute-name='example']"` ). This will return a JQuery object that contains all of the elements that match the specified element type and attribute name/value. jQucry also supports more complicated selectors. You can pass in compound CSS selectors, comma-separated lists of selectors, and pseudo-selectors such as `:visible`. These selectors all return JQuery objects that contain the elements that match.

> **Note**
>
> If a jQuery selector does not match any nodes, it still returns a JQuery object. The JQuery object will have no nodes in the collection and the length property of the object will be equal to zero. If you are checking to see if a selector found nodes, you must check on the length property, not on the truthiness of the JQuery object.

Once you have gotten a selection of nodes, JQuery object functions can be used to filter and refine the selection. Some of the simple functions that are very useful are `has()`, `not()`, `filter()`, `first()`, and `eq()`. All of these functions take in a selector and return a JQuery object with a filtered set of nodes. The `has()` function filters the list to contain elements whose descendants match the CSS selector that's provided to `has()`. The `not()` function filters the JQuery object's nodes to only contain nodes that do not match the provided CSS selector. The `filter()` function filters the nodes to only show nodes that match the provided CSS selector. `First()` returns the first node in the JQuery object's internal node list. The `eq()` function returns a JQuery object containing the node at that index. Complete, in-depth documentation on these methods and other filtering methods can be found on the JQuery website.

## Traversing the DOM

Once nodes have been selected with jQuery selectors, we can traverse the DOM to find more elements. DOM nodes can be traversed in three directions: to the parent nodes, to the child nodes, and to the sibling nodes.

Traversing parent nodes can be done in many ways, but the simplest ways are by calling one of four functions on the JQuery object. The first is a way to traverse parent nodes is by calling the `parent()` function. This function simply returns a JQuery object that contains the original node's parent node. The second function is the `parents()` function. This function takes in a CSS selector and returns a JQuery object containing the matching nodes. `parents()` traverses up the DOM tree, selecting any parent node, up to the head of the tree, that matches the provided query criteria. If no criteria is given, it selects all of the parent nodes. The third parent traversing function is the `parentsuntil()` function. It also takes in a CSS selector and returns a JQuery object. This function traverses up the parent tree, selecting elements until it reaches an element that matches the provided selector. The node that matches the provided selector is not included in the new JQuery object. The final method is the `closest()` method. This function takes in a CSS selector and returns a JQuery object containing the first parent node to match the provided selector.

> **Note**
>
> `Closest()` always starts searching at the node contained in the JQuery object it is called on. If the selector passed in to `closest()` matches that node, it will always return itself.

Traversing child nodes can be done easily in two ways: `children()` and `find()`. The `children()` function takes in a CSS selector and returns a JQuery object of nodes are direct descendants, and match the selector, of the node it was called on. The `find()` function takes in a CSS selector and returns a JQuery object of any descendent node in the DOM tree, including nested children, that match the provided CSS selector.

Traversing sibling nodes can be done in the simplest way with the `next()`, `prev()`, and `siblings()` functions. `next()` gets the next sibling and `prev()` gets the previous sibling. Both functions return the new node in the JQuery object. `Siblings()` takes in a CSS selector and selects an element's siblings in both directions (previous and next) that match the provided selector. `Prev()` and `next()` also have similar functions: `prevAll()`, `prevuntil()`, `nextAll()`, and `nextuntil()`. As you might expect, the `All` functions select all previous or next nodes. The `until` functions select nodes, until but not including the node that matches the provided CSS selector.

## Modifying the DOM

Now that we can select DOM nodes, we need to learn how to modify and create them. To create a node, we can simply pass an HTML string into the selector function. JQuery will parse the HTML string and create the nodes in the string. This is done like so: $( '<div>' ). The HTML string will be parsed for the div element and a JQuery object will be returned containing that element.

To add elements to the DOM, we can use the append(), before(), and after() functions. The append function takes in a JQuery object and appends it to the children of the JQuery object that append was called from. It then returns a JQuery object containing the node the append() function was called on. Before() and after() function in a similar way. They both take in a JQuery object and insert it before or after the nodes contained in the JQuery object they are called on.

To remove DOM nodes, we can use the remove() and detach() function. Remove permanently removes the nodes that match the CSS selector passed in to the function. Remove() returns a JQuery object containing the removed nodes. All event listeners and associated data are removed from the nodes. If they are returned to the DOM, the listeners and data will have to be reset. Detach() removes nodes but persists events and data. Like remove(), it returns the detached nodes in a JQuery object. Detach() should be used if you plan on returning nodes to the page eventually.

Modifying nodes with JQuery is very simple. Once we have selected nodes, traversed the tree, then filtered the selection to a single node, we can call JQuery object functions to modify things like attributes and CSS. To modify attributes, we can use the attr() function. Attr() takes in two values. The first is the name of the attribute to be modified. The second value sets what the attribute equals to. To modify an element's CSS, we can use the css() function. This function takes in two parameters. The first parameter is the CSS property to be modified. The second parameter value sets what the CSS property equals to. Both of these functions can also be used as get functions. If a second value is omitted, the attr() and css() functions will return the value of the attribute or CSS property instead of setting it.

# Chaining

Most jQuery object functions return jQuery objects. This allows us to chain calls together and not separate each function call with a semicolon and newline. When chaining jQuery functions, jQuery tracks changes to the selector and nodes in the jQuery object. We can use the end() function to restore the current selection to its original selection. An example of this is shown in the following snippet:

```
$( "#myList" )
    .find( ".boosted" ) // Finds descendents with the .boosted class
    .eq( 3 ) // Select the third index of the <li> filtered list
        .css( 'background-color', 'red' ) // Set css
        .end() // Restore selection to .boosted items in #myList
    .eq( 0 )
        .attr( 'age', 23 );
```

**Snippet 3.31: Chaining and .end()**

# jQuery Events

As discussed previously in the DOM *Events* section, any responsive and functional web page must rely on events. jQuery also provides a simple interface for adding event handlers and handling events.

## Registering Handlers

Registering events with jQuery is very simple. The jQuery object provides many ways to register events. The simplest way to register an event is with the on() function. On() can be called with two different sets of data.

The first way to set up an event listener is by calling on() with four arguments: **events**, **selector**, **data**, and **handler**. Events is a space separated string of event types and optional namespaces (click hover scroll.myPlugin). A listener will be created for each event that's provided. The second argument is selector. It is optional. If a CSS selector string is provided, the event listeners will also be added to all descendants of the selected elements that match the selector. The third argument is data. This can be anything and is optional. If data is provided, then it will be passed to the event object in the data field when the event is triggered. The final argument is the handler function. This is the function that will be called when the event triggers.

The second way to set up an event listener is by calling on() with three arguments: **events**, **selector**, and **data**. Much like the first method, events specifies the events that listeners will be created for. However, in this case, events is an object. The key is that the event name, which a listener will be set up for and the value is the function that will be called when the event fires. Like the first method, the selector and data arguments are optional. They both function the same way as the first method.

To remove an event listener, we can use the off() method. The simplest way to remove event listeners with off is by providing the name of the event we want to remove listeners for. Like on(), we can provide the event types in a space-separated string or through an object.

## Firing Events

jQuery provides an easy way to fire events from JavaScript: the trigger() function. The trigger() function should be used to fire an event and takes in the event type and an unlimited number of extra parameters. The event type is the type of event that will be triggered. The extra parameters are passed to the event handler function and are passed in as arguments after the event object.

## Custom Events

Custom events in jQuery are very simple. Unlike custom events with Vanilla JavaScript, in jQuery, to set up an event handler for a custom event, all we need to do is create a listener with the on() function, with the event type as the custom event. To fire the event, we simply need to fire it with trigger(), with the event type as the custom event.

## Activity 3: Implementing jQuery

You want to make a web app that controls your home's smart LED lighting system. You have three LEDs that can be individually turned on or off, or all toggled together. You must build a simple HTML and jQuery interface that shows the on state of the lights and has buttons to control the lights.

To build a functioning application with JQuery, perform the following steps:

1. Set up a Node.js project with npm run init on the command line and install jQuery.

2. Create an HTML file that loads the jQuery scripts.

3. In the HTML file, add three divs that start as white.

4. Add a toggle button above the divs and a button after each div.

5. Set up event listeners for click events for each button.

6. The toggle button should change the color of all divs. Other buttons should change the color of the associated div.

   On a color change, swap the color between black and white

**Code**

**Outcome**

Figure 3.12: After step 4 output

Figure 3.13: After step 6 output

You have successfully utilized jQuery to build a functioning application.

> **Note**
>
> The solution for this activity can be found on page 285.

## Summary

Web development revolves around the Document Object Model and the Event object. JavaScript is built to quickly and efficiently interact with the DOM and DOM events to provide us with powerful and interactive web pages. In the first topic of this chapter, we covered the DOM tree and discussed the ways to navigate and manipulate the DOM. In the second topic of this chapter, we discussed the JavaScript Event object, showed how to interact with DOM events, and demonstrated how to set up handlers to catch events. In the final topic of this chapter, we discussed the jQuery module. We discussed the jQuery object and jQuery selector, and showed how to use jQuery for DOM manipulation and event handling. With the topics learned in this chapter, you should be prepared to begin writing your own powerful and interactive web pages.

In the next chapter, you will analyze the benefit of tests and build code testing environments.

# 4

# Testing JavaScript

**Learning Objectives**

By the end of this chapter, you will be able to do the following:

- Analyze the benefit of tests
- Explain the various forms of code testing
- Build code-testing environments
- Implement tests for your JavaScript code

This chapter will cover the concepts of testing, test frameworks, and how to work with the different ways to effectively testing code.

# Introduction

In the first chapter, we covered many of the new and powerful features released in ES6. We discussed the evolution of JavaScript and highlighted the key additions in ES6. We discussed scope rules, variable declaration, arrow functions, template literals, enhanced object properties, destructuring assignment, classes and modules, transpiling, and iterators and generators. In the second chapter, we covered JavaScript's asynchronous programming paradigm. We discussed the JavaScript event loop, callbacks, promises, and the async/await syntax. In the third chapter, we learned about the Document Object Model (DOM), the JavaScript Event object, and the jQuery library.

In this chapter, we will learn about testing code and code-testing frameworks in JavaScript. In the first topic, we will introduce testing and discuss test-driven development. Then, we will discuss applying test-driven development and several different ways you can test your code and applications. In the final topic, we will discuss several JavaScript code-testing frameworks that you can use to build powerful tests for your code.

# Testing

Testing code is a lot like going to the gym. You know it is good for you. All of the arguments make sense, but getting up and starting down the road to fitness is difficult. The initial rush feels amazing; however, it is closely followed by sore muscles and you begin to wonder if it was really worth it. You take an hour or more out of your day but all you have to show for it is sore arms and legs. But, after a few weeks, it gets easier. You start to notice the benefits of working out.

Much like going to the gym, you have probably heard how important testing code can be. Writing tests is an integral part of writing good and sustainable code. It can be difficult when you first start writing tests. Writing your first tests and having them run successfully brings a thrill or rush, but after a day or two of taking an hour out of your work day to write tests, you begin to wonder if it is really worth it. But you stick with it. After several weeks, it becomes less tedious and you begin to notice the small benefits testing your code brings.

In this chapter, we will discuss the reasons to test code, the types of tests you may need to implement, and some JavaScript frameworks you may use to implement and run your tests.

## Reasons to Test Code

There are many reasons to test your code. These reasons include program correctness, agile development, code quality, bug catching, legal liability, gratification, and many more. We will briefly discuss each of the listed
reasons and explain their benefits.

1. **Correctness**

   The simplest and most important reason to test code is that testing code checks for code correctness. Intelligently written tests will test all the logic in your code against predetermined input values and their corresponding output values. By comparing the program's output with the expected output, we can verify that code works as expected, catching semantic or syntactic errors before they are integrated into code.

2. **Agile Development**

   Testing code makes the development process more agile. The **Agile Development Cycle** is one of the most popular and hottest development
   styles, and is being adopted by software companies including Lockheed Martin, Snapchat, and Google. Agile development relies on short duration goals. Changing old and tested code is a very slow process. If any old code needs to be refactored or needs to have features added or removed, we would need to go through the entire process of testing it again. With written code tests, we can automate them, and expedite the testing process, and save hours of time over doing manual tests. This could be the difference between meeting our Agile sprint goals and missing a deadline.

   > **Note:**
   >
   > The Agile Development Cycle focuses on short sprints to design, implement, and release new features. These sprints are usually two or three weeks in length. This short and speedy development strategy allows you to build a large product in smaller parts and manage potentially changing requirements.

3. **Bug Catching**

   Testing code will allow you to find bugs earlier in the development cycle. Tests should be performed before integration into a product or module. This means that any bugs found by the tests will be found and fixed before they are integrated into a product. Debugging a module that has already been fully integrated into an application is much more difficult than debugging a module that is still in development. Writing and running tests before integration will allow you to find and fix these bugs before they interact with other code, saving large amounts of time. Catching errors before integration and pushing correct working code is one of the most important skills a developer can have, and code testing can greatly improve this skill.

4. **Code Quality**

   Code tests increase the quality of written code. When writing code with tests, we must design and implement our code explicitly with these tests in mind. Writing good tests helps us to think more completely about the problem we are trying to solve and the way we are going to go about solving the problem; we must consider things such as edge cases and design a good implementation that meets the test's requirements. Writing tests will help you better understand the design and implementation of your code, which will
   result in higher quality and better thought out code.

5. **Legal Liability**

   Writing tests can help prevent and mitigate legal liability. In many jurisdictions and market areas, vendors are required to ensure or prove that the provided software is of marketable quality. A documented test process has the potential to limit your legal liability in some cases. This may prevent you from being sued for a software bug. In the worst of cases, a well-documented testing process can also be provided to prove that the software bug involved in litigation did not arise through malpractice. This could reduce your punitive damages or personal responsibility.

6. **Gratification**

   The final reason to test code is often overlooked by most people. Testing code can be very gratifying. Tests can give you instant visual feedback about the correctness of your code. Seeing green check marks across the board is very satisfying. Releasing code that you know is well written and well tested, and will perform flawlessly, is very satisfying. Knowing your code is well tested can help you be confident about the release when the deadline comes up.

## Test-driven Development

**Test-driven development** (**TDD**) is a form of software development focused around writing tests before implementing code. It is generally an Agile cycle and is one of the simplest ways to integrate tests into your code. TDD is a software development process that is built around a short and simple development cycle. In its most basic form, the cycle consists of adding a test that defines how the new function should work, and then writing code until the test's requirements are met. This cycle is repeated until all functionality has been added.

Test-driven development requires that the automated tests are created by the developer. These tests should well define the code's requirements and should be defined before any code is written. The tests should cover all expected or potential use cases, especially edge cases. The passing of the tests will inform the developer when development is complete.

> **Note:**
>
> An edge case is a situation that occurs at the extremes of operating parameters. In code, an edge case refers to valid input values that could require special handling. For example, the Fibonacci sequence algorithm ($F(n)=F(n-1)+F(n-2)$) requires special handling if the sequence value is 0 or 1.

TDD allows developers to break their code into small and manageable steps when necessary. This is possible because TDD requires that each function and feature added must have tests. We can write one small test, then write the code that makes that test pass. Large features and functions can be broken down into small pieces and built in increments. This can greatly help with understanding all the parts of a problem.

TDD can also promote more modular and reusable code. Each piece of code must be tested, and large pieces of code can be broken down into smaller parts. This can lead to smaller, more focused classes and functions, and fewer cross-dependencies between code files. These smaller parts can be wrapped in a module with their tests and shared through a program. Updates to the module can simply be verified for correctness by running the attached test suite.

## TDD Cycle

The TDD cycle is generally a sequence of six steps:

1.  **Add a test:** In TDD, every new feature should begin with test writing. To write a new test, you must clearly understand the feature's specifications and requirements. The requirements for the feature must be thought out and broken into testable pieces that can be written as tests one at a time.

2.  **Run all tests and see if any fail:** To check if the new test passes, the test should obviously fail because the feature we are adding has not been implemented yet. If the test does not fail, then the feature already exists or the test was written incorrectly. This serves as a sanity check of the written test. The test should fail for the intended purpose and serves to help check that the intended logic is being tested.

3.  **Write code to fix tests:** The code does not need to be perfect at this stage. The test may be fixed in an inefficient way but this is acceptable because it can be refactored later in the process.

4.  **Run tests and make sure they pass:** The tests should all pass, including all the previously added tests. If new code has broken a test that previously passed, changes can be reverted to figure out what the breaking change may have been.

5.  **Refactor/clean up code:** If any code cleanup is needed, it can be done in this step. Here, you can improve the implementation of the newly added code or fix any tests that may have broken when adding new code. After any refactoring, you should run the tests again to make sure all changes were correct. Repeat the refactor and run the test step as needed until the refactor is correct.

6.  **Repeat:** Add a new test and repeat the TDD cycle until the feature has been fully implemented and tested.

Test-driven development is a powerful way to ensure that all code is tested but it can lead to several pitfalls if the developers are not conscientious. TDD can be difficult to use when a full stack or functional test is required. A full stack or functional test is a test of multiple parts of a technology stack at once. Tests that require user interface elements, database calls, or network calls can be very difficult to write. Typically, outside world interaction for a test in your code can be spoofed by using mock data or network calls.

TDD can also begin to break down if tests are not run frequently or are poorly maintained. If tests are abandoned and never run, or only run infrequently, the entire purpose of TDD breaks down. The features added to a program are designed with tests in mind, and the tests are used to validate that the features are properly implemented. If the tests are never run, the entire purpose of TDD is ignored. Tests that are poorly maintained also prevent TDD from being effective. Poor maintenance can occur through either not being updated to meet adjusted feature requirements, or through not having new tests added that outline the requirements of new features. Poorly maintained tests will not properly inform you of whether the code written is performing in the way we want it to.

TDD can also fall prey to poorly or lazily written tests. If tests are too coarse, they will not be able to find bugs in the code. The tests must be written with enough specificity to test each bit of logic independently from the others. On the other end of the spectrum, if trivial tests are added, we waste time in our TDD Agile process. If tests are written that are trivial or that duplicate previous tests, we will decrease our development efficiency.

Finally, TDD can break down if any members of the team do not adopt the development strategy. If only part of a development team writes the tests before the addition of new code, we will only be able to test and validate a small part of the code base. For TDD to have the best results, it has to be fully adopted by all members of a development team.

## Conclusion

Testing your code is the best way to ensure that it functions in the intended way. If you do not currently test your code, it can be very difficult to get started implementing tests; however, it should be done. Testing your code can make your code more correct, easy to write, and of higher quality.

Test-driven development is one of the simplest ways to begin integrating tests in a project. TDD revolves around writing tests that outline the requirements of any feature or function added before any implementation code is written. It forces the developer to understand exactly how each feature will be implemented. TDD is a simple six-step process: add a test, run tests, write code, run tests, refactor, repeat. This process ensures that each small piece of a feature gets tested.

## Exercise 24: Applying Test-Driven Development

You have been tasked to write a Fibonacci number generator. Use the test-driven development cycle to write tests and develop the Fibonacci algorithm. You can use the Fibonacci code written in *Chapter 1: Introducing ECMAScript 6*, Activity I, for reference (it may or may not need to be modified). You should write tests for the n=0 condition, then implement the n=0 condition, then write tests for and implement the n=1 condition, then write tests for and implement the n=2 condition, and finally the n=5, n=7, and n=9 conditions. If the test passes, log Test passed. Otherwise, throw an error.

To develop and test an algorithm using TDD, perform the following steps:

1.  By hand, calculate the values for the Fibonacci sequence at n=0, n=1, n=2, n=5, n=7, and n=9.

2.  Write a function called fibonacci that recursively calculates the Fibonacci sequence value where the value takes in a variable i and checks if i<=0.

    If it is, return 1, then it checks if i==1.

    If it is, then it returns 1. Otherwise, it recursively gets the Fibonacci value.

    It then returns fibonacci(i-1) + fibonacci(i-2).

3.  Write a general testing function called test that takes in two arguments: a calculated value (value) and an expected value (expected).

4.  Check whether the two values are different. If they are, throw an error.

5.  If the two values are the same, print the Test passed message.

6.  For each condition to test (calculated in step 1, n=0, n=1, n=2, n=5, n=7, and n=9), write a test for the test condition using the test function.

7.  Call the test function and pass in the value returned from the fibonacci function and the value calculated manually.

8.  Run the tests.

9.  If the test fails, fix the bugs in the fibonacci function.

10. Run the test again until the bugs are fixed.

11. If the test passes, continue to the next test condition.

12. If the test fails, fix the bug and rerun the tests.

## Code

index.js

```
function fibonacci( i ) {
  if ( i <= 0 ) {
    return 0;
  } else if ( i === 1 ) {
    return 1;
  } else {
    return fibonacci( i - 1 ) + fibonacci( i - 2 );
  }
}
function test( value, expected ) {
  if ( value !== expected ) {
    throw new Error( 'Value did not match expected value' );
  } else {
    console.log( 'Test passed.' );
  }
}
test( fibonacci( 0 ), 0 );
test( fibonacci( 1 ), 1 );
test( fibonacci( 2 ), 1 );
test( fibonacci( 5 ), 5 );
test( fibonacci( 7 ), 13 );
test( fibonacci( 9 ), 34 );
```

https://bit.ly/2n5CNv0

Snippet 4.1: Testing code

**Output**

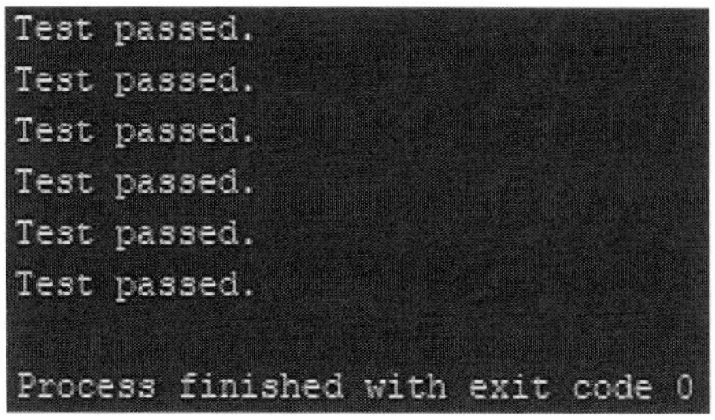

Figure 4.1: Fibonacci test

You have successfully applied test-driven development to develop and test an algorithm.

# Types of Testing

Software testing comes in many different forms. In this section, we will discuss the different methodologies for testing code and cover the most common types of code tests.

## Black Box and White Box Testing

There are two methodologies to testing code, black box and white box. The term **black box** signifies a system where the internal workings are not known. The only way the system can be observed is through its inputs and outputs. A **white box** system is a system where the internal workings are known. It can be observed through its inputs, outputs, and exact internal workings. Black box and white box systems could be anything from a software program, to a mechanical device, or any other system.

**Black box testing** refers to software testing when the internal structure or implementation of the code is not known to the tester. We are only able to observe the inputs to, and outputs from the code system. **White box testing** refers to software testing when the internal structure or implementation is known to the tester. We are able to observe the inputs and outputs' and exactly how the internal state changes at every step of the program. Nearly all forms of code testing are based on black box or white box testing principles. A visualization showing black box versus white box is shown in the following figure:

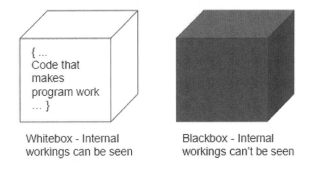

Figure 4.2: Black box and white box visualization

We will discuss three types of tests: **unit tests**, **functional tests**, and **integration tests**. Unit tests are designed to verify all pieces of testable code against the intended purpose. They test the smallest pieces of logic to ensure implementation correctness. Functional testing is designed to confirm functionality of a feature or component. Integration tests are designed to test integrated components to verify they work as intended together in an integrated system. These three types of code tests provide a good foundation from which you can approach testing code.

## Unit Tests

**Unit testing** is one of the most common forms of testing. Unit tests are used to ensure that a specific piece of functionality of a function has met the requirements. Unit tests are generally built from a white box testing perspective and we will discuss unit tests in this chapter, assuming that the internal functionality of the code is known. While unit tests can be built from a black box perspective, this is closer to functional testing and will be talked about more in the next section.

A unit test is simply a test that tests a piece of code in the smallest unit possible. A "unit" of code is a small piece that is logically isolated from other parts of code. In other words, it is a piece of code that does not logically depend on other parts of the code. The unit of code can be updated without affecting the way the code around it functions. For example, consider the code shown in the following snippet:

```
function adjustValue( value ) {
  if ( value > 5 ) {
    value--;
  } else if ( value < -5 ) {
    value++;
  }
  return value
}
```

**Snippet 4.2: Code unit example**

The function adjustvalue() takes in a number. If the number is greater than 5, it subtracts 1 from the number, and if the value is less than -5, it adds 1 to the number. We can break this code snippet into three logical units as follows:

1.  The first unit is the if statement that checks if the value is greater than 5 and the decrement operator (value--).

2.  The second unit is the else if statement that checks if the value is less than -5 and the increment operator (value++).

3.  The third unit of logic is the return statement. Changing any one of these three logic units does not affect the logical structure of the code around it.

We can create a unit test for each of these units to ensure that they function correctly. Our unit tests should test only one unit of code at a time. For this example we will need 3 unit tests. We will build tests to check the return value, the greater than 5 condition, and the less than -5 condition. To test the return condition, we simply need to pass in a value less than or equal to 5 and greater than or equal to -5. The value returned should be the same as the value passed into the function. To test the greater than 5 condition, we must pass in a value greater than 5. We know that the value returned must be 1 lower than the value entered. To test the less than condition, we must pass in a value less than -5. We know that the value returned should be 1 higher than the value entered. These three unit tests can be put into a code file and run after we make modifications to our code.

Unit tests should be run as frequently as possible. The unit test should be put into files and run whenever any code logic is changed. Minor changes in the logic of a piece of code can result in major changes in the results. Continuous testing will help to ensure that no small bugs creep through the cracks. Many companies have automated testing systems that will run unit tests automatically on a Git repository commits or on a version release. This automated testing can be very good for helping to track down the commit and change that broke the code. This can drastically cut down on debug time and effort.

## Exercise 25: Building Unit Tests

You have been tasked with building unit tests for a piece of code. To complete this assignment, follow these instructions:

1.  Reference the file provided in `exercises/exercise25/exercise.js` and look at the function titled `fakeRounding`. We will build unit tests for this function.

2.  In that file, write a general testing function called **test** that takes in two arguments: a calculated value (`value`) and an expected value (`expected`). Check whether the two values are different. If they are, throw an error.

    If the two values are the same, print the test passed message. You may use the test function from *Exercise 24* if you wish.

3.  Reference the `fakeRounding` function, line by line, and analyze what the function does to the input and the resultant output.

    It obtains the decimal part of the absolute value of the number passed in. It returns the input rounded up to the nearest integer if the decimal is <=0.5. Next, it returns the input rounded down to the nearest integer if the decimal is >0.5.

4.  Write tests to check the following cases using the **test** function we created. Calculate the expected value from the provided input.

Write tests for multiple inputs, 0, 0.4999, 0.5, 0.5001, -0.4999, -0.5, and -0.5001:

**Code:**

solution.js

```
test( fakeRounding( 0 ), 0 );
test( fakeRounding( 0.4999 ), 1 );
test( fakeRounding( 0.5 ), 1 );
test( fakeRounding( 0.5001 ), 0 );
test( fakeRounding( -0.4999 ), 0 );
test( fakeRounding( -0.5 ), 0 );
test( fakeRounding( -0.5001 ), -1 );
```

Snippet 4.3: Unit testing

https://bit.ly/2Fjulqw

**Output:**

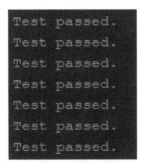

Figure 4.3: Unit Test

You have successfully built unit tests for a piece of code.

## Functional Testing

**Functional testing** is a black box testing method done to determine whether a component of an application is working to the defined specification. Functional tests are generally more complex than unit tests. Where unit tests test the logic of the functions inside of a component, functional tests are designed to test whether the component meets the specifications defined in the specification sheet or data sheet. For example, if we had a form on a web page that only accepted numbers, we may do functional tests with numbers and strings to ensure that the number-only spec was met correctly.

Functional testing can be broken down into five steps:

1. Determine functionality
2. Create input data
3. Determine output data
4. Compare input and output
5. Fix bugs

The first step to building functional tests is determining the functionality that needs to be tested. Functional tests generally test for the main functionality, error conditions, usability, and many others. It is often easiest to determine what tests need to be built by looking at the feature/component specification or data sheet. You can take the required program behavior and error handling for the component from the data sheet, and break it into a series of tests.

Once you have decided what functionality needs to be tested and how you will go about testing that functionality you must create input data to test with. The input data required for tests is heavily dependent on the component or feature being built, and therefore can be difficult to generalize for the purposes of a textbook. However, you should test with both values that you expect the program to accept and values that may be unexpected for the program. For example, if we are creating an email input form, we should test the input field with both a valid email (xxxx@yyy.zzz) and an invalid email (.23..3.2). When generating arbitrary test data, it is often a good idea to test with non-sequential values in arrays, strings, or other data structures. Using random values can help you discover logic errors.

Once you have determined the input data required for your tests, you must figure out the expected output from the feature. This part of the process is arguably the most important and should not be rushed. Output values should NEVER be calculated by putting the input through the program being tested. This will result in a tautology when running the tests and no bugs will be found. I have seen many tests fail because the programmer did not properly calculate the expected output values and the tests were invalid.

Once the output values have been determined, we are ready to run our tests. The input values should be run through the feature or component and compared against the output values. A test passes if the output values from the component match the expected output values calculated in the previous step. If the values do not match, the test did not pass and a bug needs to be fixed.

The final step in the process is bug fixing. If a test does not pass, then there is a bug somewhere in the component. Once the bugs have been fixed, the test can be re-run. If all of the tests pass for all of the functionality being tested, the component may be considered ready for integration.

Building tests can be one of the most difficult parts of functional testing. There are two different types of tests that we need to build: positive and negative tests. Positive tests test the expected program use flows and negative tests test the unexpected use flows.

Positive tests are relatively easy to generate. Any action you might want or expect a user to do can be turned into a positive test case. For example, clicking a button on an application or entering information into a text field. These two use cases can be turned into a functional test for clicking the button and a functional test for typing in the text field. Since positive tests are designed to test the expected program flow, they should use valid and expected data. In a case where a test does not use data but instead uses some other functionality, such as a user's mouse click, we would only need to write positive tests for the expected behaviors.

Negative tests are more difficult to create. They require much more creativity to build and implement effectively because you must come up with weird ways to break your own code. It can often be difficult to anticipate how a user may misuse a feature. Negative tests are designed to test error paths and failures. For example, if we intend a user to click a button on our website, it may be prudent to write negative tests for the double-click condition. A double-click is unexpected behavior and may result in a form resubmission if not properly accounted for. Negative tests are essential to fully testing a feature.

## Integration Tests

Integration tests are a step back from functional tests. Integration tests are designed to test how modules and components work when they are fully integrated. Unit tests test functions one by one. Functional tests test full components or modules one by one. Integration tests test the combined components to make sure they interact with each other correctly. Integration tests are generally more complex than unit or functional tests. Integration tests can be written for something as simple as an individual web page once all the components have been built and integrated together, or for something as complex as a full frontend application with an API, multiple servers, and databases once all of the individual components are prepared and combined. Integration testing is often the most difficult and time consuming form of testing.

**Integration testing** can be simplified and thought of like the process for manufacturing a ballpoint pen. The cap, body, ink, ballpoint, and tail cap with clip are all components of a ballpoint pen. They are all manufactured and tested separately to ensure that each component meets the specifications set for it. When the pieces are ready, they are put together for an integration test that will test whether the components function correctly together. For example, our integration test may test whether the ballpoint fits into the ink cartridge, the ink and ballpoint fit into the pen body, or the cap fits onto the body or not. If one of these tests fail, the integrated system (ballpoint pen) will not function to spec and one or more components must be updated.

There are several methods to use to go about integration testing. They are big bang testing, bottom-up testing, top-down testing, and sandwich testing. Each has its advantages and disadvantages.

Big bang testing consists of combining all of the components at once and then running your tests. It is called **big bang testing** because you throw everything together at once and get an explosion of (likely) failed integration tests. **Big bang testing** is very convenient for small systems that do not have very many component-to-component interactions. When applied to large systems, big bang testing can often break down. The first breakdown is that fault localization can be much more difficult in a very large and very complex system. If finding the source of a bug takes a long time, our test cycle will be very slow. The second breakdown is that some links between components can be missed and not tested because of the complexity of the system. If there are hundreds of component links that need to be tested, it can be difficult to keep track of them all if they are all linked at once. The third fault in big bang testing is that integration tests cannot start until all modules or components are designed and fully built. Since you must combine all the modules at once, a delay in one module pushes back integration testing for the entire system.

The second form of integration testing is **bottom up testing**. In **bottom up testing**, we must imagine the hierarchy of our system as a tree. We start by integrating the bottom layer of modules first. Then, once all the tests pass, we add the next layer of modules or components, until we have the full system being tested. To test in this manner, we must use drivers to simulate the upper layers and make calls to the modules or components in the bottom layers we are testing. Drivers are simply bits of code that simulate higher-level modules and the calls they make to lower-level modules for the purpose of tests. Bottom up testing has two main benefits. The first is that fault localization is very easy. Modules are integrated from the lowest level up. If a newly integrated module fails, then we can quickly pinpoint and blame the module that needs fixing. The second benefit is that there is no wasted time waiting for all modules to be developed. If the modules are also developed in a bottom up approach, we can simply add them to the integration tests once they are ready. We can integration test as pieces are ready, instead of waiting until the entire system is built. Bottom up testing has two main disadvantages. The first is that it can be difficult to create an early working prototype. Since modules are built and integrated from the bottom up, the user-facing features and modules are generally the last to be implemented and tested. It can be difficult to have an early prototype since the prototype components are generally ready last. The second disadvantage is that critical components and modules at the top level that control app flow are tested last and may not be tested as fully as the modules tested first. For large integrated systems, I generally believe that bottom up testing is better than big bang testing.

The third form of integration testing is **top down testing**. In **top down testing**, we must imagine our system hierarchy as a tree. We start by integrating the top layers of the system first. These are generally user-facing components and program flow modules. Top down testing requires the tester to build stubs to simulate the functionality of the modules at lower levels. The stubs imitate the undeveloped modules so that the modules being tested can make the calls they need to make. Top down testing has three major advantages. Like bottom up testing, the first major advantage is that fault localization is very easy, and we do not need to wait for the entire system to be built before we can start integration tests. Components can be added one at a time once they are built. The second advantage to top down testing is that an early prototype can be created very easily. The user-facing and most critical components are built and tested first, so it is very easy to integrate those into a prototype for early demos. The final major advantage is that critical modules are tested on priority. The critical modules are built first and therefore tested more frequently and usually more completely. Top down testing has two major drawbacks. The first is that many stubs are needed. Each module or component at a lower level must be built into a stub for testing. This can require a large amount of extra code to be written. The second disadvantage is that modules at lower levels are built and tested last. Generally, they are not as thoroughly tested.

The final form of integration testing is **sandwich testing**. <u>**Sandwich testing**</u> is a combination of the top down and bottom up approaches. The most important and lowest-level modules are built and integrated at the same time. This approach has the benefit of providing a more general and big bang-like integration testing approach, while maintaining the benefits of both top down and bottom up testing. The largest drawback to sandwich testing is that both stubs and drivers need to be built. It can sometimes be difficult to follow what is a stub or a driver if the system is very convoluted.

## Building Tests

Building tests can seem like a very daunting process. It can be very difficult to come up with an entire test suite from scratch. Test-driven development, however, provides us with a very good starting point for creating tests. As outlined previously, in the *Test-driven Development* section, building tests should always start with writing a requirements sheet.

The requirements sheet is a data sheet for the function, feature, or entire system being built. The requirements sheet should break down the requirements for the feature into a very detailed and specific list. Writing requirements sheets for software applications is out of the scope of this book, but we will walk through a brief example. Imagine that we have been tasked to build a Facebook-style comment creation component. The component must have a text field with a character limit and a button that posts the comment. The two general requirements we can easily build from this scenario are a character limit for our text field and a button that makes an API call after a click event. These two requirements can then be refined into the following list of requirements:

1. The text field must accept user-typed characters.

2. No characters can be added to the text field when the text field contains 250 or more characters.

3. Any characters in the text field may be deleted by pressing the Backspace key.

4. The button must respond to an `onclick` event.

5. On a click event, the component must make a call to the API with the test field data.

This is not a full list of requirements for the feature or the components in the feature, but for this example, it is sufficient. With these requirements, we can begin to write our tests.

We can begin to write tests, going item by item through our requirements list. Each requirement should be broken down into one or more tests. Each test should test exactly one thing and have a very specific success criterion.

The first requirement is that the text area must accept user-typed characters. If we press a key on the keyboard, the character pressed should be added to the text area, so our first test should be pressing a key on the keyboard and verifying that the same character was added to the text area.

The second requirement states that no characters can be added to the text field when the text field contains 250 or more characters. This can be broken into two tests: when the text area has 250 characters, no key presses can add to the text area, and when the text area has more than 250 characters, no key presses can add to the text area.

The third requirement states that any characters in the text field may be deleted by pressing the backspace key. This requirement can be converted into a test quite easily. We must test that if the backspace key is pressed, a character is removed from the text area. To properly test edge cases, we should run this test four times: once with an empty text area, once with a text area with more than 0 but fewer than 250 characters, once with 250 characters, and once with more than 250 characters. Testing all of the operating conditions for our text area (even the test case with more than 250 character that we never expect to reach) will ensure that no failure can occur.

The fourth requirement states that the button must respond to an on-click event. This test is very easy to write. We simply need to add a test where the user clicks on the button. The final requirement states that a click event on the button must call the API. We can easily turn this into a test by simulating the on-click event and ensuring that the website makes the API call with the correct data.

We have outlined the list of five requirements in a series of tests. These tests can now be compiled together and written in code form in a test file. This test file will be used to verify that the requirements outlined in our requirements sheet are properly met.

## Exercise 26: Writing Tests

Your team has been tasked to build a registration page for your newsletter. The registration page must have three text fields for name, email, and age, as well as a **Submit** button. Your registration page must accept a name between 1 and 50 characters (inclusive), an email between 1 and 50 characters (inclusive, and email format not validated), and the user's age (must be older than 13 years old). When the **submit** button is pressed, the user information must be validated (against the specification provided in the preceding section). If any part of the specification is not met, throw an error in the browser console. Write a very basic specification sheet detailing the requirements for each input and the submit button, then build tests from the specification sheet.

Implement the page (use exercises/exercise26/exercise.html as a starting point) and perform the tests manually from the UI. The starter file contains hints for the tests you must write. Write the specification sheet and tests before opening the starter file.

To build a basic specification sheet and run tests from the specification sheet, perform the following steps:

1.  Write the specification sheet by taking each sentence that contains specification information in the scenario description and break it into one or more requirements.

2.  Decompose the specification sheet into manual UI tests by taking each item on the spec sheet and write one or more tests for it.

3.  Open the starter HTML file at exercises/exercise26/exercise.html.

4.  Add the three input fields with the IDs name, email, and age. This is shown in the following figure:

Figure 4.4: Data sheet (after step 4)

5.  Add the **Submit** button to the HTML document and have it call the validate function on click.

6.  In the validate function, get the name text field by email id and save its value in the name variable.

    Get the email text field by id and save its value in the email variable.

    Get the age text field by id, get its value, parse the value for a number, and then save the parsed value in the age variable.

    Check the conditions on the specification sheet that relate to the name field. Also check if the name doesn't exist, or is false, and throw an error if it does not. Check if name length <= 0 or > 50, then throw an error if it is.

    Check the conditions on the specification sheet that relate to the email field. Also, check if the email doesn't exist, or is falsy; throw an error if it is. Check if email length is <=0 or > 50, then throw an error if it is.

    Check the conditions on the specification sheet that relate to the age field. Also, check if age doesn't exist, or is falsy; then throw an error. Check if age < 13 and throw an error if it is.

    Log the user details (name, email, and age) to the console.

7. For each test you wrote in the specification sheet, test it manually. Fill in the values in the text fields and then click **Submit**.

   Compare the errors logged to the console against the expected result of the test.

   If a test fails, then update the validate function to fix the bug and rerun the test.

## Code

solution.html

```
<body>
  <input type="text" id="name" value="Name">
  <input type="text" id="email" value="Email">
  <input type="text" id="age" value="Age">
  <button onclick="validate()">Submit</button>
  <script>
    function validate() {
      const name = document.getElementById( 'name' ).value;
      const email = document.getElementById( 'email' ).value;
      const age = parseInt( document.getElementById( 'age' ).value, 10 );
      if ( !name ) {
        throw new Error( 'Must provide a name.' );
      } else if ( name.length <= 0 || name.length > 50 ) {
        throw new Error( 'Name must be between 1 and 50 characters.' );
      }
      if ( !email ) {
        throw new Error( 'Must provide an email.' );
      } else if ( email.length <= 0 || email.length > 50 ) {
        throw new Error( 'Email must be between 1 and 50 characters.' );
      }
      if ( !age ) {
        throw new Error( 'Must provide an age that is also a number.' );
      } else if ( age < 13 ) {
        throw new Error( 'Age must be at least 13.' );
      }
```

```
console.log( 'User details:

Name: ${name}

Email: ${email}

Age: ${age}' )

    }

  </script>

</body>
```

**Snippet 4.4: Testing front-end input code**

https://bit.ly/2n5E7OJ

## Output

```
⊗ ▸ Uncaught Error: Email must be between 1 and 50 characters.
      at validate (writing tests soluti…avdhobms9c15jsj8:26)
      at HTMLButtonElement.onclick (writing tests soluti…favdhobms9c15jsj8:7)
⊗ ▸ Uncaught Error: Must provide an email.
      at validate (writing tests soluti…avdhobms9c15jsj8:24)
      at HTMLButtonElement.onclick (writing tests soluti…favdhobms9c15jsj8:7)
⊗ ▸ Uncaught Error: Must provide an age that is also a number.
      at validate (writing tests soluti…avdhobms9c15jsj8:31)
      at HTMLButtonElement.onclick (writing tests soluti…favdhobms9c15jsj8:7)
⊗ ▸ Uncaught Error: Must provide a name.
      at validate (writing tests soluti…avdhobms9c15jsj8:18)
      at HTMLButtonElement.onclick (writing tests soluti…favdhobms9c15jsj8:7)
⊗ ▸ Uncaught Error: Name must be between 1 and 50 characters.
      at validate (writing tests soluti…avdhobms9c15jsj8:20)
      at HTMLButtonElement.onclick (writing tests soluti…favdhobms9c15jsj8:7)
⊗ ▸ Uncaught Error: Must provide an email.
      at validate (writing tests soluti…avdhobms9c15jsj8:24)
      at HTMLButtonElement.onclick (writing tests soluti…favdhobms9c15jsj8:7)
⊗ ▸ Uncaught Error: Email must be between 1 and 50 characters.
      at validate (writing tests soluti…avdhobms9c15jsj8:26)
      at HTMLButtonElement.onclick (writing tests soluti…favdhobms9c15jsj8:7)
⊗ ▸ Uncaught Error: Must provide an age that is also a number.
      at validate (writing tests soluti…avdhobms9c15jsj8:31)
      at HTMLButtonElement.onclick (writing tests soluti…favdhobms9c15jsj8:7)
  User details:
      Name: Zach
      Email: test@test.com
      Age: 123
```

**Figure 4.5: Data sheet (final Output)**

You have successfully built a basic specification sheet and run tests from the specification sheet.

# Test Tools and Environments

Testing tools, frameworks, and environments are designed to make testing code simpler and quicker. There are many testing frameworks available for JavaScript and the most popular will be mentioned briefly. We then dive deeper into one of the frameworks and demonstrate how to use the framework to write good tests.

## Testing Frameworks

You will need to select a testing framework based on the types of tests you wish to conduct. JavaScript is generally tested in one of three ways: **general test**, **code coverage tests**, and **user interface tests**. When selecting a framework, you must decide what you are testing and how you wish to go about it.

General tests will include your unit tests, functional tests, and integration tests. It is a sort of catch-all for your tests. The most popular frameworks for tests are **Mocha**, **Jasmine**, and **Jest**. Jest is used by Facebook and is one of the simpler frameworks to set up. Mocha is the most popular testing framework available for JavaScript and it will be covered in much more detail later in this section.

Code coverage tests are used to help check test completeness. Code coverage can be defined as the percentage of your code base covered, or tested, by your automated tests. Code coverage can be used as a general guideline for the completeness of your code tests. In theory, the more code coverage your application has, the more complete and better the tests. However, in practice, having 100% code coverage does not mean that the tests for the code are well thought out and valid. It just means that every code path is referenced somehow in a test. It is more important to write well thought out tests than throw together useless tests that hit every line of code. The most popular and simplest code coverage library is **Istanbul**. It is compatible with many testing frameworks and can be easily worked into most testing suites. If you need a third-party library for testing code coverage, I recommend using Istanbul.

The final form of tests is **User Interface** (**UI**) tests. Like general tests, we can break UI tests into integration, functional, and unit tests. However, UI tests are generally not included under general tests because they require special and more complex frameworks. To perform UI tests, we must load the user view and simulate user interactions. Some of the more common UI test frameworks are Testcafe, WebdriverIO, and Casper.

## Mocha

**Mocha** is a framework for testing JavaScript in Node.js. It is a simple library designed to simplify and automate the testing process. Mocha is designed to be simple, flexible, and extendable. My company uses Mocha for unit, functional, and integration tests. We will discuss some of the benefits to using Mocha over other frameworks, cover how to set up and run your first tests with Mocha, and explain some of the advanced functionality Mocha offers.

> **Note**
>
> The full documentation for Mocha can be found at https://mochajs.org/.

There are many benefits to Mocha. As stated earlier, Mocha is the most popular testing framework for Node.js. This immediately gives Mocha its largest advantage: Mocha has the largest development community. This is important for support and extensions. If you run into issues with your Mocha tests, this community can provide extensive support. The Stack Overflow community is prompt in answering questions about Mocha. The Mocha community also has built many plugins or extensions for unique test scenarios. If your project has unique testing needs, it is likely that a plugin has been built to suit your needs.

Aside from the large community support, Mocha also provides advantages such as simple setup, assertion, and simple asynchronous testing. Setting up Mocha can be done through the command line with npm. With any testing framework, we want to make sure that setting it up does not take too much of our time. Mocha also allows for the use of assertion modules. While not necessary, if your team wants to approach testing from an assertion standard, Mocha allows you to install and import many JavaScript assertion libraries. Finally, Mocha is designed for asynchronous tests. With any JavaScript testing module, we must rely on asynchronous support to write complete tests. Mocha is designed to work with callbacks, promises, and the ES6 async/await syntax. It can easily be integrated into most backend setups.

## Setting Up Mocha

Installing Mocha is done with the npm command `npm install -g mocha`. This command will install Mocha globally on your system. Any Node.js project will now be able to use Mocha to run tests. Once installed globally, we will be able to run tests from the command line with the `mocha` keyword.

Once mocha has been installed on our system, we must add it to a project. If you do not have a Node.js project, create a path to the desired project directory and initialize the project with npm init. This is the same command used in *Chapter 1* to set up a project when we were discussing transpiling and Babel. The npm init command will create a file called package.json. After we have created our JavaScript project, we need to create our project files. Create a file called index.js and a file called test.js. index.js will contain our project code and test.js will contain our test code.

In the package.json file, there will be a field called scripts. To run our tests from npm, we must add a field to the scripts object. Replace the scripts object with the code shown in the following snippet:

```
"scripts": {
    "test": "mocha ./test.js"
}
```

Snippet 4.5: Test script in package.json

The code in the preceding snippet adds a script called test to the package object. We can run this script with the npm run test command. When we run this command, it calls the mocha keyword with the ./test.js parameter. The mocha testing framework is run with the tests contained in the test.js file. We are now ready to start adding tests to test.js.

Mocha organizes tests with the describe and it keywords. Both are functions that take in a string as the first parameter and a function as the second parameter. The describe function is used to group tests together. The it function is used to define a test. The function argument for describe() contains test declarations (with it()) or more description functions. The function argument for it() contains the test function to be run.

You can think of the describe function as a way to describe and group together a group of tests. For example, if we have a group of tests that all test a function called calculateModifier, we might group the tests together with a description using the describe function: describe( 'calculateModifier tests'. () => { ... } ). This groups the tests contained in the function under the description calculateModifier test.

You can think of the it function as a way to define a test in the form "it should ...". The string input to the it function describes the test, usually what the test is trying to accomplish. The function argument contains the actual test code. For example, if we want to define a test that checks whether two values are equal, we can use the it function to do this: it( 'should have two inputs that are equal'. () => { ... } ). The description tells us what should happen and the code to check the values will go in the function argument.

## Mocha Basics

Understanding the basics of tests, we can look at the Mocha starter documentation and see the code shown in the following snippet:

```
var assert = require('assert');
describe('Array', function() {
  describe('#indexOf()', function() {
    it('should return -1 when the value is not present', function() {
      assert.equal([1,2,3].indexOf(4), -1);
    });
  });
});
```

Snippet 4.6: Mocha basics

What do you think this code snippet is doing? First, we describe a set of tests with the description Array. Inside the function argument of the first describe block, we have another describe block. This new block describes a set of tests with the description #indexOf; because these describe blocks are nested, we can assume that we are testing the indexOf functionality of an array. Inside the second describe block, we define a test with the it function. We define a test that says it should return -1 when the value is not present. As expected from the description of the test, we would expect the indexOf function to return the value -1 if the value is not present in an array. In this example, we use the assert library to assert that the expected value of -1 is equal to the actual value. The assert library is not strictly necessary, but makes this example simpler to understand.

## Exercise 27: Setting Up a Mocha Testing Environment

The aim is to set up a Mocha testing environment and prepare a test file.
To complete this assignment, follow these steps:

1. Run npm init to create a package.json file in the exercise directory.

2. Run npm install mocha -g to install the testing package.

3. Create a file called test.js where our tests will go.

4. Add a script to the package.json file that runs the mocha test suite on the test.js file.

5. Inside the `test.js` file, add a `describe()` block that describes tests as **My first test!**

6. Inside the `describe` block's callback, add a test with `it()` that passes and has the description **Passing test!**

7. Run the tests by calling the `npm` script added to `package.json`.

**Code:**

test.js

```
describe( 'My first test!', () => {
  it( 'Passing test!', ( done ) => done( false ) );
} );
```

**Snippet 4.7: Mocha basics**

https://bit.ly/2RhZNAy

**Output:**

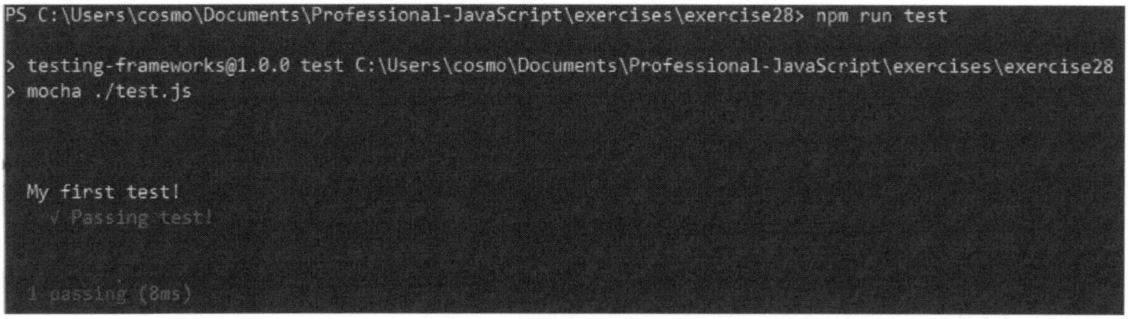

```
PS C:\Users\cosmo\Documents\Professional-JavaScript\exercises\exercise28> npm run test

> testing-frameworks@1.0.0 test C:\Users\cosmo\Documents\Professional-JavaScript\exercises\exercise28
> mocha ./test.js


  My first test!
    √ Passing test!


  1 passing (8ms)
```

**Figure 4.6: Mocha Testing**

You have successfully set up a Mocha testing environment and prepared a test file.

## Mocha Async

Mocha supports asynchronous tests as well as synchronous tests. In the example shown in snippet 4.6, we perform synchronous tests. To support asynchronous tests, all we need to do is pass a done callback parameter into the function parameter of the `it()` function: `it( 'description', ( done ) => {} )`. This tells mocha to wait until the done callback is called before proceeding to the next test. The done parameter is a function. If a test succeeds, done should be called with a falsy value (no error). If done is called with a truthy value, mocha will interpret that value as an error. It is best practice to pass an error object into the done callback but any value that evaluates to true will tell Mocha that the test failed.

Asynchronous tests are performed synchronously by Mocha in the order in which they are defined in the test file. The tests may query resources asynchronously, but the next test will not begin running until the previous test has completely finished (done has been called). Running tests synchronously is important. Even though running tests synchronously may result in longer testing times, it allows us to test asynchronous systems that may rely on some shared state. For example, we can test systems such as databases and database interfaces with Mocha. If we need to perform an integration test that tests the process of adding to and removing from a database, we can create a test to add an item to the database and a test to remove the added item from the database. If the tests run these two asynchronously, we might run into timing issues. Due to network lag, or some other unexpected error, the remove operation may be processed before the add operation and the tests would fail. Mocha prevents the need to debug problems like this by forcing tests to run synchronously.

## Mocha Hooks

For more complex tests, Mocha allows us to attach hooks to our tests. **Hooks** can be used to set up preconditions and post-conditions to our tests. In simpler terms, hooks allow us to set up before and clean up after tests. Mocha provides the following hooks: before, after, beforeEach, and afterEach. Hooks take in two arguments, a description and a callback function argument. This function argument can accept one parameter—a done function. An example of the syntax for the hooks is shown in the following snippet:

```
describe( 'Array', () => {
   before( 'description', done => { ... } );
   after( 'description', done => { ... } );
   beforeEach( 'description', done => { ... } );
   afterEach( 'description', done => { ... } );
} );
```

**Snippet 4.8: Mocha hooks**

Hooks are only run before or after the tests in the describe block they are contained within. The before hooks are run once before any of the defined tests are started. They can be used to set up a general shared state between tests. The beforeEach hooks are run before each test starts, inside the describe block. They can be used to set or reset a shared state or set of variables required for each test. The after hooks are run once after all tests have finished running. They can be used to clean up or reset a state shared between tests. The afterEach hook is run after each test completes but before the next starts. It can be used to clean up or reset test-specific shared states.

## Activity 4: Utilizing Test Environments

You have been tasked to upgrade your Fibonacci sequence test code to use the Mocha test framework. Take the Fibonacci sequence code and test the code you created for *Activity 1: Implementing Generators* and upgrade it to use the Mocha test framework to test the code. You should write tests for the n=0 condition, implement it, then write for tests and implement the n=1 condition. Repeat this for n=5, n=6, as well as n=8. If the it() test passes, call the done callback with no argument, otherwise call the test done callback with an error or other truthy value.

To write and run tests using the Mocha test framework, perform the following steps:

1. Set up the NPM project and install the mocha module.

2. Add a test script to the package.json that runs mocha and the tests in test.js.

3. Create an index.js file with a Fibonacci sequence calculator function. Export this function.

4. Create test.js, which tests the Fibonacci sequence function using the mocha framework. Test fibonacci for n=0, n=1, n=2, n=5, n=7, and n=9.

**Output**

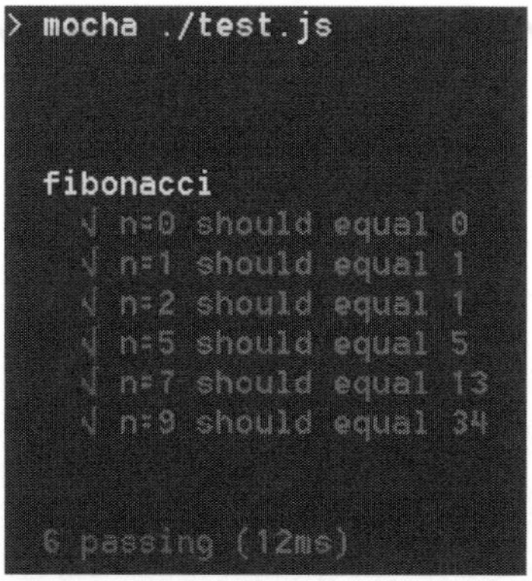

Figure 4.7: Testing the Fibonacci sequence with Mocha

You have successfully utilized the Mocha test framework to write and run tests.

> **Note**
>
> The solution for this activity can be found on page 288.

## Summary

Code testing is one of the most important skills a developer can have. Testing code is like going to the gym. You know it's good for you, but it can often be difficult to begin. In this chapter, we discussed the reasons to test code, several types of code tests, and several JavaScript code testing frameworks. Code tests need to be done to ensure program correctness. Test-Driven Development is one of the simplest ways to begin integrating tests into a project. TDD revolves around writing tests that outline the requirements of any feature or function added, before any implementation code is written. There are many forms of code tests. In this chapter, we covered unit tests, functional tests, and integration tests. These types of code tests are the most common and are generally built from one of two methodologies: black box and white box. Functional, unit, and integration tests can all be built in many of the frameworks covered in the previous topic.

In the next chapter, we will cover the functional programming coding principle and define object-oriented programming and functional programming.

# 5

# Functional Programming

**Learning Objectives**

By the end of this chapter, you will be able to do the following:

- Explain functional programming
- Implement the key concepts of functional programming
- Apply functional programming concepts to your code
- Build new code bases in the functional programming style

This chapter explains types of programming, including Object-oriented programming and Functional Programming, and how to work with different types of functions.

## Introduction

In the first chapter, we covered many of the new and powerful features released in ES6. We discussed the evolution of JavaScript and highlighted the key additions in ES6. We discussed scope rules, variable declaration, arrow functions, template literals, enhanced object properties, destructuring assignment, classes and modules, transpiling, and iterators and generators.

In the second chapter, we covered JavaScript's asynchronous programming paradigm. We discussed the JavaScript event loop, callbacks, promises, and the async/await syntax.

In the third chapter, we learned about the Document Object Model (DOM), the JavaScript Event object, and the jQuery library.

In the fourth chapter, we discussed testing JavaScript code. We covered the reasons for testing and ways to go about adding tests to code. Then, we discussed different types of code tests and how they can be applied to your code base. Finally, we discussed various JavaScript code-testing frameworks and how tests can be built in them.

In this chapter, we will cover the functional programming coding principles. In the first topic, we will define Object-oriented programming and functional programming, discuss the differences between the two, and outline the reasons why we use functional programming. Then, in the subsequent sections, we will discuss each of the key concepts of functional programming. For each key concept, we will outline the definition and show its application to functional programming.

## Introducing Functional Programming

There are many different ways to approach software design and construction. The two most well-known design philosophies, or programming paradigms, are **Object-oriented programming (OOP)** and **Functional Programming (FP)**. A programming paradigm is a way of thinking about software design and construction. Programming paradigms are based on several defining principles and are used to organize and characterize the design and construction of software applications. Functional Programming is a programming paradigm focused on building software through expressions and declarations. In this section, we will discuss the very basics of Object-Oriented Programming and Functional Programming, and compare the two programming paradigms.

## Object-Oriented Programming

**Object-Oriented Programming (OOP)** is a programming paradigm based on objects and statements. Objects are programming abstractions used to organize pieces of an application. In OOP, objects usually contain and store data in attributes, have procedures they can run in methods, and have some notion of **this** or **self**, a way for the object to reference itself. Generally, objects come in the form of classes. A **class** can be thought of as the definition of an object, with its attributes, methods, and **this** scope. An **object** is the instantiation of a class. In OOP, statements are instruction-driven code. This will be covered more in the *Declarative Versus Imperative* topic. Many programming languages work well for OOP software development. The most popular OOP languages are C++, Java, and Python.

## Functional Programming

**Functional Programming (FP)** is a programming paradigm based on expressions and declarations instead of objects and statements. In short, this means that FP relies on functions instead of objects to organize code and build applications. Functional Programming is thought to have originated from lambda calculus, which was created in the 1930s. Functional Programming relies on seven key concepts: **declarative functions**, **pure functions**, **higher order functions**, **shared state**, **immutability**, **side effects**, and **function composition**. Each of these concepts will be covered in a subsequent topic in this chapter.

Functional Programming is designed to be more concise, predictable, and testable. These benefits, however, can result in FP code being denser than other coding paradigms. Some of the most common Functional Programming languages are JavaScript, PHP, and Python.

# Declarative Versus Imperative

There are two general ways to think about writing code: **Declarative** and **Imperative**. Code written in the Functional Programming paradigm should be declarative.

**Declarative code** is code that expresses the logic of a computation without describing its control flow. Imperative code is code that uses statements to change a program's state.

These definitions are difficult to understand if you have never studied declarative and imperative code before. Declarative code is generally used with Functional Programming and imperative code is generally used with Object-Oriented Programming. There is no "right answer" when deciding which coding style to use; they both have their trade-offs. However, declarative code fits the Functional Programming paradigm better than imperative.

## Imperative Functions

**Imperative code** is most common in OOP. The technical definition is complicated, but we can simplify it. An imperative approach to coding is about HOW you solve the problem. Consider finding a table at a restaurant. You approach the host/hostess and say "I see that the table in the corner is empty. My wife and I are going to walk over and sit down." This is an imperative approach because you describe exactly how you are going go from the host/hostess to getting a table for your party.

## Declarative Functions

Declarative programming is most common in FP. The declarative approach to coding can be simplified as WHAT we need to do. Consider the restaurant example from the previous paragraph. A declarative approach to getting a table would be to approach the host/hostess and say "table for two please." We describe what we need, not every step we will take to get the table. Declarative programming is the act of conforming to the mental model of the developer rather than the operational model of the machine. From these definitions and metaphors, we can conclude that declarative programming is an abstraction of some imperative implementation.

Now, let's move from the metaphor to actual code. Consider the code shown in the following snippet:

```
function addImperative( arr ) {
  let result = 0;
  for ( let i = 0; i < arr.length; i++ ) {
    result += arr[ i ];
  }
  return result;
}


function addDeclarative( arr ) {
  return arr.reduce( ( red, val ) => red + val, 0 );
}
```

**Snippet 5.1: Declarative versus imperative functions**

In the preceding snippet, we create two functions to add the values in an array. The first function, `addImperative`, is an imperative approach to this problem. The code states exactly how the array will be added, step by step. The second function, `addDeclarative`, is a declarative approach to the same problem. The code states how the array will be added. It abstracts out much of the imperative solution (`for` loop) by using the JavaScript array reduce operation.

The simplest way to begin writing declarative code instead of imperative code is by creating functions. These functions should abstract away the step-by-step nature of the imperative parts of your code. Consider array operations such as `find`, `map`, and `reduce`. These functions are all array member functions that are declarative. They abstract away the step-by-step nature of iterating over an array. Using them will help introduce declarative concepts into your code and reduce some of the imperative code that you write.

## Exercise 28: Building Imperative and Declarative Functions

Your research team has obtained a list of values from your latest experiment; however, due to a calibration error, only some of the data can be used and any data that can be used needs to be scaled. You must build a utility function that takes in an array, filters out any values less than or equal to 0, scales the remaining values by multiplying them by 2, and returns the final results. First, build an imperative function to do this, then build a declarative function to do the same thing.

To create functions using imperative and declarative coding practices, perform the following steps:

1. Define a function called `imperative` that takes the following approach:

   Take in an array argument called `arr`. Create an array called `filtered` that will hold the filtered values.

   Create a `for` loop to step through the input array, `arr`. For each item, check the array item value. If greater than 0, push the value to the filtered array.

   Create a `for` loop to step through the filtered array. For each item, multiply it by 2 and save it back in the filtered array in the same index.

   Return the filtered array.

2. Define a function called `declarative` that does the following:

   Filter the input array with `Array.filter()`. In the filter's `callback` function, check whether the value is greater than 0. If it is, return true; otherwise, return false.

Chain a map call to the `filter` output.

Map the filtered array with `array.map()`.

In the callback, multiply each value by 2.

Return the modified array.

3. Create a test value array with values from -5 to +5.

4. Run `imperative` with the values array and log the output.

5. Run `declarative` with the values array and log the output.

## Code

`index.js`

```
function imperative( arr ) {
  const filtered = [];
  for ( let i = 0; i < arr.length; i++ ) {
    if ( arr[ i ] > 0 ) {
      filtered.push( arr[ i ] );
    }
  }
  for ( let j = 0; j < filtered.length; j++ ) {
    filtered[ j ] = 2 * filtered[ j ];
  }
  return filtered;
}


function declarative( arr ) {
  return arr.filter( v => v > 0 ).map( v => 2 * v );
}
```

Snippet 5.2: Imperative and declarative code comparison

## Outcome

```
//Test values
const values = [ -5, -4, -3, -2, -1, 0, 1, 2, 3, 4, 5 ];
console.log( imperative( values ) ); // Output: [ 2, 4, 6, 8, 10 ]
console.log( declarative( values ) ); // Output: [ 2, 4, 6, 8, 10 ]
```

Figure 5.1: Test values output

```
[ 2, 4, 6, 8, 10 ]
[ 2, 4, 6, 8, 10 ]

Process finished with exit code 0
```

Figure 5.2: The modified array output

You have successfully utilized imperative and declarative coding practices to write functions.

## Pure Functions

**Pure functions** are a key component of Functional Programming. A pure function can be defined as a function that does not have any effect on or make use of any state outside of the function. A function must meet three key criteria to be considered pure:

- A function must always return the same output, when given the same inputs.

- A function must have no side effects.

- A function must have referential transparency.

### Same Output Given Same Input

Given a set of input values, a pure function must always return the same value when provided those input values. This sounds much more complicated than it is. Simply put, the output of a pure function cannot change unless the input values are changed. This means that a function's internal code cannot depend on any program state outside of the function. A pure function cannot use any variable from outside the function to make calculations or code path decisions. An example of this is shown in the following snippet:

```
const state = { prop1: 5 };


function notPure () {
    return state.prop1 > 0 ? 'Valid': 'Invalid';
```

```
}

function pure( val ) {
   return val > 0 ? 'Valid': 'Invalid';
}


notPure(); // Expected output: 'Valid'
pure( state.prop ); // Expected output: 'Valid'
```

Snippet 5.3: Relying on an external state

In the preceding snippet, we create a variable called state with the prop property set
to 5. We then define two functions that return the strings valid or Invalid, depending
on a value comparison. In the first function, notPure, we check the prop value of the
state and return a value based on that. In the second function, pure, we check the
value passed into the function to decide what to return. The first function is not a pure
function. It relies on a state outside of the function to determine the return value of
the function. The second function is pure because it relies on the input value of the
function, not the global state variable.

## No Side Effects

A pure function must have no side effects. This simply means that a pure function
cannot modify any objects or values passed in by reference. Side effects will be
discussed in more detail in the *Side Effects* topic. In JavaScript, only objects and arrays
can be passed into functions by reference. A pure function cannot modify these objects
or arrays in any way. If your function needs to update or modify an array or object
internally, we must first create a copy of the array/object. It is important to note that, in
JavaScript, copying an object or array only copies the first level of the entity. This means
that if an array or object has arrays or objects nested in it, these nested references will
not be copied. When the copied object is by reference by reference, the nested objects
will not have been copied, and will also be passed. This means that a nested reference,
if not explicitly copied, can cause a side effect. To properly copy an object, we must
create a deep copy. A deep copy of an object is a copy that duplicates all nested
references. This can be done recursively or through the Node.js deepcopy module. An
example of side effects is shown in the following snippet:

```
function notPure( input ) {
   input.prop2 = 'test';
}

function pure( input ) {
```

```
    input = JSON.parse( JSON.stringify( input ) );

    input.prop2 = 'test';

    return input;

}
```

**Snippet 5.4: Avoiding side effects**

In the preceding snippet, we define two functions, notPure and pure. Both functions add a property to the input object passed into the function. The impure version of the function (notPure()) modifies the input object in place. Because objects are passed by reference, this update will be seen in all other scopes where the object is used. This is a side effect. The pure version of the function (pure()) creates a deep copy of the object with JSON operations and then adds a new property to the new object and returns the new object. Since the object was cloned, the original object is not modified. No side effect is created.

## Referential Transparency

**Referential transparency** is a property of pure functions that makes figuring out the function behavior simpler. If a function has referential transparency, a call to that function can be replaced with the function call's resultant value (the value returned by the function) without changing the meaning of the code. In short, this means that functions should return values that make sense in the context of the code they are being used in, and they should not depend on or modify states outside of the function.

Writing pure functions gives us two key benefits:

The first is that pure functions are very easy to unit test. Pure functions do not rely on external states, so there is no other context to consider when writing tests. We only need to consider the input and output values.

Second, pure functions make code simpler and more flexible. Pure functions do not rely on outside states and do not create side effects. This means that they can be used in any special context. They can be used in more places and are therefore more flexible.

## Exercise 29: Building Pure Controllers

You have been hired as a developer to upgrade an online store's shopping cart implementation. Build a function to add items to the shopping cart. Your function should be pure. You can assume there is a global array, called cart, that contains the shopping cart. The function should, at a minimum, take in an item (string) and a quantity (number). Create the function in the provided file (exercise-test.js) with the function name addItem(). The file will have basic tests to test purity.

To build part of an application with pure function concepts, perform the following steps:

1. Open the test file at **exercises/exercise29/exercise-test.js**.

2. Create a function called addItem that takes in three parameters: cart, item, and quantity.

3. Duplicate the cart passed into the function and save the duplicated value into a variable called newCart. Duplicate the cart with one of the following methods:

   Use JSON operations for the simplest duplication: JSON.parse( JSON.stringify( cart ) ).

   Step through the original cart array with a loop and push each item to a new array.

   Use cart.map( () => {} ) since all items in the array are simple types.

   Use the rest/spread operator, newCart= [ ...cart ], because all items are simple types.

4. Push the item passed into the function, onto the cart array, quantity number of times.

5. Return the newCart array.

6. Run the code provided in exercise-test.js.

   If an error is thrown, fix the bug in the code and run the test again.

## Code

exercise-solution.js

```
function addItem( cart, item, quantity ) {
  // Duplicate cart
  const newCart = JSON.parse( JSON.stringify( cart ) );
  newCart.push( ...Array( quantity ).fill( item ) );
  return newCart;
}
```

Snippet 5.5: Function purity testing

https://bit.ly/2n2TxJG

**Output**

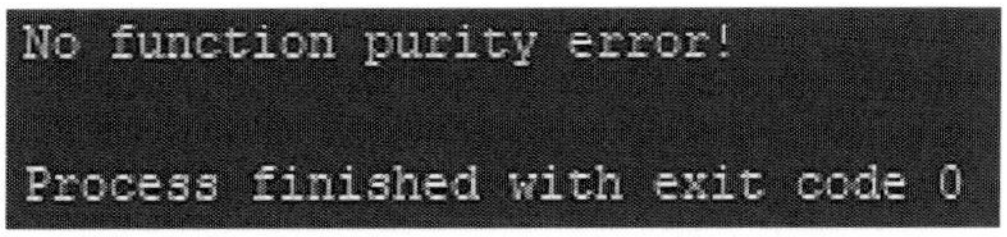

**Figure 5.3: Returning the new cart array**

You have successfully applied the concept of pure functions to build part of an application.

# Higher Order Functions

As we learned in the first topic, a higher order function is a function that either takes another function in as an input argument or returns another function as the return value. Nearly all asynchronous code in JavaScript makes use of higher order functions by passing callback functions in as input arguments. Aside from their prolific use in JavaScript, higher order functions are a key part of Functional Programming and are used for three key benefits: abstraction, utilities, and complexity reduction.

Higher order functions are very important for abstraction. Abstraction is a way to hide the internal workings or details of a procedure. For example, consider the process of cooking a meal from a recipe. A recipe may require you to chop a food item. What is chopping? It is an abstraction of an action. The action and steps to complete the action are to take a knife, place it over the food item, and press downward. Then, move the knife a short distance along the food item and repeat the process until no large pieces remain. Chopping is an abstraction of this action. It is simpler and quicker to say "chop the carrot" instead of the long-form description. As with preparing food, code uses abstraction to wrap a complicated procedure and hide the internal workings of the code.

Higher order functions can be very useful for creating functional utilities. As programmers, we often create utility functions that are designed to perform an action on a set of values. Often, we want to maximize flexibility and create functions that work over a wide range of potential input values or formats. Creating higher order utility functions that take in some parameters and return a new function can be a great way to do this. These functions are often called closures in JavaScript. Consider the functions shown in the following snippet:

```
function sortObjField1( field ) {
  return function ( v1, v2 ) {
    return v1[ field ] > v2[ field ];
  }
}
```

```
function sortObjField2( field, v1, v2 ) {
  return v1[ field ] > v2[ field ];
}
```

Snippet 5.6: Higher order utilities

In the preceding snippet, we have created two utility functions for sorting arrays of objects by the value stored in the specified field. The utility functions both need the field to be specified. Where they differ is the return value. sortObjField1 is a higher order function that takes in the field name and returns a closure function. The closure function takes in the two objects we are trying to sort and returns the sorting value. The second helper function, sortObjField2, takes in the field and the two objects at once and returns the sorting value. The higher order utility function is much more powerful because we do not need to know all of the values at the same time. We can pass sortObjField( 'field' ) as a parameter to another function to be used in another part of the program.

Higher order functions are also very useful for reducing complexity. Code that is longer and more complex is more prone to having bugs. Higher order functions abstract away the internal workings of complex parts of the code and can use utility functions to reduce the lines of code that need to be written. Both of these effects will reduce the size of your code base and therefore reduce the complexity. Making the code simpler will help to reduce the time you must spend fixing bugs.

## Exercise 30: Editing Object Arrays

The aim is to apply the concepts of higher order functions to edit arrays of objects. To edit the arrays using the necessary functions, perform the following steps:

1.  Create an array called data that contains the following data: [ { f1: 6, f2: 3 }, { f1: 12, f2: 0 }, { f1: 9, f2: 1 }, { f1: 6, f2: 7 } ].

2.  Create a function called swap that takes in two arguments, key1 and key2.

3.  Add a return statement to the swap function. The return statement should return a function. This function should take in one argument, obj.

4.  Inside the returned function, using array destructuring, swap the values of key1 and key2 stored in obj.

    Hint: Use [a, b] = [b, a] to swap values with array destructuring.

5.  Return the modified object, obj, from the function.

6. Edit the data array by calling the `map` function on `data`. Pass a call to swap, with the parameters `f1` and `f2`, as the argument for the map function.

   Hint: `data.map( swap( 'f1', 'f2' ) );`

7. Log the output of the call to `data.map()`.

## Code

**index.js**

```
const data = [ { f1: 6, f2: 3 }, { f1: 12, f2: 0 }, { f1: 9, f2: 1 }, { f1: 6, f2: 7 } ];
function swap( key1, key2 ) {
 return obj => {
   [ obj[ key1 ], obj[ key2 ] ] = [ obj[ key2 ], obj[ key1 ] ];
   return obj;
 }
}
console.log( data.map( swap( 'f1', 'f2' ) ) );
```

https://bit.ly/2D0t70k

## Output

```
[ { f1: 3, f2: 6 },
  { f1: 0, f2: 12 },
  { f1: 1, f2: 9 },
  { f1: 7, f2: 6 } ]
```

Figure 5.4: Final Output

You've successfully applied the concepts of higher order functions to edit arrays of objects.

## Shared State

A **shared state** is any variable, object, or memory space that exists in a shared scope. Any non-constant variable used by multiple separate scopes, including the global scope and closure scopes, is considered to be in a shared state. In functional programming, shared states should be avoided. A shared state prevents a function from being pure. When the shared state rule is violated and the program modifies a variable, a side effect is created. In OOP, shared states are often passed around as objects. OOP functions may modify the shared state. This is very much against functional programming rules. An example of a shared state is shown in the following snippet:

```
const state = { age: 15 }

function doSomething( name ) {

   return state.age > 13 ? '*{name} is old enough' : '*{name} is not old
enough';

}
```

**Snippet 5.7: Shared state**

In the preceding example, we have a variable in the global scope called **state**. In our function called doSomething, we reference the variable state to make a logical code decision. Since the **state** variable was defined outside of the scope of our doSomething function and is not an immutable object (an object whose state cannot be modified after it has been created), it is considered a shared state. This is something that should be avoided in Functional Programming because it prevents our functions from being pure.

Shared states must be avoided for several reasons. First, a shared state can make it difficult to understand a function. To truly understand how a function works and what the output results will be given an input, we must understand the entire state that the function operates under. If our function uses a shared state, we have a much more complex state to understand before we can properly understand the function. It is very difficult to understand a shared state in detail. To properly understand a shared state, you must understand how the state is updated and how it is used in every function it is shared with.

While it may not sound like a major drawback at first, not understanding how our functions work will result in slower development, more bugs, and inadequate testing. Shared states slow down development simply because we must take more time to understand the functions that rely on them. If we do not take the time to understand the shared states and functions that rely on them, then it is likely that we will not write code that is efficient and bug-free. This will obviously lead to more time spent debugging and refactoring code. Functions that are not fully understood tend to be more bug-ridden. If we do not fully understand how the function needs to operate under all of the possibilities and limitations defined in the shared states, it is likely that we will forget to handle edge cases in our development. If these bugs are not found, then faulty code could be released. Finally, not understanding functions makes it nearly impossible to fully test a function. To fully test any function, we must understand exactly how it will operate under all conditions, or in other words, under all states it could be called under.

## Exercise 31: Fixing Shared States

The aim is to refactor code to remove shared states. To properly refactor the code, perform the following steps:

1. Open the file at exercises/exercise34/exercise.js. You will be updating this file to solve the exercise.

2. Run the code in the file opened in *step 1* and observe the output.

3. Update the getOlder function declaration to take in a parameter called age.

4. Update the body of getOlder to return age+1 or ++age instead of modifying the global variable.

5. Update the formatName function declaration to take in two parameters, first and last.

6. Update the body of formatName to return the Mrs. ${first} ${last} string, where first and last are the values stored in the input parameters first and last.

7. Update the call to the getOlder function and pass in person.age as the parameter. Save the returned value into person.age.

8. Update the function call to formatName and pass in person.firstName and person.lastName as the parameters. Save the value returned in person.name.

9. Run the code and compare the output to the output from *step 2*. They should be the same.

## Code

solution.js

---

```js
const person = { age: 10, firstName: 'Sandra', lastName: 'Jeffereys' };
function getOlder( age ) {
  return ++age;
}
function formatName( first, last ) {
  return `Mrs. ${first} ${last}`;
```

```
}
console.log( person );
person.age = getOlder( person.age );
person.name = formatName( person.firstName, person.lastName );
console.log( person );
```

https://bit.ly/2Cz-yoC

**Output**

```
{ age: 10, firstName: 'Sandra', lastName: 'Jeffereys' }
{ age: 11,
  firstName: 'Sandra',
  lastName: 'Jeffereys',
  name: 'Mrs. Sandra Jeffereys' }
```

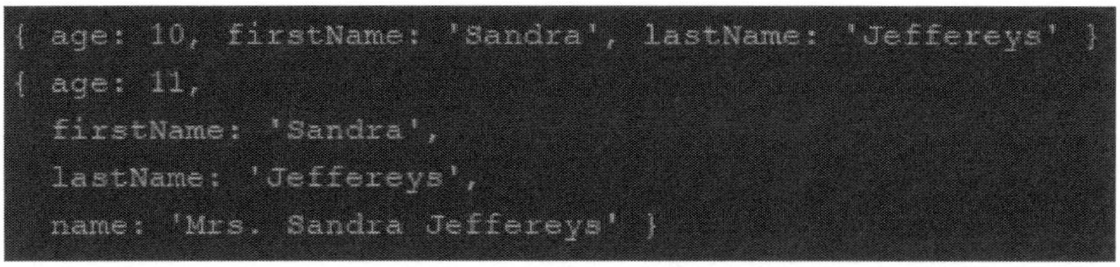

Figure 5.5: Final Output

You've successfully managed to refactor code to remove shared states.

## Immutability

Immutability is a very simple concept but very important to Functional Programming. The textbook definition of **immutability** is simply "something that is not changeable." In programming, we use the word to mean objects and variables whose state cannot be changed after they have been created.

In software development, values can be passed into functions by reference. When a variable is passed by reference, it means that a reference to the memory location (a pointer) is passed instead of the serialized value of the object contained at that location in memory. Since all of the pointers for a variable passed by reference point to the same block of memory, any update to the value of the variable passed by reference will be seen by any pointer pointing to that block of memory. Any variable passed by reference instead of by value can be considered a shared state, since it can be modified by multiple separate scopes. It is important to write functions that prevent the mutation of data because any change to values passed by reference will act as a change to the shared state. Modifying the variables passed by reference will violate the principles of Functional Programming and will lead to side effects.

In JavaScript, the concept of immutability generally applies to variables that are passed into, and returned by, functions. In JavaScript, simple types (string, number, bool) are passed by value, and complex types (objects, arrays, and so on) are passed by reference. Any changes to these complex data types will affect all occurrences because they are all essentially just pointers to the same block of memory.

JavaScript support for immutability is not very complete. JavaScript does not have built-in immutable arrays or objects. It is important to note that the variable creation keyword, const, will not create an immutable object or array. As discussed in the very first chapter, const simply locks the name binding so that the name binding cannot be reassigned. It does not prevent the object referenced by the variable from being modified. Immutable objects in JavaScript can be created in two ways: with the freeze function and with third-party libraries.

Immutable objects can be created with the freeze function. freeze is a function on the global Object prototype ( Object.freeze() ). It takes in a single argument, the object to be frozen, and returns that same object. Freeze prevents anything from being added to, removed from, or modified in the object. If an array is frozen, it will lock the element values and prevent elements from being added to or removed from the array. It is important to note that the freeze function is only a shallow freeze. Objects and arrays nested as properties (in objects) or elements (in arrays) will not be frozen by the freeze function. If you want to fully freeze all nested properties, you must write a helper function that traverses the object or array tree, freezing each nested level, or find a third-party library. The use of Object.freeze() is shown in the following snippet:

```
const data = {
  prop1: 'value1',
  objectProp: { p1: 'v1', p2: 'v2' },
  arrayProp: [ 1, 'test', { p1: 'v1' }, [ 1, 2, 3 ] ]
};
Object.freeze( data );
Object.freeze( data.objectProp );
Object.freeze( data.arrayProp );
Object.freeze( data.arrayProp[2] );
Object.freeze( data.arrayProp[3] );
```

Snippet 5.8: Freezing an object

## Immutability in JavaScript

Several third-party libraries exist to add immutable functionality to JavaScript. There are two libraries that are generally accepted as the best immutability libraries in JavaScript. They are **Mori** and **Immutable**. Mori is a library that brings ClojurScript's persistent data structures and immutability to JavaScript. **Immutable** is Facebook's implementation of an immutability library with a JS API that brings many immutable data structures to JavaScript. Both libraries are considered to be very efficient and are commonly used in many large projects.

> **Note**
>
> For more information about Mori and Immutable, along with full documentation, see the library pages at https://github.com/swannodette/mori and http://facebook.github.io/immutable-js/.

There is one final way to obtain immutability in JavaScript; however, it is not true immutability. To avoid using third-party libraries or freezing any object or array passed to a function, we can simply create a copy of any variable passed by reference and modify the copy instead of the original. This will prevent the shared state issue of passing data by reference, but it comes with a memory efficiency and inefficiency trade-off. Simply assigning the reference to a new variable will not duplicate the data. We can duplicate an object or array in one of three ways—with a third-party library, by traversing the object tree, or by using JSON operations.

Third-party libraries exist to create deep copies of objects. This is generally the simplest approach to copying objects. We can also traverse the object's tree and copy every value and property into a new object. This will generally require us to write and test our own function. Finally, we can use the JSON operations stringify and parse to duplicate an object. This is done by first stringifying an object, then parsing the string (`JSON.parse( JSON.stringify( obj ) )`). JSON operations are usually the simplest approach to duplicating objects, but they come with the most drawbacks and limitations. If the object has non-JSON-compatible properties, such as functions or classes, this approach will not work. It is also very inefficient to convert the entire object into a string and then parse that entire string into an object. For small objects, this may not affect performance, but if you must copy a large object, it is not recommended that you use this method because it is a blocking operation.

# Side Effects

A **side effect** is any secondary effect or reaction that comes from an action we take. Side effects can be either good or bad, but are generally unintended. In functional programming, side effects are any state change that can be seen outside of a function call, with the exception of the function return value. According to the rules of functional programming, functions are not allowed to modify any states outside of the function. If the function modifies a state, intentionally or unintentionally, this is considered a side effect because it breaks the tenets of functional programming.

Side effects are bad because they make a program more complex. As discussed earlier, shared states increase program complexity. Side effects in functions modify shared states and therefore increase complexity. Side effects, intentional or otherwise, can make code much harder to test and debug. The following list shows a simple breakdown of the most common causes of side effects in JavaScript:

- Modifying any external state (variable)

  The two variable types include global variables and variables in the parent function scope.

The first bullet in this list should be self-explanatory from the definition of FP side effects. A change to any external state, including any variable outside of the function's scope, is a side effect. It does not matter what level of scope the variable has. It can be in the global scope or anywhere up the parent function scope tree; any change to a variable not directly scoped in the function is considered a side effect.

- Input/output

  The list includes logging to a console, writing to a screen or display, file I/O operations, network operations, HTTP requests, message queues, and database requests.

The second bullet point in the side effect list is not as intuitive. Consider I/O operations for a moment. What do they do? They modify some external resource. This could be the contents of the console, the view or display shown on a web page, a file in the filesystem, or an external resource only accessed over the network. These external resources are not directly scoped to the block of code that is modifying them, and they can be modified and viewed from other completely unrelated applications. By definition, resources such as the filesystem and console are shared states. Modifications to these resources count as side effects.

- Starting or ending external processes

The third bullet point in the side effect list is similar to the second. Starting an external process, such as a helper thread to offload some large, synchronous amount of work, creates a side effect. When we start a new process, we are directly changing the state of our system. A new thread is created and it is outside of the scope of the function that created it. By definition, this is a side effect.

- Calling any other function with side effects

The fourth item in the side effect list is also less intuitive. Any function that calls a function with a side effect is considered to have a side effect. Consider a program setup where function A calls function B, and function B causes a change to the global state. This change to the global state can be prompted by either a direct call to function B or by calling function A, which eventually calls function B and changes the state. Since a call to function A will still result in a global state change, even though the code in function A does not directly modify the global state, function A is still considered to have a side effect.

While writing FP code, we must consider the following questions:

If any I/O operation causes a side effect, how can we apply FP principles to writing useful code without side effects? Since I/O operations cause side effects, won't every network call or file system operation used in our code cause a side effect? Yes. Side effects from I/O will be caused and they are unavoidable. The solution to this issue is to isolate side-effect code from the rest of the software. Any code that has a side effect or relies on modules or operations with side effects (database operations and so on) must be isolated from code that does not. This is usually done with modules. Most frontend and backend frameworks encourage us to separate state management from the rest of our code by using modules. Code that causes side effects is removed and put into its own module so that the rest of the code base can be tested and maintained without side effects.

## Avoiding Side Effects

It is almost impossible to write a full application without side effects. Web applications/ servers must handle/make HTTP requests - side effect by definition. In order to achieve this, you can do the following:

- Isolate code with side effects from the rest of the code base.

- Separate state management code and code with side effects from the rest of application.

These methods make testing and debugging easier.

# Function Composition

**Function composition** is the final key to understanding functional programming. Function composition takes many of the concepts learned in this chapter and nicely wraps them in the core of functional programming. The widely used definition of function composition is that function composition is a mathematical concept that allows you to combine multiple functions to create a new function. This definition tells us what function composition is, but doesn't really give us any sense of how to compose functions or why we need to use it.

As we know from the definition, function composition is the act of combining functions to create a new one. What does this mean exactly? In mathematics, we often see functions composed like so: $f(g(x))$. If this is not familiar to you, in the expression $f(g(x))$, we pass the variable x into the function g and then pass the result of $g(x)$ into the function f. The expression $f(g(x))$ is evaluated from the inside out, from right to left, in the order x, g, f. Every instance where the input parameter is used in function g, we can substitute in the value of x. Every instance where the input parameter is used in function f, we can substitute in the value of $g(x)$. Now, let's consider this method of function composition with code. Consider the code in the following snippet :

```
function multiplyBy2( c ) {
  return 2 * c;
}


function sumNumbers( a, b ) {
  return a + b;
}


const v1 = sumNumbers( 2, 4 ); // 2 + 4 = 6
const v2 = multiplyBy2( v2 ); // 2 * 6 = 12
const v3 = multiplyBy2( sumNumbers( 2, 4 ) ); // 2 * ( 2 + 4 ) = 12
```

Snippet 5.10: Function composition

In the preceding snippet, we create a function to multiply a value by 2 and a function to add two numbers. We can use these functions to calculate a value in two ways. First, we use these functions independently, one at a time. This requires us to create a variable and save the output of the first function, call the second function with that value, and then save the result of the second function into a variable. This requires two lines of code and two variables. Our second option for calculating a value is by using function composition. We simply need to call one function inside the input argument of the second function and save the resultant variable. This requires one line of code and one variable. As we can see from the code in the snippet, using function composition will help simplify our code and reduce the number of lines of code we need to write.

Function composition is very useful for reducing the number of lines of code we need to write, as well as reducing the complexity of our code. When writing code in the Functional Programming paradigm, it is important to recognize instances when we can use function composition to our advantage.

## Activity 5: Recursive Immutability

You are building an application in JavaScript and your team has been told it cannot use any third-party libraries for security reasons. You must now use FP principles for this application and need an algorithm to create immutable objects and arrays. Create a recursive function that enforces the immutability of objects and arrays at all levels of nesting with `Object.freeze()`. For simplicity, you can assume there are no null value or classes nested in the objects. Write your function in `Lesson 5/topic f - immutability/activity-test.js`. This file contains code to test your implementation.

To force immutability in objects, perform the following steps:

1. Create a function called `immutable` that takes in a single argument, `data`.

2. Freeze the `data` object.

3. Loop through object values and recursively call the immutable function for each.

**Code**

**Outcome**

**Figure 5.6: Returning the new cart array**

You have successfully demonstrated forcing immutability in objects.

> **Note**
>
> The solution for this activity can be found on page 291.

## Summary

**Functional Programming** is a programming paradigm that focuses on expressions and declarations to design an application and build a code base. Functional Programming is one of the hot new programming styles and is considered the best style for programming in JavaScript. Functional Programming can help our JavaScript be more concise, predictable, and testable. Functional Programming is built on seven key concepts: declarative functions, pure functions, higher order functions, shared state, immutability, side effects, and function composition.

**Declarative functions** focus on what the solution or goal is, instead of how we get the solution. Declarative functions are designed to abstract away a lot of the imperative approach to code. They help developers code more in keeping with the mental model of the developer, instead of the operational model of the machine running the code.

**Pure functions** are intended to make our code easier to test, easier to debug, and more flexible and reusable. All functions we write in JavaScript should strive to be pure. Pure functions must always return the same output value when given the same input values. They cannot cause any side effects by modifying external states and must have referential transparency.

**Higher order functions** are one of the most common types of functions used in JavaScript asynchronous programming. A higher order function is any function that takes a function as an input and returns a function as an output. Higher order functions are very useful for abstraction of code, complexity reduction, and utility function creation and management. They are the key to closures, which allow us to be very flexible with our code.

**Shared states** are one of the most important things to avoid in Functional Programming. A shared state is any non-constant variable or non-immutable object or memory space that exists in a shared scope. The shared scope could be a global scope or any scope up the parent function scope tree. Shared states prevent functions from being pure and can result in more bugs, inadequate testing, and slower development.

**Immutability** is the lack of ability to change something. In JavaScript, all variables that are passed by reference should be made immutable. Changes to mutable variables passed by reference can cause side effects and unintentionally modify states that are not supposed to be shared. Immutability in JavaScript can be obtained with the `Object.freeze()` function, third-party libraries, and JSON operations.

**Side effects** in JavaScript are any state change that can be seen from outside of a function call, excluding the function's return value. A side effect can be caused by any modification to a shared state variable, any I/O operation, any external process execution, or by calling any function with a side effect. It can be very difficult to fully eliminate side effects from JavaScript applications. To minimize the effect of side effects, we must isolate any code with a side effect from the rest of the code base. Code that causes side effects should be moved into modules for isolation purposes.

**Function composition** is the final key concept of Functional Programming. We can create complicated and powerful functions simply by combining simpler functions in new ways. Function composition is designed to help abstract and reduce the complexity of our code.

In the next chapter, you will be introduced to the basic concepts of server-side JavaScript and build a Node.js and Express server.

# The JavaScript Ecosystem

## Learning Objectives

By the end of this chapter, you will be able to do the following:

- Compare the different JavaScript ecosystems
- Explain the basic concepts of server-side JavaScript
- Build a Node.js and Express server
- Build a React frontend website
- Combine a frontend framework with a backend server

The final chapter covers the JavaScript Ecosystem in detail, and teaches the students how to work with different features and sections of Node.js, as well as the Node Package Manager (NPM).

# Introduction

**In** *Chapter 5, Functional Programming*, we covered the **Functional Programming paradigm**. We covered **Object Oriented Programming** and Functional Programming, discussed the differences between the two, and outlined the reasons why we should use functional programming. In the second section, we discussed the key concepts of functional programming and demonstrated how they are applied to JavaScript code.

The JavaScript ecosystem has grown immensely over the past 10+ years. JavaScript is no longer a programming language to be used for adding flair, such as animations, on top of a basic HTML web page. JavaScript can now be used to build full backend web servers and services, command-line interfaces, mobile apps, and frontend sites. In this chapter, we will introduce the JavaScript ecosystem, discuss building web servers in JavaScript with Node.js, and discuss building websites with JavaScript using the React framework.

# JavaScript Ecosystem

There are four main categories of the JavaScript ecosystem that we will discuss: **frontend**, **command-line interface**, **mobile**, and **backend**.

- Front-end JavaScript is used for user-facing websites.

- Command-line interface (CLI) JavaScript is used for building command-line tasks to assist developers.

- Mobile development JavaScript is used to build mobile phone apps.

- Backend JavaScript is used to build web servers and services.

For a language that was created originally to embed simple applications in browsers, JavaScript has come a long way.

## Frontend JavaScript

**Frontend JavaScript** is used for creating complicated and dynamic user-facing websites. Websites such as Facebook, Google Maps, Spotify, and YouTube rely heavily on JavaScript. In frontend development, JavaScript is used to manipulate the DOM and handle events. Many JavaScript libraries, such as jQuery, have been created to increase the efficiency and ease of JavaScript DOM manipulation by wrapping the DOM manipulation APIs of each browser into a standardized API. The most prevalent DOM manipulation library is jQuery, which was discussed in *Chapter 3, DOM Manipulation and Event Handling*. JavaScript frameworks have also been created to more seamlessly integrate DOM manipulation and events with the HTML design aspect. Two of the most common JavaScript frameworks for frontend development are **AngularJS** and **React**. AngularJS was built by and is maintained by Google, and React was built by and is maintained by Facebook.

Facebook and Google manage bug fixes and version releases for their respective frameworks. React will be discussed in more detail in a later section of this chapter.

## Command-Line Interface

**Command-line integration (CLI)** JavaScript is generally used to create utilities to assist developers with repetitive or time-intensive tasks. CLI programs in JavaScript are generally used for tasks such as linting code, starting a server, building releases, transpiling code, minifying files, and installing development dependencies and packages. JavaScript CLI programs are generally written in Node.js. Node.js is a cross-platform environment that allows developers to execute JavaScript code outside a browser. Node.js will be discussed in more detail in a later section of this chapter. Many developers rely on CLI utilities in their day-to-day development.

## Mobile Development

**Mobile development** with JavaScript is quickly becoming mainstream. Since the rise of smartphones, mobile developers have become a hot commodity. While JavaScript cannot be run natively on most mobile operating systems, frameworks exist that allow JavaScript and HTML to be built into Android and IOS phone apps. The most common frameworks for JavaScript mobile development are Ionic, React Native, and Cordova/PhoneGap. These frameworks all allow you to write JavaScript to build the framework and logic of an application and then compile the JavaScript down to the native mobile operating system code. Mobile development frameworks are very powerful because they allow us to build full mobile applications in our preferred JavaScript.

## Backend Development

**Backend development** with JavaScript is generally done with Node.js. Node.js can be used to build powerful web servers and services. As stated earlier in this topic, Node.js and its application to backend server development will be discussed in more detail in a later section of this chapter.

The JavaScript ecosystem is very extensive. It is possible to write nearly any sort of program in JavaScript. Despite the number of frameworks and the capabilities of modern JavaScript, it is important to remember that a framework does not replace a good understanding of core JavaScript. Frameworks nicely wrap core JavaScript to allow us to perform powerful tasks like building mobile and desktop applications from it, but if the core principles of JavaScript and asynchronous programming are not well understood, flaws may begin to appear in our applications.

# Node.js

**Node.js** (Node for short), which was developed in 2009 by Ryan Dahl, is the most popular out-of-browser JavaScript engine. Node is an open source, cross-platform JavaScript runtime environment that was based on Chrome's V8 JavaScript engine. It is used to run JavaScript code outside of the browser for non-client, side applications.

Like Google's V8 JavaScript engine in Chrome, Node.js uses a singly-threaded, event-driven, asynchronous architecture. It allows developers to use JavaScript's event-driven programming style to build web servers, services, and CLI tools. As discussed in *Chapter 2, Asynchronous JavaScript*, JavaScript is a non-blocking and event-driven programming language. JavaScript's asynchronous nature (a single-threaded event loop), along with Node's lightweight design, allows us to build very scalable network applications without worrying about threading.

> **Note**
>
> As discussed in *Chapter 2, Asynchronous JavaScript*, JavaScript is single-threaded. Synchronous code running on a single thread is blocking. CPU-intensive operations will block events as I/O file system operations and network operations.

## Setting Up Node.js

Node.js can be downloaded from the Node.js website, which can be found at https://nodejs.org/en/. There are two versions available for download: the **Long Term Support (LTS)** version and the current version. We recommend that you download the LTS version. The current version has the latest features available, which may not be completely bug-free. Be sure to follow your operating system's specific instructions for installing Node. An installer file can be downloaded for all three of the major operating systems, and Node.js can be installed with many package managers. Node.js installation debugging is outside of the scope of this book. However, installation tips and debugging tips can be found easily with a Google search.

> **Note**
>
> Node.js's download link is as follows: https://nodejs.org/en/download/.

Once Node.js has been downloaded and installed, it can be run from the terminal with the `node` command. Executing this command with no arguments following it will run the Node.js terminal. JavaScript code can be typed directly into the terminal, just like a browser's debug console. It is important to note that there is no state carry over between terminal instances. When the terminal instance running the Node.js command-line closes, all computation will stop, and all memory being used by the Node.js command line process will be released back to the OS. To run a JavaScript code file with Node.js, simply add the file path directly after the `node` command. For example, the following command will run the file at the `./path/to/file` location with the filename `my_file.js`: `node ./path/to/file/my_file.js`.

## Node Package Manager

Node.js is an open source platform. One of Node's largest assets is the availability of open source third-party libraries, called modules. Node uses the **Node Package Manager (NPM)** to handle the installation and management of the third-party modules that are used by an application. NPM is usually installed with Node.js. To test whether NPM was installed correctly with your installation of Node, open a terminal window and run the `npm -v` command. If NPM is correctly installed, the current version of NPM will be printed in the terminal. If NPM did not install with Node, you may have to rerun the Node.js installer.

> **Note**
>
> The NPM documentation for all the functionality not covered in this section can be found at https://docs.npmjs.com/.

In *Chapter 1, Introducing ECMAScript 6*, we learned about ES6 modules. It is very important that we make a distinction between ES6 modules and Node.js modules. Node.js modules were created well before ES6 and vanilla JavaScript's support for modules. While Node.js modules and ES6 modules are used for the same purpose, they do not follow the same technology specification. Node.js modules and ES6 modules are loaded, parsed, and built differently. Node.js modules are loaded from the disk synchronously, parsed synchronously, and built synchronously. No other code can run before the modules have been loaded. Unfortunately, ES6 modules are not loaded in the same way. They are loaded asynchronously from disk. The two different module loading methods are not compatible. At the time of writing this book, Node.js support for ES6 modules is in beta and is not enabled by default. Support for ES6 modules can be enabled, but we recommend that you use standard node modules until full support for ES6 modules is released.

NPM packages are installed via the command line with the `npm install` command. You can use this command to either add a specific package to the project or install all missing dependencies. If no arguments are given to the install command, `npm` will look in the current directory for a `package.json` file. Inside the `package.json` file, there is a `dependencies` field that contains all of the dependencies that have been installed for the Node.js project. NPM will run through the dependency list and verify that each package specified in this list is installed. The dependency list in `packages.json` will look similar to the code that's shown in the following snippet:

```
"dependencies": {
  "amqplib": "^0.5.2",
  "body-parser": "^1.18.3",
  "cookie-parser": "^1.4.3",
  "express": "^4.16.3",
  "uuid": "^3.3.2"
}
```

Snippet 6.1: Dependency list in package.json

The dependencies field in `package.json` lists the NPM modules that have been installed for the project, along with the version number. In this snippet, we have the `amqplib` module installed at version `0.5.2` or higher, the `body-parser` module installed at `1.18.3` or higher, and several others. NPM modules follow semantic versioning. The version number is expressed by three numbers, separated by periods. The first number is the major version. Increases in the major version number indicate major changes that break backwards compatibility. The second number is the minor version. Changes to the minor version number indicate a release of new features that do not break backward compatibility. The final number is the patch number. Increases to the patch number indicate a bug fix or small updates to a feature. Increases in patch number do not include new functionality and do not break backwards compatibility.

> **Note**
>
> More information about semantic versioning can be found at https://www.npmjs.com/.

To install a module, you can add an argument to the `npm install` command after the word *install* (for example, `npm install express`). The argument can be either the package name, a Git repository, a **tarball**, or a folder. If the argument is a package, NPM will search through its list of registered packages and install the package that matches the name. If the argument is a Git repository, NPM will attempt to download and install the files from the Git repository. If the proper access credentials are not provided, the installation may fail.

> **Note**
>
> See the NPM documentation for how to install packages from private git repositories.

If the argument is a tarball, NPM will unpack the tarball and install the files. A tarball can be installed through a URL that points to the tarball or through a local file. Finally, if the argument that's specified is a folder on the local machine, NPM will attempt to install an NPM package from the specified folder.

When installing packages with NPM, it is important to consider how the package will be installed. By default, packages are installed in the local project scope and not saved as project dependencies. If you are installing an NPM package that you want saved in `package.json` as a project dependency, you must include the `--save` or `-s` argument after the package name in the install command (for example, `npm install express -s`). This argument tells NPM to save the dependency in `package.json` so that an `npm install` command at a later time will install it.

NPM packages can be installed in two scopes: the **global scope** and the **local scope**. Packages installed in the local scope, or local packages, can only be used inside the Node.js project where they are installed. Packages installed in the global scope, or global packages, can be used by any Node.js project. Packages are installed locally by default. To force a module to be installed globally, you can add the `-g` or `--global` flag to the `npm install` command after the package name (for example, `npm install express -g`).

It is not always apparent where you should install a package, but you can follow the following general rule of thumb if you are unsure. If you are going to use the package in a project with the `require()` function, install the package locally. If you plan on using the package on the command line, install the package globally. If you still cannot decide and need to use the package in a project and on the command line, you can simply install it in both places.

## Loading and Creating Modules

Node.js uses the **CommonJS** style module specification as the standard for loading and working with modules. CommonJS is a project that's designed to specify a JavaScript ecosystem for JavaScript outside the browser. CommonJS defined a specification for modules that was adopted by Node.js. Modules allow the developer to encapsulate functionality and expose only the desired parts of the encapsulated functionality to other JavaScript files.

In Node.js, we use the require function to import modules into our code (`require('module')`). The `require` function can load any valid JavaScript file, NPM module, or JSON file. We will use the `require` function to load any NPM packages that have been installed for our project. To load a module, simply pass the name of the module as a parameter into the `require` function and save the returned object into a variable. For example, we could load the NPM module `body-parser` with the following code: `const bodyParser = require( 'body-parser' );`. This loads the exported functions and variables into the `bodyParser` object. The require function can also be used to load JavaScript files and JSON files. To load one of these files, you simply need to pass the file path into the `require` function instead of a module name. If no file extension is provided, Node.js will look for a JavaScript file by default.

> **Note**
>
> A directory can also be loaded through the require function. If a directory is provided instead of a JS file, the require function will look for a file named `index.js` in the specified directory and load that file. If that file cannot be found, an error will be thrown.

To create a module, that is, a Node.js module, we use the `module.exports` property. In Node.js, every JavaScript file has a global variable object called `module`. The `exports` field in the `module` object defines what items will be exported from the module. When a module is imported with the `require()` function, the return value of `require()` is the value that's set in the module's `module.exports` field. Modules usually export a function or an object with properties for each function or variable that's exported. An example of exporting modules is shown in the following snippet:

```
module.exports = {
    exportedVariable,
    exportedFn
}
```

```
const exportedVariable = 10;

function exportedFn( args ){ console.log( 'exportedFn' ) ;}
```

Snippet 6.2: Exporting a Node.js module

## Exercise 32: Exporting and Importing NPM Modules

To build, export, and import NPM modules, perform the following steps:

1. Create a JavaScript for our module called module.js.

2. Set the module.exports property to an object.

3. Add the exportedConstant field to the object with the value An exported constant!

4. Add the exportedFunction field to the object and set its value to a function that logs to the console with the text An exported function!

5. Create an index.js file for our main code.

6. Import the module from module.js with a require function and save it into the ourModule variable.

7. Log the value of exportedString from ourModule.

8. Call the exportedFunction function from ourModule.

## Code

module.js

```
module.js
module.exports = {
  exportedString: 'An exported string!',
  exportedFunction(){ console.log( 'An exported function!' ) }
};
```

Snippet 6.3: Exporting code as a module

https://bit.ly/2M3SIsT

index.js

```
const ourModule = require('./module.js');
console.log( ourModule.exportedString );
ourModule.exportedFunction();
```

Snippet 6.4: Exporting code as a module

https://bit.ly/2RwOIxP

## Outcome

```
An exported string!
An exported function!


Process finished with exit code 0
```

Figure 6.1: Test values output

You have successfully built, exported, and imported NPM modules.

## Basic Node.js Server

The most common application for Node.js is web servers. Node.js makes it very easy to build very efficient and scalable web servers because developers don't need to worry about threading. In this section, we will demonstrate the code that's required to make a basic web server in Node.js.

A Node.js server can be set up as either an HTTP, HTTPS, or HTTP2 server. For this example, we will create a basic HTTP server. Node.js has basic functionality for an HTTP server available through the HTTP module. Import the HTTP module with a require statement. This is shown in the following snippet:

```
const http = require( 'http' );
```

Snippet 6.5: Loading the HTTP module

This line of code will import the functionality contained in the module 'HTTP' and save it in the variable http for use later. Now that we have loaded the HTTP module, we need to choose a hostname and a port to run our server on. Since this server will only be running locally to our computer, we can use the IP address for the machine's internal local network, localhost ('127.0.0.1'), for our hostname address. We can run our local server on any network port which isn't already in use by another application.

You can choose any valid port number, but it is rare that programs use port **8000** by default, so that is what is used in this demo. Add a variable to contain the port number and hostname to your code. The full code to this point is shown in the following snippet:

```
const http = require('http');
const hostname = '127.0.0.1';
const port = 8000;
```

Snippet 6.6: Constants for simple server

Now that we have set up all of the basic parameters for our server, we can write the code to create and start the server. The HTTP module contains a function called createServer() that returns a server object. This function can take in an optional callback function that acts as am HTTP request listener. When any HTTP request comes into the server, the provided callback method gets called. We need to call the createServer function with the request listener callback so that our server can properly respond to inbound HTTP requests. This is done with the lines of code that are shown in the following snippet:

```
const server = http.createServer((req, res) => {
  res.statusCode = 200;
  res.setHeader('Content-Type', 'text/plain');
  res.end('Welcome to my server!\n');
});
```

Snippet 6.7: Creating a simple server

In the preceding snippet, we call the create server function and save the returned server into the server variable. We pass a callback into createServer(). This callback takes in two arguments: req and res. The req argument represents the incoming HTTP request and the res argument represents the server HTTP response. In the first line of code in the callback, we set the response status code to 200. A 200 status code in the response indicates that the HTTP request to the server was successful. In the line after the status code, we set the Content-Type header in the response to text/plain. This step tells the response that the data passed into it will be plain text. In the final line of the callback, we call the res.end() function. This function appends the data passed into it to the response, then closes the response and sends it back to the requester. In this snippet, we pass in the Welcome to my server! string to the end() function. The response has the string appended to it and the text is sent back to the requester. Our server now handles all HTTP calls to it with this handler.

The final step to get our mini server up and running is to call the .listen() function on the server object. The listen function starts the HTTP server on the specified port and hostname. Once the server has begun listening, it can accept HTTP requests. The code in the following snippet shows how to make the server listen to the specified port at the specified hostname:

```
server.listen( port, hostname, () => {
  console.log('Server running at http://${hostname}:${port}/');
});
```

Snippet 6.8: Server begins listening on hostname and port

The preceding snippet shows how to call the server.listen() function. The first argument passed into the function is the port number that our server will be exposed on. The second argument is the hostname that our server will be accessed from. In this example, the port evaluates to 8000 and the hostname evaluates to 127.0.0.1 (the local network for your computer). In this example, our server will be listening on 127.0.0.1:8000. The final argument passed in to .listen() is a callback function. Once the server begins listening for HTTP requests at the specified port and hostname, the provided callback function is called. In the preceding snippet, the callback function simply prints the URL that our server can be accessed from locally. You can enter this URL into your browser and a web page will load.

## Exercise 33: Creating a Basic HTTP Server

To build a basic HTTP server, perform the following steps:

1.  Import the http module.

2.  Set up variables for the hostname and port and give them the values 127.0.0.1 and 8000, respectively.

3.  Create the server with http.createServer.

4.  Provide a callback to the createServer function that takes in the arguments req and res.

5.  Set the response status code to 200.

6.  Set the response content type to text/plain.

7.  Respond to the request with My first server!

8.  Make the server listen on the specified port and host with the server.listen function.

9. Provide a callback to the `listen` function that logs `Server running at` `${server_uri}`.

10. Start the server and load the logged web page.

## Code

index.js

```
const http = require( 'http' );

const hostname = '127.0.0.1';

const port = 8000;

const server = http.createServer( ( req, res ) => {
  res.statusCode = 200;
  res.setHeader( 'Content-Type', 'text/plain' );
  res.end( 'My first server!\n' );
} );

server.listen( port, hostname, () => console.log( 'Server running at
http://${hostname}:${port}/' ) );
```

Snippet 6.9: Simple HTTP server

https://bit.ly/2sibcFw

## Outcome

```
PS C:\Users\Zach\Documents\Professional-JavaScript\Lesson 6\topic b> node ./basic-http-server.js
Server running at http://127.0.0.1:8000/
```

Figure 6.2: Returning the new cart array

← → C ⓘ 127.0.0.1:8000

⠿ Apps   G Logs Viewer - SE Dev

My first server!

Figure 6.3: Returning the new cart array

You have successfully built a basic HTTP server.

## Streams and Pipes

Streaming data can be one of the most complicated and misunderstood aspects of Node.js. Streams are also arguably one of the most powerful features Node.js has to offer. Streams are simply collections of data, just like the standard array or string. The main difference is that, with streams, all of the data may not be available at one time. You can think of it like streaming a video off YouTube or Netflix. You do not need to download the entire video before you can begin to watch it. The video provider (YouTube or Netflix) sends, or "streams", the video to your computer in small pieces. You can begin watching a part of the video without waiting for any other parts to be loaded first. Streams are very powerful because they allow the server and the client to not need to load an entire large collection of data into memory at one time. In JavaScript servers, streams are crucial to memory management.

Many of the built-in modules in Node.js rely on streams. These modules include the request and response objects in the HTTP module (`http`), the file system module (`fs`) file the cryptography module (crypto), and the child process module (`child_process`). In Node.js, streams come in four types– **readable**, **writeable**, **duplex**, and **transform**. Understanding what they do is pretty straightforward.

## Types of Streams

Data is consumed from **Readable Streams**. They abstract the loading and chunking of a source. Data is presented for consumption (use) by the readable stream, one chunk at a time. After the data chunk has been consumed, it is let go by the stream and the next chunk is presented. A readable stream cannot have data pushed into it by the consumer. An example of a readable stream is an HTTP request body.

A **readable stream** comes in two modes– **flowing** and **paused**. These modes determine the data flow of the stream. When the stream is in flowing mode, data is automatically read from the underlying stream system and is being provided to consumers. When the stream is in paused mode, data is not automatically read from the underlying system. The consumer must explicitly request data from the stream with the `stream.read()` function. All readable streams start in paused mode and can be switched to flowing by either attaching a `data` event handler, calling `stream.resume()`, or calling `stream.pipe()`. Event handlers and stream piping are covered later in this section. A readable stream can be switched from flowing to paused with the `stream.pause()` method or the `stream.unpipe()` method.

A **writeable stream** is a stream to which data can be written or pushed. **Writeable streams** abstract away the combining and handling of the source. Data is presented to the stream for consumption by the provider. The stream will consume data one chunk at a time until it is told to stop. After the stream has consumed a chunk of data and handled it appropriately, it will consume or request the next chunk of data that's available. An example of a writeable stream is the filesystem module function createWriteStream, which allows us to stream data to a file on the disk.

A **duplex stream** is a stream that is both readable and writeable. Data can be pushed in chunks by a provider to the stream or consumed in chunks by a consumer from the stream. An example of a duplex stream is a network socket such as a TCP socket.

A **transform stream** is a duplex stream that allows the data chunks to be mutated as they move through the stream. An example of a transform stream is the gzip method in Node.js's zlib module, which compresses data with the gzip compression method.

Streams load data in chunks instead of all at once, so to effectively use streams, we need some way to determine if data has been loaded by the stream. In Node.js, streams are instances of the EventEmitter prototype. Streams emit events when key events happen, such as errors or data availability. Events listeners can be attached to streams with the .on() and .once() methods. Readable streams and writeable streams have events for data handling, error handling, and steam management.

The following tables show the available events and their purpose:

## Writeable Stream Events:

| Event | Use |
|---|---|
| close | Emitted when the stream has been closed. No further events will be emitted and no further computation will occur. |
| drain | Emitted when the stream is ready to resume writing data to the specified source. |
| error | Emitted when an error occurs when writing or piping data. |
| finish | Emitted when the stream has ended and all data has flushed. All data writing has completed. |
| pipe | Emitted when the stream becomes a pipe destination. |
| unpipe | Emitted when the stream is removed from another stream's pipe destinations. |

Figure 6.4: Writeable Stream Events

## Readable Stream Events:

| Event | User |
|-------|------|
| close | Emitted when the stream has been closed. No more events will be emitted and no further computation will occur. |
| data | Emitted when the stream is giving a chunk of data to the consumer. |
| end | Emitted when there is no more data to be consumed from the stream. |
| error | Emitted when there was an error reading data or piping data. |
| readable | Emitted when data is ready to be read from the stream. |

Figure 6.5: Readable Stream Events

> **Note**
>
> These event listeners can be attached to the stream to handle data flow and manage the state of the stream. Complete documentation can be found on the Node.js site under the Stream API.

Now that you understand the basics of streams, we must implement them. Readable streams follow a basic workflow. Generally, a method that returns a readable stream is called. An example of this is the filesystem API function createReadStream(), which creates a readable stream that streams a file off the disk. After the readable stream is returned, we can begin to pull data from the stream by attaching a data event handler. An example of this is shown in the following snippet:

```
const fs = require( 'fs' );
fs.createReadStream( './path/to/files.ext' ).on( 'data', data => {
    console.log( data );
} );
```

Snippet 6.10: Using a readable stream

In the preceding example, we imported the `fs` module and call the `createReadStream` function. This function returns a readable stream. We then attach an event listener to the `data` event. This puts the stream in flowing mode, and every time a data chunk is ready, the callback provided will be called. In this example, our callback simply logs the data that the readable stream relinquishes.

Just like readable streams, writable streams also follow a pretty standard workflow as well. The most basic workflow for a writable stream is to first call a method that returns a writable stream. An example of this is the `fs` module function `createWriteStream`. After the writeable stream has been created, we can write to it with the `stream.write()` function. This function will write the data that's passed into it to the stream. An example of this is shown in the following snippet:

```
const fs = require( 'fs' );
const writeable = fs.createWriteStream( './path/to/files.ext' );


writeable.write( 'some data' );
writeable.write( 'more data!' );
```

Snippet 6.11: Using a writeable stream

In the preceding snippet, we loaded the `fs` module and called the `createWriteStream` function. This returns a writeable stream that writes data to the filesystem. We then call the `stream.write()` function several times. Each time we call the `write` function, the data we pass into the function is pushed into the writeable stream and written to the disk.

One of the most powerful features in Node.js is the ability to pipe streams. Piping a stream simply takes the source and "pipe" it to a destination. You take the data output from one stream and pipes it to the input of another stream. This is extremely powerful because it allows us to simplify the process of connecting streams.

Consider the problem where we must load a file from the disk and send it in an HTTP response to a client. We can do this in two ways. The first implementation we can build is to load the entire file into memory, then push it all at once to the client. This is hugely inefficient for our server. The second is to make use of streams. We stream the file from the disk and push the data chunks to the request stream. To do this without pipes, we must attach listeners to the read stream and catch each data chunk, then push the data chunk to the HTTP response. The pseudocode for this is shown in the following snippet:

```
const fileSystemStream = load( 'filePath' );

fileSystemStream.on( 'data', data => HTTP_Response.push( data ) );

fileSystemStream.on( 'end', HTTP_Response.end() );
```

Snippet 6.12: Sending data to HTTP response with a stream

In the pseudocode in the preceding snippet, we created a stream that loads from the specified file path. We then add an event handler for the data event and the end event. Every time the data event has data for us, we push that data to the HTTP_Response stream. Once there is no more data and the end event is fired, we close the HTTP_Response stream the data is sent to the client. This requires several lines of code and requires the developer to manage the data and data flow. We can build the exact same functionality with stream piping on a single line of code.

Piping streams is done with the Stream.pipe() function. Pipe is called on the source stream and is passed the destination stream as an argument (for example, readableStream.pipe( writeableStream )). Pipe returns the destination stream, which allows it to be used for chaining pipe commands. Using the same scenario as in the preceding example, we can simplify the pseudocode down to one line with the pipe command. This is shown in the following snippet:

```
load( 'filePath' ).pipe( HTTP_Response );
```

Snippet 6.13: Piping data pseudo code

In the preceding snippet, we loaded the file data and piped it to the HTTP_response. Each chunk of data loaded by the readable stream is automatically passed to the writeable stream HTTP_Response. When the readable stream finishes loading the data, it automatically closes and tells the write stream to also close.

## Filesystem Operations

Node's filesystem module, named '**fs**,' provides an API with which we can interact with the filesystem. The filesystem APIs are modeled around the POSIX standard. The **POSIX (Portable Operating System Interface)** standard is a standard specified by the IEEE Computer Society to help keep general compatibility between different operating system filesystems. You do not need to learn the details of the standard but understand that the fs modules follow it to maintain cross-platform compatibility. To import the filesystem module, we can use the following command: `const fs = require( 'fs' );`.

Most filesystem functions in Node.js require that you specify a path to the file that will be used. When specifying a file path for the fs module, the path can be specified in one of three ways: as a **string**, as a **buffer**, or as a **URL** object using the `file:` protocol. When the path is a string, the filesystem module will attempt to parse the string for a valid file path. If the file path is a buffer, the filesystem module will attempt to parse the contents of the buffer into a valid file path. If the path is a URL object, the filesystem will convert the object into a valid URL string and then attempt to parse the string for a valid file path. An example of the three ways to show file paths is shown in the following snippet:

```
fs.existsSync( '/some/path/to/file.txt' );
fs.existsSync( Buffer.from( '/some/path/to/file.txt' ) );
fs.existsSync( new URL( 'file://some/path/to/file.txt' ) );
```

*Snippet 6.14: Filesystem path formats*

As you saw in the preceding example, we used the `existsSync` function from the `fs` module. In the first line, we pass in a file path as a string. In the second line, we create a buffer from the file path string and pass the buffer into the `existsSync` function. In the final example, we create a URL object from the `file:` protocol URL of the file path and pass the URL object into the `existsSync` function.

File paths can be parsed as either **relative** or **absolute paths**. An absolute path is resolved from the root folder of the operating system. A relative path is resolved from the current working directory. The current working directory can be obtained with the `process.cwd()` function. Paths specified via a string or a buffer can be either relative or absolute. Any path specified with a URL object must be the absolute path to the object.

The filesystem module brings in many functions that allow us to interact with the hard disk. For a large portion of these functions, there are both synchronous and asynchronous implementations. The synchronous fs functions are blocking! It is very important to remember this when you are writing any code that uses the fs module.

> **Note**
>
> Remember the definition of blocking operations from *Chapter 2, Asynchronous JavaScript*? Blocking operations will prevent any events from being handled by the event loop.

If you use a synchronous `fs` function to load a large file, it will block the event loop. No events will be handled until the synchronous `fs` function has finished its work. Nothing else will be done by the Node.js thread, including responding to HTTP requests, handling events, or any other asynchronous work. You should almost always use the asynchronous versions of the `fs` functions. The only instances where you may need to use the synchronous version is when you must perform a file system action that must occur before ANY other operation. An example of this may be loading files that an entire system or server depends on.

## Express Server

We discussed the basic Node.js HTTP server in an earlier section of this topic. The server we created was very basic and lacked a lot of functionality that we come to expect from true web servers. In Node.js, one of the most common modules for creating minimal and flexible web servers is **Express**. Express takes a Node.js server object and wraps it in an API that simplifies functionality. Express can be installed through NPM (`npm install express --save`).

> **Note**
>
> The full documentation for Express can be found at https://expressjs.com.

The basic Express server is very easy to create. Let's look back at the basic Node.js HTTP server that we created earlier in this chapter. In the basic HTTP server example, we first created a server with the nTTP.createServer() function and passed a basic request handler. We then started the server with the server.listen() function. An Express server is created in a similar manner. Just like with the HTTP server, we must first require our modules. Add a require statement for the Express module and create variables to hold our hostname and port number. Next, we must create our Express server. This is done simply by calling the function that is imported by default from the require('express') statement. Call the imported function and save the result in a variable. This is shown in the following snippet:

> **Note**
>
> The code for the simple HTTP server can be found under the code for Exercise 33.

```
const express = require( 'express' );

const hostname = '127.0.0.1';

const port = 8000;

const app = express();
```

**Snippet 6.15: Setting up Express server**

In the preceding snippet, we imported the Express module and save it to the variable Express. We then created two constant variables – one to hold the hostname and one to hold the port number. In the final line of code, we called the function that was imported by the require statement. This creates a basic Express server with all the default parameters.

The next step we must do to replicate our basic HTTP server is to add a basic HTTP request handler. This can be done with the app.get() function. App.get sets up an HTTP GET request handler for the path provided to it. It takes in two parameters– a path and a callback. The path specifies the URL path that the handler will catch requests to. callback is the function that gets called when the HTTP request is handled. We should add a route handler for the root path of the server ('/'). This is shown in the following snippet:

```
app.get( '/', ( req, res ) => res.end( 'Working express server!' ) )
```

**Snippet 6.16: Setting up the route handler**

In the preceding snippet of code, we added a route handler with **app.get()**. We pass in the root path ('/') so that when the base ('localhost/') path is hit with an HTTP request, the specified callback will be called. In our callback, we pass in a function that has two parameters: req and res. Just like with the simple HTTP server, req represents the incoming HTTP request and res represents the outgoing HTTP response. In the body of the function, we close the HTTP response with the string Working express server!. This tells Express to use the base 200 HTTP response code and to send the text as the body of the response.

In the final step, we must take to get our basic Express server working is to make it listen for HTTP requests. To do this, we can use the **app.listen()** function. This function tells the server to begin listening for HTTP requests at the specified port. We will pass three parameters into **app.listen()**. The first parameter is the **port number**. The second parameter is the **hostname**. The third parameter is a **callback function**, which gets called once the server begins listening. Call the listen function with the correct port, hostname, and a callback that prints the URL we can access the server from. An example of this is shown in the following snippet:

```
app.listen( port, hostname, () => console.log( 'Server running at
http://${hostname}:${port}/' ) );
```

Snippet 6.17: Making the Express server listen for incoming requests

In the preceding snippet, we called the listen function. We pass in the port number, which resolves to 8000; the hostname, which resolves to '127.0.0.1'; and a callback function that logs the server URL. Once the server begins listening to HTTP requests at port 8000 on the local network, the callback function is called. Go to the URL logged to the console to see your basic server in action!

## Exercise 34: Creating a Basic Express Server

To build a basic Express server, perform the following steps:

1.  Import the express module.

2.  Set up the variables for the hostname and port and give them the values 127.0.0.1 and 8000. respectively.

3.  Create the server app by calling express() and save it to the **app** variable.

4.  Add a get request handler to the base route /.

5.  Provide the callback function that takes in req and res, and closes the response with the text Working express server!.

6. Make the server listen on the specified port and host with **app.listen()**.

7. Provide a callback to **app.listen()** that logs Server running at ${server uri}.

8. Start the server and load the specified URL in your browser.

## Code

index.js

```
const express = require( 'express' );
const hostname = '127.0.0.1';
const port = 8000;
const app = express();
app.get( '/', ( req, res ) => res.end( 'Working express server!' ) );
app.listen( port, hostname, () => console.log( 'Server running at
http://${hostname}:${port}/' ) );
```

Snippet 6.18: Simple Express server

https://bit.ly/2Qz4Z93

## Outcome

```
PS C:\Users\Zach\Documents\Professional-JavaScript\Lesson 6\topic b> node ./basic-express-server.js
Server running at http://127.0.0.1:8000/
```

Figure 6.6: Returning the new cart array

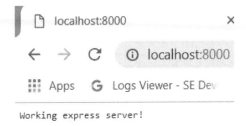

Figure 6.7: Returning the new cart array

You have successfully built a basic Express server.

## Routing

One of Express' most powerful features is its flexible routing. **Routing** refers to how a web server's endpoint URIs respond to client requests. When a client makes a request to a web server, it requests a specified endpoint (URI or path) with a specified HTTP method (GET, POST, and so on). A web server must explicitly handle the paths and methods that it will accept, along with callback functions that state how to handle the request. In Express, this can be done with the following line of code: app.METHOD( PATH. HANDLER );. The app variable is the instance of the Express server. Method is the HTTP method that the handler is being set up for. The method should be in lowercase. The path is the URI path on the server that the handler will respond to. The handler is the callback function that will be executed if the path and method match the request. An example of this functionality is shown in the following snippet:

```
app.get( '/'. ( req. res ) => res.end('GET request at /') );

app.post( '/user'. ( req. res ) => res.end( 'POST request at /user') );

app.delete( '/cart/item'. ( req. res ) => res.end('DELETE request at /cart/
item') );
```

**Snippet 6.19: Examples of Express routing**

In the preceding snippet, we set up three route handlers for our Express server. The first is set up with the .get() function. This means that the server will look for GET requests to the specified route. We pass in the base route for our server (/). When the base route is hit with a GET request, the provided callback function will be called. In our callback function, we respond with the string GET request at /. In the second line of code, we set up our server to respond to POST requests at the path /user. When a POST request hits our Express server, we call the provided callback which closes the response with the string POST request at /user. In the final line of code, we set up a handler for DELETE requests. When a DELETE request comes into the URI /cart/item, we respond with the provided callback.

Express also supports the special function app.all(). If you have worked with HTTP requests a lot, you will recognize that ALL is not a valid HTTP method. app.all() is a special handler function that tells Express to respond to all valid HTTP request methods to the specified URI with the specified callback. It was added to Express to help reduce duplicated code if a route was intended to accept any request method.

Express supports having more than one callback function for a request URI and HTTP method. To do this, we must add a third parameter to the callback function: next. next is a function, and when next is called, Express will move to the next callback handler that matches the method and URI. An example of this is shown in the following snippet:

```
app.get( '/', ( req, res, next ) => next() );
app.get( '/', ( req, res ) => res.end( 'Second handler!' ) );
```

Snippet 6.20: Multiple request handlers for the same route

In the preceding snippet, we set up two different route handlers and GET requests to the base URI. When a GET request to the base route is caught, the first handler will be called. This handler only calls the next() function, which tells Express to look for the next matching handler. Express sees that there is a second matching handler and calls the second handler function, which closes the HTTP response. It is important to note that HTTP responses can only be closed and set back to the client one time. If you set up multiple handlers for a URI server and HTTP method, you must ensure that only one of the handlers closes the HTTP request, otherwise an error will occur. The functionality provided with multiple handlers is critical for middleware and error handling in Express. These applications will be discussed in more detail later in this section.

## Advanced Routing

As explained earlier, in Express, route paths are the path URIs that it matches, along with an HTTP method, when checking which handler callbacks to call. Route paths are passed into functions, such as app.get(), as the first parameter. Express's power comes from the ability to create extremely dynamic route paths that match multiple URIs. In Express, a route path can be a string, string pattern, or regular expression. Express will parse string-based routes for the special characters ?, +, *, (), \, [, and ]. When used in string paths, the special characters ?, +, *, and () are subsets of the regular expression counterparts. The [ and ] characters are used to escape parts of a URL. They are not interpreted literally in the string. The \ character is a reserved character in the Express path parsing module. If you must use the \ character in a path string, you must escape it with the [ and ]. For example, /user/\225\5 should be written in the Express route handler as /data/[\\]225\5.

If we wish to incorporate special characters in our routes to add flexibility we can use the characters ?, +, *, and (). These characters operate the same way as their regular expression counterparts. This means that the ? character is used to symbolize optional characters. Any character or character group followed by the ? symbol will be considered optional and Express will match URIs that either match the full string literally with the optional character(s) or match the full string literally without the optional character(s). This is shown in the following snippet:

```
app.get( '/abc?de', ( req, res ) => {
    console.log( 'Matched /abde or /abcde' );
} );
```

**Snippet 6.21: Optional characters in the route path**

In the preceding snippet, we set up a GET handler for the URL path '/abc?de.' When this URL is hit, the callback is called, which logs the two possible URI match options. Since the ? character follows the c character, the c character is considered optional. Express will match both GET requests to the URI that contains or does not contain the optional character. Requests to both /abde and /abcde will match.

The + symbol is used to indicate zero or more repetitions of the character or character group it follows. Express will match a route that matches literally with the string with zero of the repeated character, and any string that contains one or more sequential repetitions of the marked character. An example of this is shown in the following snippet:

```
app.get( '/fo+d', ( req, res ) => {
    console.log( 'Matched /fd, /fod, /food, /foooooooooood' );
} );
```

**Snippet 6.22: Routing with zero or more repeated characters**

In the preceding snippet, we set up a GET handler for the URL path fo+d. When this URI is hit, the callback is called, which logs some of the matching options. Since the o character is followed by the + character, Express will parse any route with zero or more o's in it. Express will match fd, fod, food, foooooooooooood, and any other string URI with consecutive o's.

The * character functions similar to the + character, but matches zero or more repetitions of any character. Express will match routes that match literally with the string without the extra characters. One or more consecutive characters of any type are used in place of the asterisk. An example of this is shown in the following snippet:

```
app.get( '/fo*d', ( req, res ) => {
    console.log( 'Matched /fd, /fod, /fad, /faeioud' );
} );
```

**Snippet 6.23: Routing with zero or more characters**

In the preceding snippet, we set up a GET handler for the URL path `'fo*d'.` When this URI is hit, the callback is called, which logs some of the matching options. Since the o character is followed by the * character, Express will parse any route with zero or more additional characters in it. Express will match fd, fod, fad, foood, faeioud, and any other string URI with consecutive characters in place of the *. Notice the difference between the matching strings when comparing the + and * characters. The * character will match all of the strings that the + character matches, with the addition of strings with any valid character in place of the asterisk.

The final set of characters is the (). The parentheses groups a set of characters together. Grouped characters are treated as single units when used in conjunction with the other special characters (?, +, or *). For example, the URI /ab(cd)?ef will match the URIs /abef and /abcdef. The characters cd are grouped together, and the entire group is subject to the ? character. An example of this interaction with each of the special characters is shown in the following snippet:

```
app.get( '/b(es)?t', ( req, res ) => {
    console.log( 'Matched /bt and /best' );
} );
app.get( '/b(es)+t', ( req, res ) => {
    console.log( 'Matched /bt, /best, /besest, /besesest' );
} );
app.get( '/b(es)*t', ( req, res ) => {
    console.log( 'Matched /bt, /best, /besest, /besesest' );
} );
```

**Snippet 6.24: Routing with character groups**

In the preceding snippet, we set up GET request handlers for the paths b(es)?t, b(es)+t, b(es)*t. Each handler calls a callback that logs some of the match options. In the all of the handlers, the characters **es** are grouped together. In the first handler, the grouped characters are subject to the ? character and are considered optional. The handler will match URIs that contain the full string and do only contain the non-optional characters. The two options are bt and best. In the second handler, the character group is subject to the + character. URIs with zero or more consecutive repetitions of the character group will match. The match options are bt, best. besest, besesest, and any other string with more consecutive repetitions.

Express also allows us to set up route parameters in the route strings. Route parameters are named route sections, and allow us to specify sections of the route URL to capture and save into variables. The captured sections of the URL are saved into the req. params object under the key name that matches the name of the capture. URL params are specified with the : character, followed by the capture name. Whatever string falls in that part of the route is captured and saved. An example of this is shown in the following snippet:

```
app.get( '/amazon/audible/:userId/books/:bookId'. ( req. res ) => {
    console.log( req.params );
} );
```

Snippet 6.25: Routing with URL params

In the preceding snippet, we set up a get parameter for the route /amazon/ audible/:userId/books/:bookId. This route has two named parameter captures: one for userId and one for bookId. The two named captures can contain any set of valid URL characters. Whatever characters are contained between audible/ and /books will be saved into the req.params.userId variable and whatever characters are after books/ will be saved into req.params.bookId. It is important to note that the / character is what is used to split sections of the URL. The capture groups saved will not contain the / character because Express parses it as a URL separator.

Express routes can also use regular expressions in place of a path strings. If a regular expression is passed into the first argument of a request handler instead of a string, Express will parse the regular expression and any string that matches the regular expression will fire the provided callback handler. If you are unfamiliar with regular expressions, you can find many tutorials online that teach the basics. An example of regular expression paths is shown in the following snippet:

```
app.get( /^web.*/. ( req. res ) => {
   console.log( 'Matched strings like web. website. and webmail' );
} );
```

Snippet 6.26: Routing with regular expressions

In the preceding snippet, we set up a GET handler for the regular expression route /^web.*/. If this handler is matched, the server will log two examples of strings that match. The regular expression that we provided to the GET handler specifies that the URI must start with the string web and may be followed by any number of characters. This will match URIs such as /web, /website, and /webmail.

## Middleware

Express also expands on server flexibility with a feature called middleware. Express is a routing and middleware framework that has little functionality on its own. **Middleware** are functions that have access to the HTTP requests request and response objects and run somewhere in the middle of the handling sequence. Middleware can perform one of four tasks: execute code, make changes to request and response objects, end the HTTP request-response sequence, and call the next middleware that applies to the request.

> Note
>
> Middleware functions can be manually written, or they can be downloaded through third-party NPM modules. Before writing a middleware, check that the middleware does not already exist. Official middleware modules and some select popular modules can be found at https://expressjs.com/en/resources/middleware.html.

Middleware functions have three input variables: req, res, and next. Req represents the request object, res represents the response object, and next is a function that tells Express to continue to the next middleware handler. We saw the next function earlier in this section when registering multiple route handlers to one URI. The next function tells the middleware handlers to pass control to the next middleware in the handler stack. In simpler terms, it tells the next middleware to run. If a middleware does not end the request-response sequence, it must call the next function. If it does not, the request will hang and eventually time out. Middleware can be attached with the functions app. use() and app.METHOD(), where method is the lowercase HTTP method the middleware is being attached to. A middleware set up with app.use() will fire for all HTTP methods that match the specified optional path. Middleware attached with an HTTP method function will fire for all requests that match the method and specified path. An example of middleware is shown in the following snippet:

```
app.use( ( req, res, next ) => {
  req.currentTime = new Date();
  next();
} );
app.get( '/', ( req, res ) => {
  console.log( req.currentTime );
} );
```

Snippet 6.27: Setting up middleware

In the preceding snippet, we set up a middleware function using app.use(). We do not provide a path to app.use(), so all requests will trigger the middleware. The middleware updates the request object by setting the currentTime field in the request to a new date object. The middleware then calls the next function, which passes control to the next middleware or route handler. Assuming a request to the base URI, the next handler that gets hit is the registered handler, which prints the value held in req.currentTime.

## Error Handling

The final important aspect of Express is error handling. **Error handling** is the process through which Express handles and manages errors. Express can handle synchronous errors and asynchronous errors. Express has built-in error handling, so you do not need to write your own. Express's built-in error handler will return the error to the client in the response body. This may include error details such as the stack trace. If you want the user to see a custom error message or page, then you must attach your own error handler.

The built-in Express error handler will catch any error thrown in synchronous code in a route handler or middleware function. This includes runtime errors and errors thrown with the throw keyword. Express will not, however, catch errors thrown in asynchronous functions. To invoke errors in asynchronous functions, you must add the next function to the callback handler. If an error occurs, you must call next with the error you want to handle. An examples of synchronous and asynchronous error handling with the default error handler are shown in the following snippet:

```
app.get( '/synchronousError', ( req, res ) => {
  throw new Error( 'Synchronous error' );
} );
app.get( '/asynchronousError', ( req, res, next ) => {
  setTimeout( () => next( new Error( 'Asynchronous error' ) ), 0 );
} );
```

Snippet 6.28: Synchronous and asynchronous error handling

In the preceding snippet, we first created a GET request handler to the path /synchronousError. If this handler is hit, we call the callback function, which throws an error in a block of synchronous code. Since the error is thrown in a synchronous code block of code, Express automatically catches the error and passes it to the client. In the second example, we create a GET request handler for the path /asynchronousError. When this handler is hit, we call a callback function that begins a timeout and calls the next function with an error. The error occurs in an asynchronous block of code, so it must be passed to Express through the next function. When Express catches an error, either synchronously through thrown events or asynchronously through the next function, it immediately skips all applicable middleware and route handlers in the stack and jumps to the first applicable error handler.

To define our own error handler middleware function, we add it in the same way as other middleware functions, except with one key difference. Error handler middleware callback functions have four arguments in the callback instead of three. The arguments, in order, are err, req, res, and next. They are explained as follows:

- err represents the error that is being handled.
- req represents the request object.
- res represents the response object.
- next is a function that tells Express to move on to the next error handler.

Custom error handlers should be the last defined middleware. An example of custom error handling is shown in the following snippet:

```
app.get( '/', ( req, res ) => {
    throw new Error( 'OH NO AN ERROR!' );
} );
app.use( ( err, req, res, next ) => {
    req.json( 'Got an error!' + err.message );
} );
```

Snippet 6.29: Adding a custom error handler

In the preceding snippet, we added a GET request handler for the base route. When the handler is hit, it calls a callback function, which throws an error. This error is automatically caught by Express and passed to the next error handler. The next error handler is the one we defined with the **app.use()** function. This error handler catches the error and then responds to the client with an error message.

## Exercise 35: Building a Backend with Node.js

You have been tasked with building a Node.js Express server for a note taking application. The server should serve a basic HTML page (provided in the activity folder under index.html) to the base route (/). The server will need to have an API route to load a saved note from a text file in the server's local filesystem and an API route to save changes to the note to the text file on the server's local filesystem. The server should accept a GET request to the URI **/load** when loading the note and accept a POST request to the URI **/save** when saving the note. The provided HTML file will assume that these are the API paths used on the server. When building the server, you may want to use the body-parser middleware with the strict option set to false to simplify the handling of requests.

To build a working Node.js server that serves an HTML file and accepts API calls, perform the following steps:

1. Set up the project with npm init.

2. Install **express** and **body-parser** with npm.

3. Import the modules **express**, **http**, and **body-parser** saved as **bodyParser**, and **fs**, and save them in variables.

4. Create a variable called **notePath** that contains the path to the text file (**./note.txt**).

5. Log that we are creating a server.

6. Create the server app with express() and save it in the app variable.

7. Create an HTTP server from the Express app with http.createServer(app) and save it in the server variable.

8. Log that we are configuring the server.

9. Use the body-parser middleware to parse JSON request bodies.

   Tell the Express app to use the middleware with app.use().

   Pass in bodyParser.json() to the use function.

   Pass an options object into bodyParser.json() with the key/value pair strict:false.

10. Create a router to handle the routing with express.Router() and save it to the variable router.

11. Add a get route handler for the base route with router.route('/').get.

    Add a callback function that takes in req and res.

    In the callback, send the index.html file with res.sendFile().

    Pass in index.html for the first parameter and the options object {root: __dirname } for the second parameter.

12. Add a route for the /save route that accepts a POST request with router.route( '/save' ).post.

    The route handler callback should take in the parameters req and res.

    In the callback, call the fs function writeFile() with the notePath and req.body parameters and a callback function.

    In the callback function, take in the arguments err and data.

    If an err is provided, close the response with the status code 500 and the error in JSON form.

    If no error is provided, close the response with the 200 status code and the JSON of the data object.

13. Add a route for the /load route that accepts a get request with router.route( '/load' ).get.

    The route handler callback should take in the parameters req and res.

    In the callback, call the fs function readFile with the notePath and utf8 parameters, and a callback function.

    In the callback function, take in the arguments err and data.

    If an err is provided, close the response with the status code 500 and the error in JSON form.

    If no error is provided, close the response with the 200 status code and the JSON of the data object.

14. Make the express app use the router to handle requests at the base route with app.use('/', router).

15. Set the server up to listen on the correct port and hostname and pass in a callback using server.listen( port, hostname, callback ).

    The callback should take in an error parameter. If an error is found, throw that error.

    Otherwise, log the port that the server is listening on.

16. Start the server and load the URL that is running at (localhost:PORT).

17. Test the server's routing and functionality by saving a note, refreshing the web page, loading the saved note (should match what was saved before), then updating the note.

## Code

index.js

```
router.route( '/' ).get( ( req, res ) => res.sendFile( 'index.html', { root:
__dirname } ) );
router.route( '/save' ).post( ( req, res ) => {
  fs.writeFile( notePath, req.body, 'utf8', err => {
    if ( err ) {
      res.status( 500 );
    }
    res.end();
  } );
```

```
} );
router.route( '/load' ).get( ( req, res ) => {
  fs.readFile( notePath, 'utf8', ( err, data ) => {
    if ( err ) {
      res.status( 500 ).end();
    }
    res.json( data );
  } );
} );
```

**Snippet 6.30: Express server routing for complicated application**

https://bit.ly/2C4FR64

## Outcome

```
PS C:\Users\Zach\Documents\Professional-JavaScript\Lesson 6\topic b> npm start

> activity-b-nodejs-server@1.0.0 start C:\Users\Zach\Documents\Professional-JavaScript\Lesson 6\topic b
> node ./index.js

Starting HTTP server.
Configuring HTTP server.
Listening on port 8000
```

**Figure 6.8: Listening on port 8000**

test note | Load | Save

**Figure 6.9: Loading the test note**

You have successfully built a working Node.js server that serves an HTML file and accepts API calls.

# React

**React** is a JavaScript library for building user interfaces. React is maintained primarily by FaceBook. React was first created by Jordal Walke, a Facebook software engineer, and open sourced in 2013. React is designed to simplify web development and allow developers to build single-page web sites and mobile applications with ease.

> **Note**
>
> React's full documentation, along with extended tutorials, can be found at their home page: https://reactjs.org/.

React uses a declarative approach for designing a view to improve the predictability and debugging of pages. The developer can declare and design simple views for each state in the application. React will handle the updating and rendering of the views as states change. React relies on a component-based model. The developer builds encapsulated components that track and handle their own internal states. We can combine our components to make complex user interfaces, similar to how we use function composition to build complex functions from simple functions. With components, we can pass rich data types from component to component, through our application. This is allowed because component logic is written purely in JavaScript. Finally, React allows us to be very flexible in our transition into the framework. No assumptions are made about the technology stack behind the application. React can be compiled on load in the browser, on a Node.js server, or into a mobile app with React Native. This allows React to be slowly incorporated into new features without requiring existing code to be refactored. You can begin to incorporate React at any point in the technology stack.

## Installing React

React can be installed through NPM and compiled on the server or integrated into an application through script tags. There are several ways to install React and add it to a project.

The quickest way to add React to your application is to include the built-in libraries through a <script> tag. This method is generally the easiest if you have an existing project and you want to slowly start incorporating React into it. Adding React in this way takes less than a minute and can prepare you to begin adding components immediately. First, we need to add a DOM container to our HTML page where we want our React components to attach. This is generally a div with a unique ID. We then add the **React** and ReactDOM modules with script tags. Once the script tags have been added, we can load our React components with a script tag. An example of this is shown in the following snippet:

```
<div id="react-attach-point"></div>

<script src="https://unpkg.com/react@16/umd/react.development.js"
crossorigin></script>
<script src="https://unpkg.com/react-dom@16/umd/react-dom.development.js"
crossorigin></script>

<script src="react_components.js"></script>
```

Snippet 6.31: Adding React to a web page

The next simplest way to set up a React app and install React into a new project is with the React app creator. This module is a Node.js command-line interface that automatically sets up a React project with a simple predefined folder structure and the basic dependencies installed. The CLI tool can be installed with the command-line command npm install create-react-app -g. This command tells NPM to install the CLI module in the global scope so that it can be run from the command line. Once the CLI has been installed, you can create a new React project by running the create-react-app my-app-name command. The CLI tool will create a folder in the working directory with the name provided (my-app-name from the example command), install the React dependencies, and create two folders for your application's resources. The CLI tool will populate the source code folder, named src, with an example app. You can start the app with the npm start command. From this point, you can begin hacking and modifying the files to see how React works, or you can delete all the files in src and begin writing your own application.

The most difficult way to install React is to install the individual dependencies one at a time. This method provides the most flexibility and allows you to integrate React into your existing toolchain. To install React, you must install the modules react and react-dom with NPM. Both modules can be installed in the local project scope and should be saved to the package.json dependency list with the --save or -s flag. Once the modules are installed, React components can be created and built with your existing toolchain.

In this topic, we will use React with JSX. **JSX** is a JavaScript syntactic sugar and is not supported by default in browsers. JSX must be transpiled into valid JavaScript code with Babel. To finalize the setup of React, you will need to set up Babel to transpile your React and JSX code into JavaScript. If Babel has not been installed for your project, you can install it with the `npm install babel -s` command.

This will save Babel as a dependency for your project. To add the React JSX plugin to Babel, run the `npm install babel-preset-react-app -s` command. This command adds the JSX transpiling libraries for Babel. After babel has been set up, we must create a build script that we can run to transpile all of our code. In package.json, add the following line: `build": "npx babel src -d lib --presets react-app/prod`. Note that `npx` is not a typo. It is a package runner tool that comes with NPM. This line tells Babel to compile code from the `src` directory to the `lib` directory with the `react-app/prod` preset. This command should be run each time we make changes to our React code and want to reflect this in the front-end. You are now ready to start building a React application.

> **Note**
>
> You can provide the Babel setup commands stated in the previous paragraph to demonstrate how to set the project up for transpilation.

## React Basics

React is built around small encapsulated pieces of code called components. Components in React are defined by subclassing `React.Component` or `React.PureComponent`. The most common method is to use `React.Component`. In the simplest form, a React component takes in properties (commonly called **props**) and returns the view to display via a call to `render()`. Properties are defined when the components are initialized. Each component that's created must have a method called `render()` defined in the subclass. The render function returns a description of what will be rendered on the screen in JSX form. An example component declaration is shown in the following snippet:

```
class HelloWorld extends React.Component {
  render() {
    return (
      <div>
        Hello World!!! Made by {this.props.by}!!!
      </div>
```

```
    );
  }
}
ReactDOM.render(
  <HelloWorld by="Zach"/>,
  document.getElementById('root')
);
```

**Snippet 6.32: Basic React element**

In the preceding snippet, we have defined a new React component **class** called nelloWorld. This new class extend the basic React.Component. Inside the declaration, we define the render() function. The render() function returns a block of JSX that defines what will be rendered on the screen. In this block of JSX, we create a div with the text nello World!!! Made by *!!!, where the * character is replaced with the value passed in through the by property. In the final few lines, we call the ReactDom.render() function. This tells the ReactDom module to render all of the components and views we have passed into the render() function. In the preceding snippet, we passed our nelloWorld component with the property by set to Zach, and we tell the render function to attach the rendered DOM to the root element. The data that's passed into the property is passed into this.props inside our component and filled into the nello World!!! div.

> **Note**
>
> If your code base does not use ES6 or ES6 classes, you can use the create-react-class module, however, the specifics of this module are outside the scope of this book.

Congratulations! You have learned about the most basic form of React. By expanding on this one example, you can now build basic static web pages. This may not seem very useful, but it is the most basic building block of all web development.

## React Specifics

From our very basic example in the preceding snippet, we can see that React uses an odd syntactic sugar called JSX. JSX is neither HTML nor JavaScript. It is a syntax extension for JavaScript that incorporates some concepts from HTML and XML to help describe what a user interface should look like. JSX is not necessary for a React app, however it is recommended that you use it when building a React UI. It looks like a template language but comes with the full power of JavaScript. It can be compiled into standard JavaScript with the Babel React plugin. An example of JSX and the equivalent JavaScript is shown in the following snippet:

```
const elementJSX = <div>Hello, world!</div>;

const elementJS = React.createElement( "div", null, "Hello, world!" );
```

*Snippet 6.33: JSX vs JS*

In the preceding snippet, we defined a variable called **elementJSx** and saved a JSX element into it. In the second line, we created a variable called **elementJS** and saved the equivalent element into it with pure JavaScript. In this example, you can clearly see how the markdown style of JSX simplifies the approach to defining an element in JavaScript.

## JSX

**JSX** can have expressions embedded into it much like template literals in standard JavaScript. The main difference, however, is that JSX uses just curly braces ({}) to define an expression. Much like template literals, the expressions used in JSX can be variables, object references, or function calls. This allows us to use JSX to create dynamic elements in React. An example of JSX expressions is shown in the following snippet:

```
const name = "David";

function multiplyBy2( num ) { return num * 2; }

const element1 = <div>Hello {name}!</div>;

const element2 = <div>6 * 2 = {multiplyBy2(6)}</div>;
```

*Snippet 6.34: JSX expressions*

In the preceding snippet, we first created a variable called name that contains the string David and a function called multiplyBy2 that takes in a number and returns the number multiplied by 2. We then create a variable called element, and save a JSX element into it. This JSX element contains a div that contains an expression that references the name variable. When this JSX element is built, the expression evaluates the name variable to the string David and inserts that into the final markup. In the final line of code, we create a variable called element2 and save another JSX element into it. This JSX element contains a div with an expression that references the multiplyBy2 function. When the JSX element is created, the expression evaluates the code inside it and calls the function. The function return value is put into the final markup. As you can see, expressions in JSX work much like expressions in template literals.

## ReactDOM

When we create React elements, we must have some way to render them into the DOM. This was touched on very briefly in the React introduction example. In that example, we used the ReactDOM library to render the component we created. The ReactDOM object, which was imported from the react-dom module, provides DOM specific methods that can be used through your app; however, most components do need these methods. The function you will use most is the render() function. This function takes in three parameters.

The first parameter is the React element that we will rendering, or attaching, to the DOM. The second parameter is the container or DOM node that the React component will be rendered into. The final parameter is an optional callback method. The callback function will be executed after the component is rendered. For full React apps, ReactDOM.render() is usually only needed at the top level of the application, and is used to render the entire app in the view. In applications where React is being slowly incorporated into an existing code base, ReactDOM.render() may be used at each new point where a React component is being incorporated into non-React code. An example of ReactDOM.render() is shown in the following snippet:

```
import ReactDOM from 'react-dom';

const element = <div>HELLO WORLD!!!</div>;

ReactDOM.render( element, document.getElementById('root'), () => {
  console.log( 'Done rendering' );
});
```

**Snippet 6.35: Rendering elements into the DOM**

In the preceding example, we first imported the ReactDOM module. We then created a new React element with JSX. This simple element contains only a div with the text nELLO WORLD!!! inside it. We then called the ReactDOM.render() function with all three arguments. This function call is telling the browser to select the root DOM node and attach the markup rendered by our React element. When the rendering completes, the provided callback is called and the Done rendering string is logged to the console.

## React.Component

React revolves around components. As we learned earlier, the simplest way to create a new component is by creating a new subclass that extends the React.Component class. The React.Component class can be accessed through the React object that's imported from the React NPM module. When we define a React component we must, at the very least, define a render() function. The render function returns the JSX description of what the component will contain. If we wish to make more complex components, such as components with states, we can add a constructor to our component. The constructor must take in the **props** variable and it must call the **super()** function with the **props** variable. The **props** variable will contain an object with the properties assigned when creating the React component. An example of a React component with a constructor is shown in the following snippet:

```
class ConstructorExample extends React.Component{
  constructor( props ){
    super( props );
    this.variable = 'test';
  }
  render() { return <div>Constructor Example</div>; }
}
```

Snippet 6.36: React class constructor

In the preceding snippet, we created a new component called ConstructorExample. In the same snippet, we call the constructor function. The constructor function takes in one parameter, which is the object that contains the properties. In the constructor, we call the **super()** function and pass in the **props** variable. We then create a **class** variable called variable and assign the value **test**. At the end of the class, as required for all React components, we add a render() function that returns the JSX markup for the component.

## State

To add a local state to a React component, we simply initialize the variable state, in the this scope, inside the constructor (this.state = {};). The state variable is a special variable keyword name in React. Any changes to this.state will cause the render() function be called. This allows us to have the view dynamically change, depending on the current state of the component.

It is important to know three key things about the state variable. First, you should never modify the state directly with a statement such as this.state.value = 'value'. Modifying the state in this way will not result in a call to render() and a view update. Instead, you must use the setState() function. This will update the state with the data passed into the function. For example, we must set the state like so: this.setState( { name: 'Zach' } ). The second key detail is that state updates may be asynchronous. React may batch multiple setState calls into a single update to boost performance. Because of this fact, and because this.props and this.state can be changed asynchronously, we cannot rely on their values for calculating a state. If we must use the current state or current value of a property to calculate the next state, we can use a second form of setState that accepts a function instead of an object. The function will receive the previous state as the first argument and the properties object at the time the state update was applied as the second argument. This reliably allows us to use the previous state and property information for calculating the next state. Finally, state updates are merged instead of overwritten. Much like the Object.assign function, setState does a shallow merge of the state object and the new state. When setting a state, the new object will be merged with into old state object. Only the properties specified in the new state object will change. All of the properties in the old state object that are not in the new state object will be left untouched.

In React components, the property object is read-only from inside the component. This means that changes to the properties object from inside component will not be reflected to any variable inside the parent component or DOM structure. Data only flows downward. Consequently, any change to the parent component's JSX markup for the child component's properties will cause the child to re-render with the new property values. To get data to flow in an upward direction, we must pass in functions from the parent component to the child component in the form of properties. An example of this is shown in the following snippet:

```
class ChildElement extends React.Component {
  render() {
    return (
      <button onClick={this.props.onClick}>
        Click me!
```

```
        </button>
    );
  }
}
class ParentElement extends React.Component {
  clicked() { console.log( 'clicked' ); }
  render() {
    return <ChildElement onClick={this.clicked.bind(this)}/>;
  }
}
```

**Snippet 6.37: Rendering a child component**

In this snippet, we created two components. The first one is called ChildElement and the second is called ParentElement. ChildElement simply contains JSX for a button that, when clicked, calls the function that's passed in through the onClick property. ParentElement contains a function called clicked that logs to the console and, when rendered, returns JSX with a ChildElement instance. The ChildElement that's created in the JSX of ParentElement has the property onClick set to the clicked() function of ParentElement. When the button in ChildElement is clicked, the clicked() function gets called. In this example, bind the parent scope to this.clicked when we pass it into the child element (this.clicked.bind(this)). If this.clicked needs to access anything in the parent component, we must bind it's scope to the scope of the parent component. In your React applications, you can use this functionality to create upward data flow.

Handling DOM events in React is very similar to HTML DOM element event handling, with a few main differences. First, in React, event names are using camelcase instead of lowercase. This means that at each "new word" in the name, the first letter of that word is upper case. For example, the DOM event onclick becomes onClick in React. Second, in JSX, function event handlers are passed into the handler definition directly as the function, instead of as a string containing the handler function name. An example of the differences between standard HTML and React are shown in the following code:

```
<button onclick="doSomething()">HTML</button>
<button onClick={doSomething}>JSX and React</button>
```

**Snippet 6.38: JSX versus HTML events**

In the preceding snippet, we created two buttons. The first is in HTML and has an `onclick` listener attached to it that calls the `doSomething` function. The second button is in JSX format and also has an `onclick` listener that calls the `doSomething` function. Note the difference in how the listeners are defined. The JSX event name is in `camelcase` and the HTML event name is in lower case. In JSX, we set the handler function via an expression, which evaluates to the function. In HTML, we set the event handler to a string that calls the function.

> **Note**
>
> We learned in *Chapter 3, DOM Manipulation and Event Handling*, that it is a bad practice to attach events directly in the DOM. JSX is not HTML and this practice is acceptable because JSX prevents injection attacks by escaping any values embedded in JSX.

Another significant difference between React event handling and standard DOM event handling is that, in React, the event handler function cannot return false to prevent the default behavior. You must explicitly call the `preventDefault()` function on the event object.

When attaching event listeners in React, we must be careful with the `this` scope. In JavaScript, class methods are not bound to the `this` scope by default. If the functions are passed somewhere else and called from somewhere else, the `this` scope may not be properly set. You should be sure to bind the `this` scope correctly when attaching them to listeners or passing methods around as properties.

## Conditional Rendering

In React, we create distinct components to encapsulate the views or behaviors we need. We need a way to only render some of the components we have created, based on the state of the application. In React, this is referred to as **Conditional Rendering**. In React, conditional rendering works the same way as JavaScript conditional statements. We can use JavaScript's if or the conditional operator to decide what elements to render. This can be done in several ways.

Out of two simple ways, one is to have a function that returns a React element (JSX) based on the current state, while the second is have a conditional statement in JSX that returns a React element based on the current state. An example of these forms of conditional rendering are shown in the following snippet:

```
class AccountControl extends React.Component {

  constructor( props ) {

    super( props );

    this.state = { account: this.props.account };

  }

  isLoggedIn() {

    if ( this.state.account ) { return <LogoutButton/>; }

    else { return <LoginButton/>; }

  }

  render() {

    return (

      <div>

        {this.isLoggedIn()}

        {this.state.account ? <LogoutButton/> : <LoginButton/>}

      </div>

    );

  }

}
```

**Snippet 6.39: Conditional rendering**

In the preceding snippet, we created an element called AccountControl. In the constructor, we set the local state to an object that contains account information that's passed in from the property variable. The render function simply returns a div with two expressions. Both expressions take advantage of conditional rendering to display information based off of the current state. The first expression calls the isLoggedIn function, which checks this.state.account and returns either a LogoutButton or a LoginButton, depending on the current state. The second expression uses the conditional operator to check this.state.account inline and returns either a LogoutButton or a LoginButton depending on the local state.

## List of Items

Rendering lists of items in React is extremely simple. It is based on the concepts of JSX and expressions. As we learned earlier, JSX uses expressions to create dynamic code. If an expression evaluates to an array of components, all the components will be rendered as if they were added inline in JSX. We can build a collection, or array, of components, save the collection in a variable, and include the variable in a JSX expression. An example of this is shown in the following snippet:

```
class ListElement extends React.Component {

  render() {

    return (

      <ul> {this.props.items.map( i => <li>{i}</li> )} </ul>

    );

  }

}

ReactDOM.render(

  <ListElement items={[ 1, 4, 5, 5, 7, 9 ]}/>,

  document.getElementById( 'root' )

);
```

**Snippet 6.40: Rendering lists**

In the preceding snippet, we created an element called ListElement. This element simply takes in an array of items and maps the array to an array of JSX elements that contains the array item value in a <li> tag. The resulting array of list items is then returned into a <ul> tag. When JSX compiles this into HTML each item in the array is inserted, in order, into the <ul> element.

## HTML Forms

The final key concept of React that we must discuss is HTML forms. HTML forms work differently in React than other DOM elements because HTML forms track their own internal state. If we only need to handle the default behavior of a form, then we can use them off the shelf with React and have no issues. However, we run into a complication when we want to have a JavaScript handle the form submission and have access to all of the data in the form. This issue arises because both the element and React component try to track the state of the form at the same time.

The way to achieve this is with controlled components. The goal of controlled components is to remove state control from the form element and make React the controlling component. This is done by adding a React event listener for a field's value change event (onChange) and having React set its internal **state** variable value equal to the form's value. Then, React sets the value of the field equal to the value that's saved in the **state** variable. React reads any changes from the **input** field and forces the **input** field to adopt any changes that happen to the data stored in the React component. An example of this is shown in the following snippet:

```
class ControlledInput extends React.Component {
  constructor(props) {
    super(props);
    this.state = {value: ''};
  }
  handleChange(event) { this.setState({value: event.target.value}); }
  render() {
    return (
      <div>
        <input type="text" value={this.state.value} onChange={this.
handleChange.bind(this)} />
        <div>Value: {this.state.value} </div>
      </div>
    );
  }
}
```

Snippet 6.41: React component states

In the preceding snippet, we created a component called ControlledInput. This component has a state variable called value that will store the value of the text input. We create a function called handleChange that simply updates the components state by setting a value equal to the value of the read from the event. In the render function, we create a div that contains an input field and another div. This input field has its value mapped to this.state.value and an event listener that calls the handleChange function. The second div simply mirrors the value of this.state.value. When we make a change inside of the text input, the onChange listener gets called and the components state. value gets set to the current value of the input field. Whenever this.state.value gets changed, that changes gets reflected back to the input field. The component's value for this.state.value is absolute and the input field is forced to mirror it.

## Activity 6: Building a Frontend with React

The front-end team working on your note taking app from *Exercise 32* has unexpectedly quit. You must build the frontend for this application using React. Your frontend should have two views, a Home view and an Edit view. Create a React component for each view. The home view should have a button that changes the view to the edit view. The edit view should have a button that switches back to the home view, a text input that contains the note text, a **Load** button that calls the API load route, and a **Save** button that calls the API save route. A Node.js server has been provided to you. Write your React code in activities/activity6/activity/src/index.js. When you are ready to test your code, run the build script (defined in package.json) before starting the server. You can reference the index.html file from *Exercise 35* for hints on how to call the API routes.

To build a working React front-end and integrate it with a Node.js Express server, perform the following steps:

1. Open the starter activity at activity/activity6/activity. Run npm install to install the required dependencies.

2. Create a home and Editor component in the src/index.js file.

3. The home view should display the app name and have a button that changes the app state to the edit view.

4. The edit view should have a return home button that changes the app state to the edit view, a text input that is controlled by the edit view state, a **Load** button that makes a request to the server for the saved note text, and a **Save** button that makes a request to the server to save the note text.

5. In the App component, use the app state to decide which view (home or editor) to show.

**Code**

**Outcome**

# Note Editor App

Edit Note

Figure 6.10: Home view

Figure 6.11: Edit View

```
PS C:\Users\Zach\Documents\Professional-JavaScript\Lesson 6\topic c\solution> npm start

> lesson-6-topic-b@0.1.0 start C:\Users\Zach\Documents\Professional-JavaScript\Lesson 6\topic c\solution
> node ./index.js

Starting HTTP server.
Configuring HTTP server.
Listening on port 8000
```

Figure 6.12: Server view

You have successfully built a working React front-end and integrate it with a Node.js Express server.

> **Note**
>
> The solution for this activity can be found on page 293.

## Summary

The JavaScript ecosystem has grown immensely over the past 10+ years. In this chapter, we first discussed the JavaScript Ecosystem first. JavaScript can be used to build full backend web servers and services, command-line interfaces, mobile apps, and front-end sites. In the second section, we introduced Node.js. We discussed how to set up Node.js for out of browser JavaScript development, the Node Package Manager, loading and creating modules, basic HTTP servers, streams and piping, filesystem operations, and the Express server. In the final topic, we introduced the React framework for frontend web development. We discussed installing React and the basics and specifics of React.

This rounds up the book. In this book, you examined major features in ES6 and implemented these features to build applications. Then, you handled JavaScript browser events and created programs that follow the TDD pattern. Lastly, you constructed the backend framework Node.js and the frontend framework React. Now, you should be equipped with the tools to put what you have learned into practice in the real world. Thank you for choosing this advanced JavaScript book.

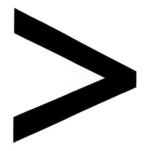

# Appendix

**About**

This section is included to assist the students in performing the activities in the book. It includes detailed steps that are to be performed by the students to achieve the objectives of the activities.

# Chapter 1: Introducing ECMAScript 6

## Activity 1 – Implementing Generators

You have been tasked with building a simple app that generates numbers in the Fibonacci sequence upon request. The app generates the next number in the sequence for each request and resets the sequence it is given an input. Use a generator to generate the Fibonacci sequence. If a value is passed into the generator, reset the sequence. You may start the Fibonacci sequence at n=1 for simplicity.

To highlight how the generators can be used to build iterative datasets, follow these steps:

1. Look up the Fibonacci sequence and understand how the next value is calculated.

2. Create a generator for the Fibonacci sequence.

3. Inside the generator, set up the default values for current and next (0, 1) using variables n2 and n1.

4. Create an infinite while loop.

5. Inside the while loop, use the yield keyword to provide the current value in the sequence and save the return value of the yield statement into a variable called input.

6. If input contains a value, reset the variables n2 and n1 to their starting values.

7. Inside the while loop, calculate the new next value from current + next and save it into the variable next.

8. Otherwise update n2 to contain the value from n1 (the next value) and set n1 to the next value that we calculated at the top of the while loop.

**Code:**

index.js

```
function* fibonacci () {
  let n2 = 0;x
  let n1 = 1;

  while ( true ) {
    let input = yield n2;
    if ( input ) {
```

```
        n1 = 1;
        n2 = 0;
    } else {
      let next = n1 + n2;
      [ n1, n2 ] = [ next, n1 ];

    }

  }

}
let gen = fibonacci();
```

**Snippet 1.87: Implementing a generator**

```
https://bit.ly/2Cv4kAi
```

**Outcome:**

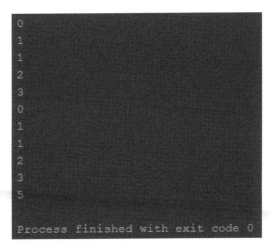

**Figure 1.19: Fibonacci sequence with a generator**

You have successfully demonstrated how generators can be used to build an iterative data set based on the Fibonacci sequence.

# Chapter 2: Asynchronous JavaScript

## Activity 2 – Using Async/Await

You have been tasked with building a server that interfaces with a database. You must write some code to look up sets and look up basic user objects in the database. Import the `simple_db.js` file. Using the `get` and `insert` commands, write the following program using the async/await syntax:

- Look up the key called `john`, the key `sam`, and your first name as a database key.
- If the database entry exists, log the `age` field of the result object.
- If your name does not exist in the database, insert your name and associate an object containing your first name, last name, and age. Look up the new data association and log the age.

For any `db.get` operation that fails, save the key into an array. At the end of the program, print the keys that failed.

**DB API:**

`db.get( index ):`

This takes in an index and returns a promise. The promise is fulfilled with the `db` entry associated with that index. If the index does not exist, the db lookup fails, or the key parameter is not specified, the promise is rejected with an error.

`db.insert( index, insertData ):`

This takes in an index and some data and returns a promise. The promise is fulfilled with the key inserted if the operation completes. If the operation fails, or there is no key or inserted data specified, the promise is rejected with an error.

To utilize promises and the async/await syntax to build a program, follow these steps:

1. Import the database API with `require( './simple_db' )` and save it into the variable `db`.

2. Write an async main function. All of the operations will go in here.

3. Create an array to keep track of the keys that cause `db` errors. Save it into the variable `missingkeys`.

4. Create a try-catch block.

   Inside the try section, look up the key `john` from the database with async/await and the `db.get()` function.

   Save the value into the variable `user`.

Log the age of the user we looked up.

In the catch section, push the key `john` to the `missingkeys` array.

5. Create a second try-catch block.

Inside the try section look up the key `sam` from the database with async/await and the `db.get()` function

Save the value into the variable `user`.

Log the age of the user we looked up.

In the catch section, push the key `sam` to the `missingkeys` array.

6. Create a third try-catch block.

Inside the try section, look up the key that is your name from the database with async/await and the `db.get()` function.

Save the value into the variable `user`.

Log the age of the user we looked up.

In the catch section, push the key to the `missingkeys` array.

In the catch section, insert your `user` object into the `db` with await and `db.insert()`.

In the catch section, create a new try-catch block inside the `catch` block. In the new try section, look up the user we just added to the db with async/await. Save the found user into the variable `user`. Log the age of the user we found. In the catch section, push the key to the `missingkeys` array.

7. Outside all of the try-catch blocks, at the end of the main function, return the `missingkeys` array.

8. Call the `main` function and attach a `then()` and `catch()` handler to the returned promise.

9. The `then()` handler should be passed a function that logs the promise resolution value.

10. The `catch()` handler should be passed a function that logs the error's message field.

**Code:**

index.js

```
const db = require( './simple_db' );
async function main() {
  const missingKeys = [];
  try { const user = await db.get( 'john' ); }
  catch ( err ) { missingKeys.push( 'john' ); }
  try { const user = await db.get( 'sam' ); }
  catch ( err ) { missingKeys.push( 'sam' ); }
  try { const user = await db.get( 'zach' ); }
  catch ( err ) {
    missingKeys.push( 'zach' );
    await db.insert('zach', { first: 'zach', last: 'smith', age: 25 });
    try { const user = await db.get( 'zach' ); }
    catch ( err ) { missingKeys.push( 'zach' ); }
  }
  return missingKeys;
}
main().then( console.log ).catch( console.log );
```

Snippet 2.43: Using async/await

https://bit.ly/2FvhPo2

**Outcome:**

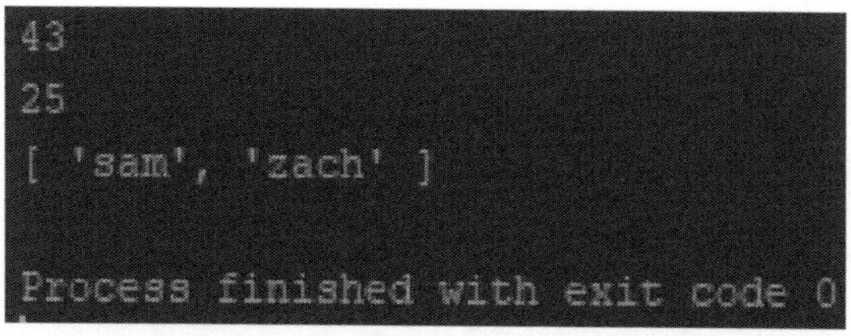

Figure 2.12: Names and ages displayed

You have successfully implemented file-tracking commands and navigated the repository's history.

# Chapter 3: DOM Manipulation and Event Handling

## Activity 3 – Implementing jQuery

You want to make a web app that controls your home's smart LED light system. You have three LEDs that can be individually turned on or off, or all toggled together. You must build a simple HTML and jQuery interface that shows the on state of the lights. It must also have buttons to control the lights.

To utilize jQuery to build a functioning application, follow these steps:

1. Create a directory for the activity and in that directory, in the command prompt, run `npm run init` to set up `package.json`.

2. Run `npm install jquery -s` to install jQuery.

3. Create an HTML file for the activity and give the HTML block a body.

4. Add a style block.

5. Add a div to hold all of the buttons and lights.

6. Add a `script` tag with the source to the `jQuery` file.

   ```
   <script src="./node_modules/jquery/dist/jquery.js"></script>
   ```

7. Add a `script` tag to hold the main JavaScript code.

8. Add a `light` class to the CSS style sheet with the following settings:

   Width and height: `100px`

   Background-color: `white`

9. Add a toggle button to the div by using the `id=toggle`.

10. Add a div to hold the lights with the id `lights`.

11. Add three divs inside this div.

> **Note**
>
> Each div should have a div with the `light` class and a button with the `lightButton` class.

12. In the code script, set up a function to run when the DOM loads:

```
$( () => { ... } )
```

13. Select all the lightButton class buttons and add on-click handler that does the following:

Stops the event propagation and selects the element target and get the light div by traversing DOM.

Check the lit attribute. If lit, unset the lit attribute. Otherwise, set it with jQuery.attr()

Change the background-color css style to reflect the lit attribute with jQuery.css().

14. Select the toggle button by ID and add an on click handler that does the following:

Stops the event propagation and selects all the light buttons by CSS class and trigger a click event on them:

**Code:**

```
activity.html
```

The following is the condensed code. The full solution can be found at activities/activity3/index.html.

```
$( '.lightButton' ).on( 'click', e => {
  e.stopPropagation();
  const element = $( e.target ).prev();
  if ( element.attr( 'lit' ) !== 'true' ) {
    element.attr( 'lit', 'true' );
    element.css( 'background-color', 'black' );
  } else {
    element.attr( 'lit', 'false' );
    element.css( 'background-color', 'white' );
  }
} );
$( '#toggle' ).on( 'click', e => {
  e.stopPropagation();
  $( '.lightButton' ).trigger( 'click' );
} );
```

**Snippet 3.32: jQuery function application**

**Outcome:**

Figure 3.14: Adding buttons after each div

Figure 3.15: Adding toggle buttons

You have successfully utilized jQuery to build a functioning application.

# Chapter 4: Testing JavaScript

## Activity 4 – Utilizing Test Environments

You have been tasked with upgrading your Fibonacci sequence test code to use the Mocha test framework. Take the Fibonacci sequence code and test code you created for Activity 1 and upgrade it to use the Mocha test framework to test the code. You should write tests for the n=0 condition, then implement the n=0 condition, then write tests for and implement the n=1 condition, then write tests for and implement the n=2 condition, and finally do so for the n=5, n=7, and n=9 conditions. If the `it()` test passes, call the `done` callback with no argument. Otherwise, call the `test done` callback with an error or other truthy value.

To utilize the Mocha test framework to write and run tests, follow these steps:

1. Set up the project directory with `npm run init`. Install mocha globally with `npm install mocha -s -g`.

2. Create `index.js` to hold the code and `test.js` to hold the tests.

3. Add the test script to `package.json` in the `scripts` field. The test should call the `mocha` module and pass in the `test.js` file.

4. Add the recursive Fibonacci sequence code to `index.js`. You can use the code built in `Exercise 24`.

5. Export the function with `module.exports = { fibonacci }`.

6. Import the Fibonacci function into the test file using the following command: `const { fibonacci } = require( './index.js' );`

7. Write a `describe` block for the tests. Pass in the string `fibonacci` and a callback function

8. Calculate the expected value by hand for each item in the fibonacci sequence (you can also look up the sequence on Google to avoid doing too much math by hand).

9. For each test condition (n=0, n=1, n=2, n=5, n=7, and n=9) do the following:

   Create a mocha test with the `it()` function and pass in a description of the test as the first parameter.

   Pass a callback as the second parameter. The callback should take in one argument, `done`.

   Inside the callback call the fibonacci sequence and compare its result to the expected value with a not equal comparison.

Call the done() function and pass in the test comparison result.

If the test fails, return done( error ). Otherwise, return done(null) or done(false).

10. Run the tests from the command line with npm run test.

## Code:

**test.js**

```
'use strict';
const { fibonacci } = require( './index.js' );
describe( 'fibonacci', () => {
  it( 'n=0 should equal 0', ( done ) => {
    done( fibonacci( 0 ) !== 0 );
  } );
  it( 'n=1 should equal 1', ( done ) => {
    done( fibonacci( 1 ) !== 1 );
  } );
  it( 'n=2 should equal 1', ( done ) => {
    done( fibonacci( 2 ) !== 1 );
  } );
  it( 'n=5 should equal 5', ( done ) => {
    done( fibonacci( 5 ) !== 5 );
  } );
  it( 'n=7 should equal 13', ( done ) => {
    done( fibonacci( 7 ) !== 13 );
  } );
  it( 'n=9 should equal 34', ( done ) => {
    done( fibonacci( 9 ) !== 34 );
  } );
} );
```

**Snippet 4.9: Utilizing test environments**

Take a look at the following output screenshot below:

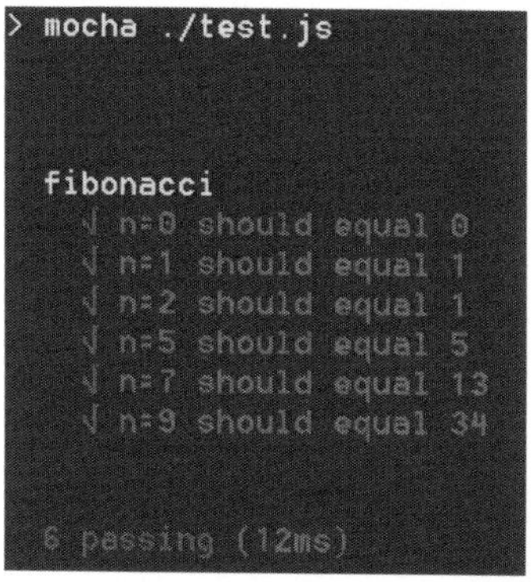

```
> mocha ./test.js


fibonacci
  √ n=0 should equal 0
  √ n=1 should equal 1
  √ n=2 should equal 1
  √ n=5 should equal 5
  √ n=7 should equal 13
  √ n=9 should equal 34


6 passing (12ms)
```

Figure 4.8 : Displaying the Fibonacci series

**Outcome**

You have successfully utilized the Mocha test framework to write and run tests.

# Chapter 5: Functional Programming

## Activity 5 – Recursive Immutability

You are building an application in JavaScript and your team has been told that it cannot use any third-party libraries for security reasons. You must now use Functional Programming (FP) principles for this application and you need an algorithm to create immutable objects and arrays. Create a recursive function that enforces the immutability of objects and arrays at all levels of nesting with `Object.freeze()`. For simplicity, you can assume that there are no null or classes nested in the objects. Write your function in `activities/activity5/activity-test.js`. This file contains code to test your implementation.

To demonstrate forcing immutability in objects, follow these steps:

1. Open the activity test file at `activities/activity5/activity-test.js`.

2. Create a function called `immutable` that takes in a single argument, `data`.

3. Check to see if `data` is not of type `object`. If it is not, then return.

4. Freeze the `data` object. You don't need to freeze non-objects.

5. Loop through the object values with `object.values` and a `forEach()` loop. Recursively call the immutable function for each.

6. Run the code contained in the test file. If any tests fail, fix the bugs and rerun the test

**Code:**

`activity-solution.js`

```
function immutable( data ) {
  if ( typeof data !== 'object' ) {
    return;
  }
  Object.freeze( data );
  Object.values( data ).forEach( immutable );
}
```

**Snippet 5.11: Recursive immutability**

Take a look at the following output screenshot below:

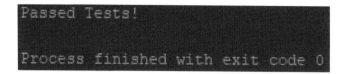

Figure 5.7 : Passed Tests output display

**Outcome:**

You have successfully demonstrated forcing immutability in objects.

# Chapter 6: JavaScript Ecosystem

## Activity 6 – Building a Frontend with React

The frontend team working on your note-taking app from Exercise 35 has unexpectedly quit. You must build the frontend for this application using React. Your frontend should have two views: a Home view and an Edit view. Create a React component for each view. The Home view should have a button that changes the view to the Edit view. The Edit view should have a button that switches back to the Home view, a text input that contains the note text, a load button that calls the API load route, and a save button that calls the API save route. A Node.js server has been provided. Write your React code in activities/activity6/activity/src/index.js. When you are ready to test your code, run the build script (defined in package.json) before starting the server. You can reference the index.html file from Exercise 35 for hints on how to call the API routes.

To build a working React frontend and integrate it with a Node.js express server, follow these steps:

1. Begin working in "activity/activity6/activity". Run npm install to install the required dependencies.

2. In src/index.js, create React components called Home and Editor.

3. Add a constructor to the App react component. In the constructor:

   Take in the props variable. Call super and pass props into super.

   Set the state object in the this scope. It must have a property called view with the value home.

4. Add a changeview method to the app.

   The changeview method should take in a parameter called view.

   Update the state with setState and set the view property of the state equal to the provided parameter view.

   In the constructor, add a line that sets this.changeview equal to this.changeview.bind(this).

5. In App's render function, create a conditional rendering based on the value of this.state.view that does the following:

   If state.view is equal to home, show the home view. Otherwise, show the editor view.

Pass the changeview function as a parameter to both views, which are <Editor changeview={this.changeview}/> and <nome changeview={this.changeview}/>.

6. In the nome component, add a goEdit() function, which calls the changeview function passed in through props (this.props.changeview). and passes in the string editor to the changeview function.

7. Create the render function in the nome component:

Return a JSX expression.

To the returned JSX expression, add a div that contains a title heading title of the app Note Editor App, and add a button that changes the view to the Edit view.

The button should call the goEdit function on click. Be sure to properly bind the this state to the goEdit function.

8. Add a constructor to the Editor component:

Take in the props parameter

Call super and pass in the props variable.

Set the state variable in the this scope equal to the {value: ''} object.

9. Add a function called handleChage to Editor:

Takes in an argument, e, that represents the event object.

Update the state with setState to set the state property value equal to the event target's value:

```
this.setState( { value: e.target.value } );
```

10. Create a save function in Editor that makes an HTTP request to the API save route.

Create a new XHR request and save it into the xhttp variable.

Set the xhttp property onreadystatechange to a function that checks if this. readyState is equal to 4. If it is not, then return. Also, check if this.status is equal to 200. If it is not, then throw an error.

Open the xhr request by calling the open function on xhttp. Pass in the parameters POST, /save, and true.

Set the request header Content-Type to application/json;charset=uTF-8 by calling the setRequestheader on the xhttp object. Pass in the values specified.

Send the JSON data of the text input with xhttp.send.

The value to which, we must send is stored in this.state. Stringify the value before sending it.

11. Create a load function in Editor that makes an HTTP request to the API load route.

    Create a new XHR request and save it into the xhttp variable.

    Save the this scope into a variable called that so that it can be used inside the xhr request.

    Set the xhttp property onreadystatechange to a function that checks if this.readyState is equal to 4. If it isn't, then return. It then checks if this.status is equal to 200. If it is not, then throw an error. It calls the setState function on the React component's scope, which is saved in the that variable.

    Pass in an object with the key value equal to the parsed response of the request. Parse the HTTP response value from the this.response variable with the JSON.parse function.

    Open the HTTP request by calling the open function on the xhttp variable. Pass in the parameters GET, /load, and true.

    Send the XHR request by calling the send() method on the xhttp object.

12. Create a gohome function in Editor.

    Call the changeview function that was passed in through the React element properties object (this.props.changeview()).

    Pass in the string home.

13. Create the render function in Editor.

    Add a button that, once clicked, calls the gohome function that contains the text Back to home. It calls the gohome function on the click event. Make sure to properly bind the this scope to the function.

    Add a text input that contains the note text. The text input loads its value from the state.value field. The text field calls the handleChange function on a change event. Make sure to properly bind the this scope to the handleChange function.

    Add a button to load the note data from the server that contains the text Load. It calls the load function on the click event. Be sure to properly bind the this scope to the load function call.

Add a button to save the note data to the server that contains the text Save. It calls the save function on the click event. Be sure to properly bind the this scope to the save function call.

Be sure to bind the this state properly to all listeners.

14. Test the code when ready by doing the following:

Running npm run build in the root project folder to transpile the code from JSX.

Running npm start to start the server.

Loading the URL specified when the server start (127.0.0.1:PORT).

Testing the view changes by clicking the **Edit** and Back to home buttons.

Testing the save functionality by entering text into the text input, saving it, and checking the text file that was created in the folder to see if it matches.

Testing the load functionality by entering text into the text file, loading it, and making sure that the value in the text input matches the value in text file.

A condensed snippet is provided in the following snippet. Refer to activities/activity6/solution/src/index.js for the full solution code.

Index.js

```
class Editor extends React.Component {
  constructor( props ) { ... }
  handleChange( e ) { ... }
  save() { ... }
  load() { ... }
  goHome() { ... }
  render() {
    return (
      <div>
        <button type="button" onClick={this.goHome.bind( this )}>Back to home</button>
        <input type="text" name="Note Text" value={this.state.value} onChange={this.handleChange.bind( this )}/>
        <button type="button" onClick={this.load.bind( this )}>Load</button>
        <button type="button" onClick={this.save.bind( this )}>Save</button>
```

```
        </div>
    );
  }
}
class Home extends React.Component {
  goEdit() { ... }
  render() {
    return (
      <div>
        <h1>Note Editor App</h1>
        <button type="button" onClick={this.goEdit.bind( this )}>Edit Note</
button>
      </div>
    );
  }
}
//{...}
```

**Snippet 6.42: React component**

https://bit.ly/2RzxKI2

**Outcome:**

Take a look at the output screenshots here:

# Note Editor App

Edit Note

**Figure 6.13 : Edit view**

Figure 6.14 : Server view

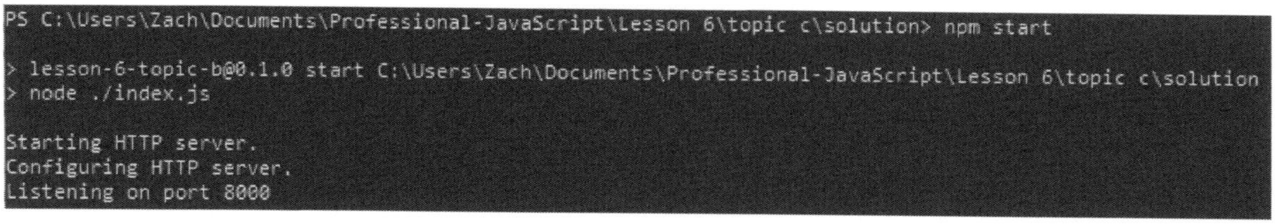

Figure 6.15 : Running the server to test code

You have successfully built a working React frontend and integrated it with a Node.js express server.

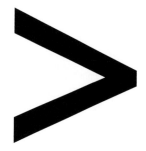

# Index

**About**

All major keywords used in this book are captured alphabetically in this section. Each one is accompanied by the page number of where they appear.

Printed in Great Britain
by Amazon

67394028R00188